Hemingway: THE INWARD TERRAIN

Hemingway: The Inward Terrain

RICHARD B. HOVEY

University of Washington Press
Seattle and London

TO MARCIA WITH LOVE

Forsan et haec olim meminisse iuvabit

There is but one way left to save a classic: to give up revering him and use him for our own salvation.

Ortega y Gasset

Foreword

Mr. Hovey's epigraph from Ortega poses the main issue behind this book. What use are we to make of Hemingway? Does he come off better as a statue or as a man? Recent information about his miserable last years has helped to dim the Tarzan image that Alfred Kazin already found wearisome a quarter-century ago, but where the fiction is concerned it is still common practice to take the hypermanly code of stoic fatalism at face value. The critic's job seems to be to find out how Hemingway would have wanted us to read his stories, and above all to avoid sympathizing with the wrong characters. Thus the most respected of Hemingway critics assures us that *The Sun Also Rises* has "sturdy moral backbone" because it is so faithful to its "moral norm of . . . healthy and almost boyish innocence of spirit," coming down good and hard on neurotics like Lady Brett, Mike Campbell, and Cohn while placing in "high and shining relief" such models of innocence as Jake, Bill Gorton, and Pedro Romero. Such a view preserves the locker-room Hemingway by passing over everything that is problematic and irresolute in his novel. The question is whether it is worthwhile to start over with more psychological frankness and less eagerness to take Hemingway's defensive stance as the whole truth about his art.

In setting out in this direction, Richard Hovey courts ridicule from the still thriving Hemingway cult and from reviewers who cling to the curious idea that one can say penetrating things about a text without implying anything about the limitations of the mind that produced it. Literary commentary continues to pretend that an author's unconscious fantasies, even such obvious and persistent and determinative ones as Hemingway's, are "merely of biographical interest," that is, of no interest, while his declarations about the good life are accepted as the basis for close reading. What is lost in accuracy of statement seems to be recouped in specious dignity; the critic is spared the embarrassment of asking what morbid feelings in himself are touched by his author's strain of fear and gloom.

Mr. Hovey, in contrast, would like us to consider that a writer can be morbid and major at the same time—that a pathetic and at times sinister code of bravado and a desperate moral confusion can go into the making of brilliant art. This seems paradoxical only until we have grasped that fiction begins in fantasy, not in moralism. The Hemingway code is very much a part of his net effect, but it is only a part; his energy and urgency come from the deeper realm explored in this book. As for Hemingway's dignity, Mr. Hovey rightly insists that we can measure it only after appreciating the mental terrors he really faced.

Richard Hovey is not anxious to play rhetorical tricks on the reader. His evidence is laid out straightforwardly and in great detail, with a minimal recourse to psychoanalytic terms. It is hard to see how anyone could resist the general drift of his argument—anyone, that is, who grants that Hemingway's inner battles are worth reconstructing and that the tools for doing so lie ready at hand. I suspect that more than a few readers who doubt whether this can or should be done will have changed their minds before they finish this patient and extraordinarily sensible book.

FREDERICK C. CREWS

Berkeley, California
November, 1967

Preface

The purpose of this book is to get into perspective certain central but often underestimated truths about the writings of Ernest Hemingway. In searching out these truths I found myself going against a tide of opinion. For it seems to me that too many scholar-critics who interest themselves in the works of Hemingway are less concerned with the potency of life in them than with various other matters. Doubtless these other matters have their uses and values, and one may be grateful for them. In the agglomerate, though, and viewed from certain angles, our academic labors begin to look like a rather oddly shaped and bigger-than-life-size monument.

One trouble with this Hemingway monument is that it is inspired pervasively by a legend, a legend close to us all and familiar to the world: the bronzed god of the moderns, the big, strong, romping fighter, soldier, sportsman, lover, drinker, *bon vivant*, and conqueror of fear; besides, the artist unswervingly dedicated to his calling; beyond that, a man with the courage to be himself and the daring to live life as he chose. If sophisticates smiled that the colors were too vivid, they were fascinated nonetheless. And we are hardly to blame if we liked and wish to preserve the legend. It remains attractive. It was animated by a personality whose power both in his life and in his writings has been nearly irresistible. We needed a hero; the legend was not without its foundation in fact; and it has been thrust on us from all sides.

Moreover, Hemingway himself invited us to believe it. He was a great debunker but never of his publicized image. The fiction with its autobiographical import, the intruding of the legendary personage upon his writings by the 1930's, the relentless publicity, and those countless news photos he permitted over three decades—all that not only points to his uncanny knack for helping a legend grow around him; it also suggests a straining to keep it alive. Did he, we wonder, strive to sell that image to the public? Or was he trying to believe in it himself? Either way, we sense that between the legend in the popular media and Hemingway's own self-image more and more parallels developed as time passed.

If ever a writer had problems over his self-image, he was Ernest Hemingway. Surely that question needs to be gone into. Yet much of the commentary is based, wittingly or not, on Hemingway's own self-image—or at least colored by it. It is as if among the authorities a consensus had been reached, suppressing debate about essentials. Join the monument makers and you are encouraged in a variety of endeavors—so long as you proceed within certain hard and fast lines. You may anatomize the Hemingway technique, dissect his symbols and stylistics, computerize his vocabulary or syntax, peer at him through the lenses of mythopoesis, build outworks upon his ontology and superstructures above his metaphysics, erect steeples atop his theology, and so on and on. In sum, we may be arriving at an Establishment Hemingway.

The advantages are numerous. With Hemingway institutionalized, he is not hard to live with. The fundamentals settled now, we need only refine upon our refinements, assured that what we are not yet certain about, our methodologies will in time take care of. We are thus spared many difficulties—like reading him afresh and comprehensively or putting him to the test of our own good judgment. Soon we may be able to get by with little insight, less intuition, and sometimes no common horse sense at all. So, our progress in fabricating a sort of marvel: round the base, in chaste low relief, memorials to the more newsworthy escapades of the career; rising above it, a marble colossus of the super-well-adjusted man, model of middle-class normality, exemplar of classic virtues, in essence maybe a neo-orthodox Christian of, say, vintage 1950's. Of course I have caricatured. In teasing my colleagues I am playing a game as old as Lucian's. If we care for truth, though, what may be no laughing matter is that our authorized version of Hemingway might eventuate in a nearly scandalous misrepresentation.

To be sure, my sketch of the commentators, academic and otherwise, is far from inclusive. Aside from the simplistic or overingenious performances of pedantry and aside from the products of bedazzled adulation or of its spiteful opposite, we have the work of those who could be satisfied only with the realities of Hemingway's art and mind. Some of these excellent critics have, out of sympathy, tried to undercut the legend. And some, alive to the strange power of his art, have sought for its inner stresses and had notable success in elucidating them. Such critiques, however, are mostly in the form of essays and reviews and chapters scattered over the decades; and since, for all their substance and cogency, they never quite became the dominant mode in Hemingway studies, one is tempted to say they belong to a kind of underground tradition. I have at any rate drawn from them, gratefully, and put their findings into a sort of order. As to the book-length studies, even the best of these, I believe, take us only part of the way. For all their critical expertise and their sometimes considerable psychological acumen, they never thoroughly examine the Hemingway self-image. That problem sticks with us, as does the legend.

Even as I write, it is being expanded, complicated, and broadcast by A. E. Hotchner's *Papa Hemingway*. We may label that best-seller irresponsible in its methods, problematic in its ethics, dubious in its data, naïve in its hero worship. But after every subtraction is made, Hotchner's book leaves us with evidence enough that a desperate man, sick in mind and heart, wore until the last the mask of Hemingway-living-out-the-legend. Only the innocent can suppose that these agonies struck Hemingway out of the blue and by sheer chance in old age. The story behind them needs someday to be told. That is the province of the biographer; and this book confines itself to the published works.

Still, much of the essential story emerges plain to see in those very writings. It is there in his crotchets and moods and opinions and ironies and passions. It is bodied forth in his plots, characters, themes, and images. The wonder is that we have missed so much of it—have applauded his heroics and ignored his essential courage in living it and telling it. Maybe we academics have too little heart for the terribly human and intensely lived life which was Hemingway's and which is his work? That life is intense because it was and is a drama. It is a drama because it was full of conflict, especially inner conflict. It is exciting because the conflict became ever more desperate. It takes on tragic meanings because its protagonist must fight against demons that step by step make inroads upon his art and finally destroy its creator. This inward drama gives to the writings their fire and dark power. This is the urgency which moves us and makes Hemingway so compelling a figure. By no means is this all of Hemingway—and I am far from encouraging the sensationalism which dogged his life and still clings to his memory. But to see into and make sense out of the world of his fiction we must be aware of this inner drama. And it cannot be dismissed by anybody seriously trying to understand Hemingway and to value rightly what he has left us.

But so far no one has given us a book which, breaking the spell of the legend and refusing to accept at face value the self-image, has attempted to dig out through the canon the origins and movements of that inner drama; considered the relations between Hemingway's literary triumphs and his disasters; hunted for the links between these and the private man; inquired how he really followed his fated vocation as artist; and asked what use to us now are his words and deeds.

That is admittedly a big order—virtually an impossible one at present. If, inevitably, I flirt with unsuccess, my hope is that we are raising a few of the right questions. The quest promises no hard certitudes and no easy finalities. The venture is, frankly, not always a pleasant business. It means striking some nerves—some universal human ones as well as certain professorial ganglia. It means admitting we do have a Hemingway question and possibly reopening the debate about his stature. It means looking once again—and this time directly and closely—at the actual emotions in his works. It means letting in more light on the old dark places. Whatever else it means, this much is obvious: something like a pathography has to be brought to bear along with the more traditional ways of interpreting Hemingway's writings.

My particular approach to the man and his books is in part psychological. My task has been both simplified and complicated because as a writer Hemingway stays so close to the facts of the life he himself lived and knew first-hand. Granted, we should not confuse his various protagonists and narrators with their creator himself. But with Hemingway it is far more misleading to separate the man from his works. His ephemera aside, he has seldom, if ever, written except out of experience directly encountered and emotions deeply felt. So far as I have been able to sketch a map of Hemingway's inward terrain, I have found Freud the best guide for marking certain recurrent features along the trip.

That does not demand of the reader that he follow at every turn my sometimes seemingly subtle arguments, nor that he accept all of my premises. Besides, since pinning well-known Freudian labels can help us so little, I submit my readers to a minimum of doctrine and jargon. Anyway, their interest and mine is less in the letter of such terminology than in the workings of spirit it points toward. In some quarters the Freudian cartography will raise an outcry—out of benighted habit or private anxiety rather than from understanding. For them, the reply is that I have never presumed to get at *the whole truth* of Ernest Hemingway; and that any reduction of so eminent and complex an artist to some pat formula I, too, regard as the acme of stupidity and arrogance. Readers already disposed to entertain Freud's views of the psyche may complain that I have not gone far enough. To them I can only say it is beyond my ambition to work out every Freudian implication in Hemingway's art. I am making no contribution to psychology; I hope only that I have been enough of a psychologist to read Hemingway well. Insofar as I outline a "case," my interest in the symptoms is literary not clinical. Emphatically, it is nowhere my intention to argue, as to Hemingway or any other creative personality, that with less neurosis we could be certain of more and better art.

Rather, at every point I have intended to supply an abundance of evidence and allow that to speak for itself, without, I trust, any important omissions or distortions or forcing of data to fit preconceptions. I am far less concerned with unraveling the recondite than with following a first rule for any searcher: never overlook the obvious. So, if readers of various persuasions object, their troubles will be, I hope, less with my hypotheses than with the undeniable import of Hemingway's text.

Surely one reason why we are right to trouble ourselves so over Hemingway is his immeasurable influence. Besides what other writers have learned from him, two generations of readers around the globe have not only been delighted and disturbed by the force of his art; consciously or not, they have also gained from his vision of reality a certain style, certain feelings and attitudes about how to live in a threatening world. Thus far has Hemingway been a moralist, a moralist we can neither dodge nor shrug off. A remark made recently by Lionel Trilling about the literature of our century tells us why we cannot ignore Hemingway in the conduct of life: "We set great store by the unillusioned militancy which deals violently with the specious good." Hemingway's militancy can seldom be questioned, and we share his rage against the specious good. The word to be examined, though, is "unillusioned." We can trust his eye, his ear, his nerves, his recording hand; but we need also to decide for ourselves whether he saw steadily and whole those sectors of reality he made his own. Because we are so involved in his testimony on the human condition, we ask, how well did Hemingway understand himself and thus his fellow creatures?

If my inquiries lead toward a re-examination of the Hemingway self-image—and momentarily disquiet a few monument builders—that may be so much to the good. In our best moments, is it not the superbly human we all love rather than the gigantic? Is it not David we care for more than Goliath, who, after all, was a Philistine? And if I have sometimes had to turn a harsh light on this writer's books and have had only middling luck in wrestling with shadows no human life can escape, I have worked always in the faith that what is best in Hemingway will endure and prevail.

R. B. H.

University Park, Maryland
October, 1966

Acknowledgments

Portions of this book have appeared in *University Review, College English, Literature and Psychology, Discourse,* and *Forum.* I gratefully acknowledge permission to use them here, where they appear in revised form. Thanks are due to Charles Scribner's Sons, to The Executors of The Ernest Hemingway Estate, and to Jonathan Cape Limited for their permission to quote generously from the works of Ernest Hemingway. I also wish to thank the former members of the General Research Board of the University of Maryland for summer grants. My indebtedness to many scholars and critics is suggested throughout the Notes and Bibliography.

The warmest thanks go to those persons who in their different ways made this book possible: To my graduate students in English 242, whose response made our Hemingway studies more than merely academic. To my friends, Dr. and Mrs. George W. Rucker, whose encouragement came when it was needed. To undergraduate Gary Kenyon, who did careful work on the quotations. To my colleague, George A. Panichas, whose hospitality of spirit made the long trek easier. To the memory of my teachers, Drs. Hubertis M. Cummings, Frank Wadleigh Chandler, Robert Shafer, and Theodore Spencer. To the memory of Bill

ACKNOWLEDGMENTS

Milton and Weldon Werfelman, who in World War II suffered wounds comparable to Hemingway's on the Italian front in 1918 —and were not so lucky. To Leonard F. Manheim, who gave the manuscript his expert reading and has often been a help in a difficult discipline. To Frederick C. Crews, who brought sympathy and uncommon intelligence to his critique of more than one version of this book and whose faith in the project never wavered. Finally, to my wife, Marcia Johnson Hovey, who has been not only an editor but virtually my collaborator.

R. B. H.

Author's Note

Page references to quotations from Hemingway's work are cited within my text proper. Unless otherwise indicated, all such citations are from the following titles, in every instance the publisher being Charles Scribner's Sons of New York: *The Short Stories of Ernest Hemingway*, 1953, Modern Standard Authors; *The Torrents of Spring* in *The Hemingway Reader*, ed. Charles Poore, 1953; *The Sun Also Rises*, 1926 and 1954, Student's Edition; *A Farewell to Arms*, 1929 and 1957, Scribner Library; *Death in the Afternoon*, 1932; *Green Hills of Africa*, 1935, Scribner Library; *To Have and Have Not*, 1937; *For Whom the Bell Tolls*, 1940, Scribner Library; *Across the River and into the Trees*, 1950; *The Old Man and the Sea*, 1952, Scribner Library; *A Moveable Feast*, 1964; *By-Line: Ernest Hemingway: Articles and Dispatches of Four Decades*, ed. William White, 1967.

Contents

Hemingway: THE INWARD TERRAIN

Chapter I

A Tragic Adventure:
The First Forty-five Stories

Though there is room enough for debate about Hemingway's stature as a novelist, his pre-eminence as a writer of short stories can hardly be challenged. But our estimate of these is based largely on only a handful, in particular the stories most often anthologized. To range further and read straight through as a kind of unit all of the first forty-five—those he wrote during his most productive decade and included in *In Our Time* (1925), *Men Without Women* (1927), and *Winner Take Nothing* (1933)—is to have a rather startling experience.

One of the reasons is that we have become habituated to certain truisms about Hemingway's fiction. We have long paid homage to the style: the marvelous concision, the deceptive simplicity, the cunning obliqueness of its effects, the steely control over some inner fury. We have come to recognize that most of the stories are like lyric poems: the response of a private consciousness to the shocks of experience. As to the Hemingway technique—that unerring choice and patterning of outward realities which point to and make us feel but almost never explain the inward reality—familiarity with these methods has not staled our amazement at such hard-won originality. We take for granted the Hemingway preoccupation with violence, war, and death. And we know the ingredients of heroism he prescribed for these agonies: courage in the midst of danger, "grace under pressure," competence in and dedication to one's job, integrity, self-reliance, and stoicism of the sort that is embarrassed by emotional sloppiness. In enduring pain and facing death, his heroes, we might say, achieve a sort of self-definition. Most readers also agree that Hemingway's treatment of love is confined to the simple, sensual, and primitive when he is not boyishly romantic. Rightly, many of these truisms go unquestioned. Some of them, though, greatly oversimplify his accomplishment. For one thing—as all but one of the novels testify—Hemingway from start to finish has been as much preoccupied with the life of love as with death by violence.

That fact is undeniable in his stories. In these he has provided a more diverse and sometimes more penetrating account of the ways of Eros than he has generally been credited with. Of the first forty-five stories, over two thirds deal with varieties of love experience; in the rest physical violence or death becomes central. By my own count—and my classification makes no pretense of being air-tight or subtle or without overlapping, since several stories contain more than one theme—five of them are about unhappy first love; another five treat the frustrations of marriage; two apiece concern the death of a wife, link childbirth with dying, consider reluctance to become a father; four include victims of venereal disease; six focus on homosexuality; one involves self-emasculation; and nearly ten are devoted to unsatisfactory relations between parents and children. Naturally, other statisticians will arrive at other statistics. But whatever else we want to make of them, we can hardly deny that in these stories love is regularly the loser.

The question is, why? Why cannot the people of these stories avail themselves of love as at least a temporary stay against whatever is hurting or destroying them? Why are these Hemingway protagonists so often without love, or so maimed in their ability to love? It is not Prufrockian self-doubt that undoes them; and it is rarely their entanglement in a mechanized, convention-ridden society which thwarts them. Something else is the enemy. Toward discovering that something else, and for light on the question of why pain so regularly dominates pleasure in the Hemingway universe, we have to concentrate on his treatment of both love and death. Though at first such a focus appears narrow, it can take us far, if only because those two great facts of human existence are present in nearly everything Hemingway has written. What is striking is that a similar darkness permeates his view of both Eros and Thanatos. What we have yet to study through the whole Hemingway canon is his singular and characteristic interweaving of the erotic with pain-wounds-and-death—a twining of opposites so close and persistent that Eros itself seems the friend of Thanatos.

These terms, of course, have been appropriated by psychoanalysis; and perhaps more than any other modern thinker Freud has explored the mysteries they point to, in particular the close union of these opposites. We need not be concerned here with the problematic status of Freud's theory of a death instinct, nor committed to any specific theory of instincts. The helpful thing about Freudian psychology is that it makes the clearest sense out of the warring and confused impulses in all of us: our loving against our hating, our urges to give and receive both pleasure and pain, our mingled impulses simultaneously to create and destroy. So, my use of the two terms is not meant to be rigidly Freudian, still less dogmatic. Rather, *Thanatos,* as it appears in these pages, refers to the fact of death, surely; but also to all those actions, emotions, fantasies, predispositions, drives which push us to hate, inflict pain, and destroy—and so can lead to death. By *Eros,* I do not designate eroticism in our common usage of that term, nor love in an exclusively sexual sense; instead the word points to all aspects of human love. The premises are Freudian inasmuch as they hold that love, like all other emotions, has its deepest roots in sexual energy.

To find our way into the emotional texture of Hemingway's

imagination calls for examining some of these love-and-death enigmas. That, at any rate, is the aim of my survey of his short stories. I propose that we take them up one by one as so many instances of love experienced, or of violence or death encountered. At the outset, my categorizing may appear crude; the order in which the stories are considered and the patterns traced through them may seem unorthodox; the sophisticated may suppose they are being offered mere summaries of what they already know; and others may complain that the summaries are incomplete. Such objections must be risked, I feel, if we are to break through our ritualized reading of Hemingway—to relax a little in our scrutiny of his surfaces and forms so that we can listen more attentively to his silences. Those silences make the drama and his meanings, in the tension between stated fact and passionate implication. Evidently, for neither the uninitiated nor the blasé reader is there any more workable way than to move step by step from the rather simple to the complex and even mysterious, steadily accumulating the facts from the text and painstakingly structuring the argument upon that evidence. The promise is a fresh and valid reassessment of Hemingway's achievement in a genre where he is still supreme.

To begin, then, with the stories of first love. Hemingway's attitude here mingles sunshine and shadow. Such love has a chance for happiness, it seems, but only if it is simple and primitive. Of these five, the lightest in heart is "Ten Indians," perfect in tone, warm and humorously poignant in its nostalgia. It is about a very young Nick Adams on his summer vacation in Michigan and how he feels "hollow and happy inside himself to be teased" by a good-hearted neighbor family because he has an Indian girl. After a "swell Fourth of July" with these farm people, Nick returns to his own family's cottage. There his father tells him he saw his girl "thrashing around" with another boy. Nickie hides his tears from his father; and when he goes to bed he tells himself, "If I feel this way my heart must be broken" (p. 336). Finally he forgets Prudence and falls asleep. The

been hurt in his ability to love. He has a special reason why he will not go to the trouble of seeking a girl: "He did not want any consequences. He did not want any consequences ever again. He wanted to live along without consequences" (p. 147).

If wedlock is no cure for a man's troubles and only brings "consequences," the narrator of "In Another Country" gains a sudden revelation that even a happy marriage might bring something worse. It might inflict an unbearable wound on a man's heart. The setting is a Milan hospital, where the wounded and mutilated come daily for therapy. One patient is a sardonic Italian major, a former fencing champion, now with a mangled hand. When one day the narrator says he hopes to marry, the major becomes angry and calls him a fool. "A man must not marry," he says. "He should not place himself in a position to lose. He should find things he cannot lose" (p. 271). Later he apologizes: "I would not be rude. My wife has just died. You must forgive me." Then the major, who has so far been bitterly tight-lipped, breaks into tears. "I am utterly unable to resign myself," he says (p. 272), and leaves the hospital. Such grief is searing. The story is powerful and makes its point—at least to the narrator: married love is too risky; it would be terrible if the wife you loved would die.

At the other extreme is the grotesquerie of "An Alpine Idyll." Again we have a widower. This time he is a superstolid Swiss peasant whose wife died during the winter and whose body he could not bring into the valley for parish burial until the spring thaw opened the roads. When the priest asks why the corpse's face looks so bad, the husband finally gets out the truth. The comic horror is that he had put her body in the woodshed; when it became rigid he placed it vertically against the wall there; as the mouth dropped open, he had hung a lantern from her jaw when he worked in the shed at night. Cheerful searchers after symbols might be moved by this instance of a wife who, even after death, gives light to her husband in his labors. The explanation Hemingway offers, however, is through a comment made by one of the two American ski companions who hear this tale. They were tired of skiing; they had been up in "the unnatural high mountain spring" too long. "Too damn long," John said. "It's no good doing a thing too long" (p. 345). So we must conclude: husband and wife can live together too long; then habit and routine may anesthetize their love—may well dehumanize it.

In these four accounts, the narrator looks at married love from the outside and dislikes and fears what he sees. The next group of stories also deals with married couples, and in each we see their relationships more directly.

The least in this group is "Out of Season." A miniature of a world at sixes and sevens, this is one of Hemingway's less successful stories. The setting is Cortina in the Italy of Mussolini; and the narrative concerns a fishing trip which is ruined partly by lack of equipment, more by worry over violating game laws, but most by a sullen and complaining wife. The political situation is epitomized by the fishing guide. Peduzzi is a veteran of World War I; and though a sponger and a ne'er-do-well, he is good-hearted. He has also become an outcast in his own home town. If, like him, the Americans are outcasts in Italy, they also feel alienated toward each other. The political troubles underscore the marital ones. And of course we have to conclude that wives do spoil the fun of men who want to go fishing.

In another story of marital dissatisfaction, "Cat in the Rain," Hemingway develops a mere anecdote into a telling insight. An expatriate couple is passing a rainy day in their hotel room, and the wife's attention is caught by a cat outside seeking shelter. The sight stirs her maternal instincts and intensifies her awareness of her own plight. She wants the cat, and she wants other things, too—to grow her hair longer so she will stop looking like a boy, to have some new clothes, and to serve dinner with her own silver and candles. Her husband, who is reading, is irritated at her interruption. She does not get what she really needs, but at least she gets the cat. The gracious old *padrone* at the hotel—a sort of father figure who can make the wife feel "very small and at the same time really important" (p. 169)—has the maid deliver it to their room. Our sympathy in this story is all with the wife whose womanhood is being denied her.

Two of the stories concern divorce or separation. In "A Canary for One" we have another expatriate couple, this time riding a train from Italy to Paris. Traveling in their compartment is a middle-aged American lady—whom we will later give the fuller consideration she deserves. We sense something wrong from the way the husband-narrator so painstakingly holds on to circumstantialities. Flatly he records the cheerless sights he sees through the window, seeming most interested in a farmhouse that is on fire and three railroad cars that have been wrecked. With the same numb attention to detail he listens to the "very wholesome" lady from New York chatter to his wife about how she prevented her daughter from marrying a Swiss. The lady is sure that only American men make good husbands. The irony of the story is doubled when we reach the final sentence. As the train enters the Paris station, the reader learns: "We were returning to Paris to set up separate residences."

The second story that includes divorce is the triptych, "Homage to Switzerland." Its three parts begin with almost identical situations: in each an American man is waiting in a Swiss railway station for the Simplon-Orient Express, which is an hour late. In Part I, "Portrait of Mr. Wheeler in Montreux," a very unpleasant traveler flirts with the waitress, offering her a sizable sum to go upstairs with him. The woman is annoyed and disgusted. Mr. Wheeler gets his pleasures in this fashion and considers himself clever: "He was very careful about money and did not care for women. He had been in that station before and he knew there was no upstairs to go to. Mr. Wheeler never took chances" (pp. 424–25).

In Part II, "Mr. Johnson Talks about It at Vevey," the traveler is one who has taken chances and has been hurt by love.

Though he, too, jokes and flirts with the station waitress, he is kindly and harmless. He rounds up three porters whom he treats to champagne; he needs an audience so that he can talk about what is bothering him: his divorce. He talks awkwardly, and the Swiss do not understand. Suddenly he leaves them and goes outside into the snow to walk up and down the platform. He had thought that talking about it would help, but it only made him feel nasty.

The central figure in Part III, "The Son of a Fellow Member at Territet," is also hurt in his affections. This American, a Mr. Harris, is joined at his restaurant table by a pedantic gentleman who entertains an exaggerated respect for the National Geographic Society. Marking a rather tight effort to be congenial with the old fellow, Harris says that his father had been a member of the society for many years. The older man says he would like some day to meet Harris' father.

"I'm sure he would have liked to meet you but he died last year. Shot himself, oddly enough."

"I am very truly sorry. I am sure his loss was a blow to science as well as to his family."

"Science took it awfully well." [p. 434]

Only with such taut-lipped obliqueness is Hemingway at this time able to find a fictional expression for the pain of his own divorce and the shock of his father's suicide.[1]

In only one of the forty-five stories do we have a hero who is happily married. That fact, of course, is by no means central to the theme of "Fifty Grand," but it is emphatically present. Jack Brennan, the aging welterweight champion fighting his last fight, is the prototype of Harry Morgan in *To Have and Have Not*. Like Morgan, he is also a family man, devoted to his wife and daughters. During training he misses his wife miserably and is plagued with insomnia. When one of his trainers asks him what he thinks about when he cannot sleep, Brennan lists the standard middle-class worries: his wife, his children, his property, his money. He even worries about social status, not for himself but for his girls. He tells his trainer: " 'Who's your old man?' some of those society kids'll say to them. 'My old man's Jack Brennan.' That don't do them any good" (p. 312). In his way, Brennan is as close as we come in Hemingway to the American family man, the concerned husband and father who is doing a tough job in order to be a good provider.

If Hemingway's stories so seldom hint at what a workable marriage might be like, at least one of them tells us what sort of marriage he loathes. In "Mr. and Mrs. Elliot" the moralist takes over completely. The result is caricature and heavy-handed satire of the genteel, the prudish, and the priggish. Hubert Elliot, an affluent man of twenty-five, who "writes long poems very rapidly" and takes pride in his virginity, finds himself marrying a forty-year-old proprietress of a teashop— a Southern lady whom people sometimes take for Hubert's mother. In the opening sentences we learn: "Mr. and Mrs. Elliot tried very hard to have a baby. They tried as often as Mrs. Elliot could stand it" (p. 161). Such phrasing runs like a leit-motiv through the narrative. The wedding night is a farce. Hubert passes part of it walking the corridors of their hotel, where the sight of shoes outside the doors sets "his heart to pounding." Besides the fetishism, Hubert is clearly deep in his Oedipus complex. The marriage bed continues joyless and sterile, but soon he has enough poems to publish a book—at his own expense. At his wife's request, her "girl friend" joins the honeymooning couple. A nice equilibrium is achieved when the girl friend proves very efficient at typing the manuscripts; when Hubert takes to drinking wine and writing poetry at night in his own room; and when Mrs. Elliot and her girl friend share the big medieval bed. And Mrs. Elliot almost gets her baby—at least she helps Hubert remain infantile. The story has a certain bearlike power through the comic manner in which Hemingway weaves together perversion and genteel sterility, biological as well as in art and culture.

What is emotionally akin to actual sterility is dislike of

13

pregnancy. Two of the stories treat this subject. In "Cross-Country Snow" the irresponsible happiness of a skiing holiday is clouded by the fact of Nick Adams' impending fatherhood. The description of the Alpine skiing enjoyed by Nick and George is boyish in its delight; and the dialogue, with its "Gee's," is kiddish. At the inn where "the boys" go for wine and strudel, Nick at first does not notice that their waitress is pregnant, and later wonders why he missed it. He did not see it, of course, because a part of him did not want to, because unconsciously Nick does not want to recognize pregnancy. Something else is much better:

> "There's nothing really can touch skiing, is there?" Nick said.
> "The way it feels when you first drop off on a long run."
> "Huh," said George. "It's too swell to talk about." [p. 185]

The sentimentality that saturates such reluctance to grow up is embarrassing.

In the marvelous economy and precision of "Hills Like White Elephants," the man's dread and hatred of pregnancy darken into cruel narcissism. The setting, a Spanish railroad station, with a view of the Ebro, is given with an absolute minimum of essentials. As the American couple waits for a train, the woman remarks that the hills "look like white elephants." Their terse, edgy conversation, which comprises most of the story— an example of Hemingway's very best dialogue, natural-seeming, yet a poet's concentrate of implications—makes plain the double analogy: the pregnant belly and the unwanted gift. The woman is brought near to hysteria and then to silent bitterness by the man's specious plea for an abortion. He tells her that the operation is simple and that he has known a lot of people who have done it. " 'So have I,' said the girl. 'And afterward they were all so happy' " (p. 275). Our sympathy is naturally with the woman. Yet just enough ambivalence has gone into the handling of the story as to make uncannily convincing Hemingway's sketch of this quirk of masculine psychology.

14

For the Hemingway protagonist, pregnancy seems to be one of the bad accidents of living; but childbirth is worse. In the two stories on this subject, childbirth is linked with dying, as if the important thing is the coming not of new life but of death. "On the Quai at Smyrna," reported like a journalist's interview with an officer who directed the evacuation of civilians during the Greco-Turkish war, is a compact of war's horrors. The crisp, very British, cheerily professional vernacular under-scores our pain in reading it: "The worst, he said, were the women with dead babies. You couldn't get the women to give up their dead babies. They'd have babies dead for six days. Wouldn't give them up. Nothing you could do about it. Had to take them away finally" (p. 87).

To be sure, this sketch is a protest against man's inhumanity. The subjective, almost obsessive element in it, however, emerges when we think of "Indian Camp"—which happens to be the story Hemingway put next in the collected edition. It is bad enough that the Indian mother, who for two days has been screaming in labor, must undergo a caesarian with no anesthetic, with a jackknife for a scalpel, and with fishing line for surgical thread; and it is worse that little Nick Adams has to see and even assist his physician father in this anguished business. What is worst of all for the boy is to see, on the bunker above the mother, the Indian father, who has slashed his throat from ear to ear because he could not stand his wife's cries. This father had previously cut himself badly with an axe, a selfhurt that might indicate his being accident prone and to this extent perhaps guilt-laden. Anyhow, the shocks the boy undergoes are com-pounded when we realize that he catches his father making mistakes: when, with his professional manner, Dr. Adams tells Nick that the woman's screams are not important—the screams which led to the suicide; and next when, before he knows what has happened, he briskly turns to the Indian father with a little joke: "I must say he took it all pretty quietly" (p. 94). Too early in life, Nickie has seen too much suffering. He has also seen a man, through suicide, reject the role of husband and father.[2]

As to other penalties exacted by the love life, we have the stories about venereal disease. "A Very Short Story," a cold and bitter account of love lost, interests us as a sort of preliminary sketch for *A Farewell to Arms*. It is about a wounded American soldier in Italy who falls in love with his nurse and who later gets a letter from her telling him their affair is over. But the fictional account ends this way: "A short time after he contracted gonorrhea from a sales girl in a loop department store while riding in a taxicab through Lincoln Park" (p. 142).

"One Reader Writes," an even shorter sketch, is permeated with wry pity—this time for the woman. The body of the piece is a letter written by a woman to a physician who publishes a daily advice column in the newspapers. The letter writer, stupid, frightened, scarcely literate, wants to know what she should do since she has just learned that her husband, while on a four-year tour of duty in Shanghai, has contracted syphilis. We smile at this poor creature for exposing so her threadbare soul, but we also feel compassion for her.

Venereal disease figures also in an antifascist story. As Alberto Moravia will do later, Hemingway epitomizes the sickness of the body politic through the sickness of love. An account of a brief motor trip through Italy by two Americans, "Che Ti Dice la Patria" reads like a human-interest report of conditions under Il Duce.[3] Insulted by a village youngster who preens himself on the domineering hardness of fascist youth, fined by an officious bully who says their license plate is dirty, oppressed by a pair of lovers who seem very sad, the travelers stop at Spezia and go into a dismal eating place where the waitresses turn out to be whores. One, who will not leave them alone, is evidently syphilitic. When she hears them talking about Spezia, she says, "Spezia is my home and Italy is my country." "Tell her it looks like her country," Guy says (p. 295).

"A Pursuit Race" is one of Hemingway's blackest and most chilling pieces. Its protagonist is a victim of venereal disease and of things worse. William Campbell has been hired as an "advance man" for a traveling burlesque show headed for the Pacific Coast. When the show catches up with him in Kansas City, his boss finds him in bed in a hotel room. While they talk, Campbell keeps a sheet pulled over his face, as if he is a corpse; and when he insists even on talking through the sheet, he is like a gibbering ghost. Literally he loves and fawns on his sheet. He wants only to hide under it—to retreat to womblike peace. When the boss insists that Campbell is merely drunk, the man bares his forearm, covered with tiny blue puncture bruises. The manager urges him to "fight it out":

"They got a cure for that," "Sliding Billy" Turner said.

"No," William Campbell said. "They haven't got a cure for anything." [p. 353]

Plainly, Campbell symbolizes one of the damned, the irretrievably damned. What got him into his "jam," what led him so far along the way to self-destruction, he diagnoses this way:

"Stick to sheets, Billy. Keep away from women and horses and, and—" he stopped "—eagles, Billy. If you love horses you'll get horse-s——, and if you love eagles you'll get eagle-s——." He stopped and put his head under the sheet. . . . "If you love women you'll get a dose," William Campbell said. [p. 354]

In the stories so far considered, every avenue for love seems blocked or threatened. If heterosexual love is so regularly denied or thwarted, we might ask: can Eros possibly find an outlet through homosexuality? It is as if Hemingway put this question to himself. For a half dozen of the stories deal with homosexuality, a phenomenon he was drawn to in anxious, puzzled loathing. It is curious, too, that Hemingway devoted so much of his talent to this subject, because he was to remark in *Death in the Afternoon* that generally "tales of the adnormal" lack drama for the reason that they all "end much the same" (p. 180). We have already touched on lesbianism in "Mr. and Mrs. Elliot." There Hemingway considers the women ridiculous and is contemptuous of the man.

In "The Sea Change" he is less tolerant of deviates. A fine-looking, sun-tanned young couple breaks up because the woman is irresistibly drawn to a lover of her own sex. Though the woman hopes he will let her go easily, the man is evidently too hurt and shocked for that. He wants at least to put a plain label on her conduct. "Vice," he calls it. When she says that's not very polite, he changes it to "perversion."

Other samples of sexual perversion are provided in "The Light of the World." [4] Hemingway said of this story that "nobody else ever liked" it.[5] He was probably wrong. It may well become a darling among the exegetes. A variety of interpretations are possible and maybe valid. It could be called surrealistic; its treatment of the absurd invites the label of existentialist; its Biblical title and the bandying about of the names God, Mary, and Jesus will alert the neo-orthodox; its Walpurgis Night atmosphere and its talk about the death of a "god" will inspire the myth-minded. But the story, however experimental, does depict recognizable outward reality. And, whatever view we take of it, "The Light of the World" is centered on the initiation of youth into the violence and ugliness of human existence: a violence and ugliness which are part and parcel of the degradation of sexuality as well as of the weird reversal of Christian charity.

Two boys on the road, boys in their late teens, seek shelter from the cold and dark in a railroad station somewhere in Michigan. There they encounter five prostitutes and an assortment of men, white and Indian. Three of the whores are enormous; and Alice, the hugest of all, gets into an argument with another whom the narrator calls "Peroxide." With phony histrionics, Peroxide claims she has been the mistress of Steve Ketchel, a prize fighter who had been knocked out by the Negro champion, Jack Johnson. She says she was at the fight when it happened: "Steve turned to smile at me and that black son of a bitch from hell jumped up and hit him by surprise" (p. 389). Of Ketchel's subsequent career she offers this account: "His own father shot and killed him. Yes, by Christ, his own father. There aren't any more men like Steve Ketchel. . . . I knew him like you know nobody in the world and I loved him like you love God" (p. 388). This tale ends when 350-pound Alice calls Peroxide a liar and claims to be "the only one here that ever knew Steve Ketchel. . . ." The two whores squabble, each accusing the other of lying. The narrator is attracted to Alice, but when his pal, Tom, sees him eyeing her, he says, "Come on. Let's go" (p. 391).

Among the other sorry practitioners in the rites of Eros is a homosexual cook, who keeps his hands white by putting lemon juice on them. He tries to get acquainted with the boys. The story ends with the boys leaving the station. "Which way are you boys going?" the cook asks. " 'The other way from you,' Tom told him" (p. 391). The final double entendre is obvious: whatever their erotic temptations, the boys reject the homosexual way.

The story is interesting, yet requires too much puzzle solving to be wholly successful. If we wish, we can detect here certain old myths—specifically their Christian version—about the god who dies at the will of the Father God. The myth is then reduced to the squalid and violent: one prize fighter defeated by another and then killed by his own father; the women who worship the "god" being sickly whores; the one who idealizes him a fantasy-making liar. But the symbolism is overstrained, and Hemingway underscores it for us by his title. "The Light of the World," of course, is part of the account of Jesus' compassionate treatment of the woman taken in adultery. So, reminded of what Jesus had to say about love and charity, we are made aware, through this sordidness and degradation, of what in the modern world has happened to both Eros and Agape. The boys are fascinated by Eros ailing but are not seduced. Eros is both

silly and sinister. If the story is overburdened by more significances than the short narrative can gracefully bear, it is in-
disputable here that the boys glimpse a hell of adultery, forni-
cation, venereal disease, prostitution, homosexuality, and other
perversions. What is central is that love is inextricable from disease, pain, violence, and death.

Similar but bleaker for its atmosphere of threatening evil is
"The Battler." Again we have a boy on the road, Nick Adams.
Thrown off a freight train at night in swampy country, Nick
meets a couple of hoboes. One is an overpolite Negro; the other
is a former prize fighter with a sickeningly mutilated face and
still proud of his ability to "take it." The ex-fighter threatens
Nick with a beating and is thereupon neatly blackjacked by his
companion. "What made him crazy?" Nick wants to know. The
Negro explains that Ad Francis has taken too many beatings.
He adds:

Then his sister was his manager and they was always being written
up in the papers all about brothers and sisters and how she loved her
brother and how he loved his sister, and then they got married in
New York and that made a lot of unpleasantness. . . . Of course
they wasn't brother and sister no more than a rabbit, but there was
a lot of people didn't like it either way and they commenced to
have disagreements, and one day she just went off and never came
back. . . . He just went crazy. . . . She was an awful good-looking
woman. Looked enough like him to be twins. . . . [pp. 136–37]

Aside from these ambiguities about the incest motive, the behavior of the Negro who is so curiously solicitous and knows so
well how to handle the ruined man suggests that his own relationship with Francis is not normal. Nick gets away unharmed,
but he has seen enough to be thoroughly shaken: masochism,
psychosis, pain, and in the background incest and homosexuality.

In "A Simple Inquiry" homosexuality is very much in the
foreground, although Hemingway's concern is with its puzzles
and ethical ambiguities. In a military post in snow-covered hills,
an Italian major quizzes his nineteen-year-old orderly to find

out if the boy might be homosexual. When the boy protests innocence, the major dismisses him. But then the tempted officer thinks to himself: "The little devil. . . . I wonder if he lied to me" (p. 330).

For once, Hemingway seems somewhat tolerant of sexual deviation. At least he gives us indications of how homosexuality can develop among men who have been too long without women. Evidently the major has been on duty all winter at his snowed-in post. As the sun bit by bit melts a wider trench around the hut, we take the hint that bit by bit the major himself is being demoralized.⁶ We also infer the abnormality of the situation from its physical effect on the officer: the white circles around his eyes which sunglasses had protected; the rest of his face burned, then tanned, then burned again; his nose swollen, his skin peeling and blistered; and the delicate, very gentle way he spreads oil over his face. Such details make him, if not repulsive, at least ugly.

We can have no doubt that homosexuality is repulsive in "The Mother of a Queen," a character study of a bullfighter. Although he is earning fifteen thousand dollars in the Mexican rings, the bullfighter ignores requests to pay twenty dollars to insure that his mother's corpse may stay in regular burial ground. When he ignores the final notice, her grave is opened and her "remains dumped on the common boneheap" (p. 513). The young pervert's reaction is chilling in its sentimentalism: " 'Now she is so much dearer to me. Now I don't have to think of her buried in one place and be sad. Now she is all about me in the air, like the birds and the flowers' " (p. 416). Some years later, when the narrator meets him again in Madrid, he explodes: " 'All I say is you never had a mother.' . . . That's the worst thing you can say to insult a man in Spanish." The "queen," however, is not at all offended. " 'That's true,' he said. 'My poor mother died when I was so young it seems as though I never had a mother. It's very sad' " (p. 419). The story ends with the comment:

There's a queen for you. You can't touch them. Nothing, nothing can touch them. They spend money on themselves or for vanity, but they never pay. Try to get one to pay. I told him what I thought of him right there on the Gran Via, in front of three friends, but he speaks to me now when I meet him as though we were friends. What kind of blood is it that makes a man like that? [p. 419]

The insight is that a man who is abnormal in his sex life might lack normal feelings in other ways: toward money, toward himself, toward others. Although this is scarcely an adequate explanation of male homosexuality, Hemingway has in this instance penetrated further than in his other stories. At least he has probed a son's feelings toward his mother—rather lack of feelings. For everything like a normal response is blocked by a façade of grossly sentimental self-deception. Psychologically, we can say that for this matador his mother never did exist; he had, so to speak, killed her in his own heart, long ago. Unconscious rejection of his mother had thus twisted and deadened his heart. Just why Hemingway was drawn to such a special kind of bullfighter for his protagonist here may become clearer when later we consider the mother figures in his stories.

Another case history in Hemingway's own *Psychopathia Sexualis*—at times one is tempted to label some of the stories thus— is the hellish account of a sixteen-year-old boy "who sought eunuch-hood." Titled after the Christmas carol, "God Rest You Merry, Gentlemen" tells of a guilt-tormented boy who on the day before Christmas comes to a Kansas City hospital demanding that the doctors castrate him. Nothing he has done—even praying all night—helps. "Helps what?" the doctor asks. "That awful lust." Then Doc Fischer, who is intelligent and humane, tells the boy that there is nothing wrong with him. The other doctor, so incompetent that he can practice only by continually checking into an indexed vade mecum, *The Young Doctor's Friend and Guide,* calls the boy "a goddamned fool" and dismisses him with an obscene remark. Doc Fischer tries another tack with the boy: "If you are religious remember that what you complain of is no sinful state but the means of consummating a sacrament" (p. 395). The boy leaves. At one o'clock the next morning he is brought back, having cut off his penis with a razor. He may die of loss of blood. Fischer's commentary is: "The good physician here, Doctor Wilcox, my colleague, was on call and he was unable to find this emergency listed in his book" (p. 395).

Of course the entire significance of this story does not center merely in sexual self-mutilation. It is nearly overburdened with moral, even religious meanings. Obviously Hemingway is contrasting humane enlightenment with the hell-fire sort of Christianity which could make a youngster feel such self-destructive guilt over his sex urges. Obviously, too, the Jew is more of a "Christian" than Wilcox. And the unfeeling Wilcox, who in his incompetence must go by the letter of the book, is a foil to Fischer, who in his life and in his healing art is ruled by what Pascal called the *esprit de finesse*.

Nonetheless, one asks: could not all this have been set down with equal power and skill in a story dealing with another sort of situation? Why must self-emasculation be the mainspring of both the action and the emotion here? In fact, if this story has a flaw, it is that what is in the foreground is so luridly lighted up that our attention may be too readily drawn away from other things in it. Irresistibly, Hemingway seems fascinated by emasculation—which of course is the central fact of Jake Barnes's existence.

To summarize our progress through the stories, we might remark that so far Hemingway has testified thus: Eros is walled about with so many barriers, leads into so many blind alleys, seeks outlets in so many deviations, brings so many dubious "consequences," that maybe we had better have done with it altogether. At any rate, the destruction of the genitals puts an end to the matter in "God Rest You Merry, Gentlemen." To work such destruction on a part of the body is to commit a partial suicide.[7] And at this point it seems scarcely an exaggeration to assert that for Hemingway Eros is the intimate accomplice to pain and destruction. At least, we have been afforded few hints that love can ever bring pleasure or more of life. To be sure, our survey of the record Hemingway has left in his stories is by no means completed here. There are still those where Eros is conspicuous by its absence. And we have still to examine the stories which might help to explain how it comes about that in the Hemingway world love must always be a casualty.

The plight of those without love is epitomized in the haunting tale, "After the Storm." In the wake of a hurricane over the Florida keys, the hero takes to his boat to survey the sea's wreckage. In shallow water he comes upon an ocean liner sunk in quicksand. "There I was looking down through the [water] glass at that liner with everything in her and I was the first one to her and I couldn't get into her" (p. 374). The symbolism is interesting. Wrench in hand, he dives two fathoms down to the nearest porthole. There, inside, he sees the corpse of a woman, her hair floating out in the water and rings on her hand. Four more times he dives, hammering at the glass of the porthole, succeeding only in cracking it. He loses his grapple, then his wrench. "It wasn't any good diving unless you had a big hammer or something heavy enough to do good" (p. 376). By nightfall the wind rises and blows for another week. When he can go out to the wreck again, someone else has been there and has taken all that is valuable. For the impotent, for the luckless, the waters will not yield their treasure, nor the lady in the sea her secret.

Another luckless solitary is the suicidal octogenarian who sits up so late drinking in "A Clean Well-Lighted Place." The year before this story was published, Hemingway had remarked: "There is no lonelier man in death, except the suicide, than that man who has lived many years with a good wife and then outlived her" (*Death in the Afternoon*, p. 122). "A Clean Well-Lighted Place" poetizes such misery. The two waiters in the café express contrasting attitudes toward their customer. The younger

A TRAGIC ADVENTURE

man wants to get home to his wife. He is so irked by the old
man's dawdling that he is rude to him and even wishes the old
man had succeeded the week before in his attempt at hanging
himself. Though this waiter has youth and confidence and a
wife, these blessings of love have taught him neither compassion
nor awareness. The older waiter says of himself that he has
nothing but his job; yet he can sympathize with the aged
widower: "I am of those who like to stay late at the cafe. . . .
With all those who do not want to go to bed. With all those
who need a light for the night" (p. 382).

This perfect story is a synecdoche, of course, its meanings
circling outward to further ranges of suggestion. The night that
closes round the café is blackness, loneliness, emptiness, *nada*.
Feeling that cosmic chill makes the older waiter respond to the
dignity in the lonely despair of his customer; and it is he who
utters the two blasphemous prayers: "Our nada who art in
nada"; and the other, the Hail Mary: "Hail nothing full of
nothing, nothing is with thee" (p. 383). There is no God, no
father, no mother, to watch over us. But, despite the all-sur-
rounding night of *nada*—in fact, because of it—the older waiter
sees the need to share with others whatever there is of kindly
light. Whether married love has any value in our God-abandoned
world is considered in this exchange between the waiters:

"He's lonely. I'm not lonely. I have a wife waiting in bed for me."
"He had a wife once too."
"A wife would be no good to him now."
"You can't tell. He might be better with a wife." [pp. 380–81]

When we turn to the stories in which violence so predominates
as almost to eliminate love, in particular to those focused on an
encounter with death or the threat of death, the question arises:
how do these heroes get through their ordeals when love can
be no help or armor for them? Sometimes they do it heroically.
They suffer or die for a principle within themselves, a loyalty to
something spiritual, which transcends the actual world. We have
three instances of such heroism in the first forty-five stories.

25

One of these, the playlet "Today Is Friday," is about the Crucifixion. It might remind us of Anatole France's "Procurator of Judea," where the death of Jesus is a topic of conversation by urbane pagans to whom it is merely a curious incident in a busy world. But no further; for "Today Is Friday" translates the mandarin French into twentieth-century vernacular, into Hemingwayese—the hard-bitten lingo of three veterans of Rome's legions as, off-duty and "a little cockeyed on wine," they talk over their latest assignment: the execution of one Jesus of Nazareth. The theme comes in a line repeated by the "1st Soldier," the most sensitive one: "He was pretty good in there today." What has won his heart is not exactly what Christ lived for, nor the faith he died for, nor his gospel of love, nor the mystery of his sacrifice. It is, rather, his bravery in enduring the bodily agony of the cross, his style of dying. As to love, sacred or profane, there is only a bit of off-color gossip about "his girl," Mary Magdalene. On the question of woman's love as a sustaining power, we have this exchange:

> 2d Soldier—What became of his gang?
> 1st Soldier—Oh, they faded out. Just the women stuck by him.
> 2d Roman Soldier—They were a pretty yellow crowd. When they seen him go up there they didn't want any of it.
> 1st Soldier—The women stuck all right. [p. 358]

In Hemingway's scale of values, Manuel Garcia is unsurpassed as a hero. No women stand by during his ordeal; hardly anyone is even aware of it. Yet Hemingway permits us to feel more exultation in the heroism of this bullfighter than he did in the play about the crucified Nazarene. One of Hemingway's finest stories, "The Undefeated," records the great matador's most desperate performance. (The historical account appears in *Death in the Afternoon*.[8]) In the fictional version, Manuel faces worse odds: he has just come out of the hospital after a severe goring, he is too old, and he has so slipped in popular favor that he must struggle even to be signed up for a "nocturnal"—

those bullfights which pay little and are held at night for "kids and bums."

It turns out to be the bravest performance of Manuel's career. But his luck is bad. Five times he stabs the bull; five times he strikes bone; twice the bull knocks him down and almost gets him. The substitute bullfight critic of *El Heraldo* is too bored to take notes, and the crowd begins to hurl empty bottles and cushions at Manuel. When he trips over one of these on his fifth try, the bull's horn goes into his side. He refuses to go to the infirmary. Though badly gored, he succeeds in killing the bull in the proper manner.

No great cause makes Manuel Garcia a martyr. No faith illuminates him: merely his skill and courage and the absolute probity of his dedication to his hard craft.

A story similar in theme is "The Gambler, the Nun, and the Radio." Here the heroic one is an obscure Mexican gambler, Cayetano Ruiz, who is brought into a hospital in Montana with two bullet wounds in his abdomen. We get to know him through Mr. Frazer, a writer convalescent in the same hospital. Mr. Frazer is unmistakably Hemingway, who scarcely bothers to disguise his own hospitalization after an automobile accident in that state. Cayetano is a model patient: though in great pain and not expected to live, he always smiles, does not make a sound, and feels sorry for other patients; he even refuses to tell the police who shot him.

Mr. Frazer is so impressed that he tries to understand the secret of the little man's heroism. As for the pain, Cayetano tells him he could not make a fuss with so many others in his ward; besides, he considers the man who shot him at the card game only a fool. As to his occupation—well, he says he likes to gamble and thinks he is good at it, but admits he is "a poor idealist," a "victim of illusions," and has bad luck "with everything and with women." Concerning his love life and his philosophy, Cayetano can explain his cheerful, stoic pessimism only by saying he will go on slowly and hope for a change of luck. About women? "No gambler has luck with women," he tells Mr. Frazer. "He is too concentrated. He works nights. When he should be with the woman. No man who works nights can hold a woman if the woman is worth anything" (p. 484). So part of the price for this unpretentious heroism is Cayetano's lack of a love life.

Though moved by his example, Mr. Frazer needs something more to ease him through his own present pains. Cayetano has his "code." The delightfully characterized nurse, Sister Cecelia, has for her escape her obsession with the fortunes of Notre Dame's football team and her childlike yearning to achieve Catholic sainthood. Mr. Frazer has only his radio and his liquor.

The story ends with his mulling over a cliché uttered by a visitor, a misquotation about religion being "the opium of the poor." It inspires the insomniac Frazer to make his own list of opiums for the bad times: religion, music, drink, economics, patriotism, gambling, sex, liberty, bread, education. The list is long, and it was made in 1933, when Roosevelt went into office and Hitler became master of Germany. What such a mingling of private hurts and public woes spelled for Hemingway we cannot see at this point. But of this much we can be sure: his Mr. Frazer wants an escape. He can admire and love the Cayetanos of this world, but his present pain demands an immediate anodyne. Evidently, the example of the Hemingway hero is no longer enough for those who live in a loveless world.

In the other stories that center on violent death or the threat of it, the protagonist is less the heroic than the shocked and passively suffering person. In these stories, too, we begin to get some glimpses into what might have made the heart of the Hemingway hero more susceptible to the pangs and darkness of Death than to the pleasures of Eros.

Among these, the best known of course is "The Killers," a story so much dissected that little commentary is called for here. It might be remarked, though, that Nick Adams' first reaction to the gunmen who intend to kill the big Swede boxer, Ole

Andreson, is not one of evident terror. When the killers leave the lunchroom because their victim has not appeared, the youngster has nerve enough to accept the responsibility of warning Andreson and to walk the dark street to the rooming house where he lives. It is not until he finds the big fighter lying in his bed, hopeless and powerless to do anything but wait for the murdering bullets, that Nick is shattered. He goes back to the lunchroom and reports what he has seen to George and Sam:

> "I'm going to get out of this town," Nick said.
> "Yes," said George. "That's a good thing to do."
> "I can't stand to think about him waiting in the room and knowing he's going to get it. It's too damned awful." [p. 289]

The "damned" awfulness of witnessing and contemplating violent death receives its most anguished treatment in "A Natural History of the Dead," a story to be considered with *Death in the Afternoon,* where it originally appeared as an illustration of one of the themes of that strange book.

In "A Way You'll Never Be" it is Nick Adams himself who has already "got it." Having experienced in battle a death-threatening wound, Nick is in a state of shock. This is one of several autobiographical pieces in which Hemingway seeks to understand, or at least to find a way out of, the trauma his own war wound brought him.

The setting is Italy of the first World War. After an absence of some months, Nick is returning to a sector of the front where there has been a recent attack. As he goes through a landscape of the dead, he carefully notes the horrific and absurd mementos of the battlefield: corpses swollen in the heat, flies, a field kitchen, cast-off ammunition and guns, prayerbooks, letters, photographs, and papers, and many propaganda postcards showing an Austrian soldier about to rape a woman, cards apparently issued just before the attack. When he presents himself to the commanding officer, his friend Paravicini, we learn that Nick had been hospitalized with a head wound. Soon aware that the

American is hardly normal, Paravicini gets Nick to lie down in the dugout.

As soon as he does so, however, Nick is overwhelmed by the remembered terrors of an earlier battle when he had to go out without first getting "stinking" drunk. Then his recollections suddenly take another tack. And we realize that the images which now pass through Nick's damaged psyche—objectified in a head wound—are those which have repeatedly tormented his many sleepless nights:

Sometimes his girl was there and sometimes she was with some one else and he could not understand that, but those were the nights the river ran so much wider and stiller than it should and outside of Fossalta there was a low house painted yellow with willows all around it and a low stable and there was a canal, and he had been there a thousand times and never seen it, but there it was every night as plain as the hill, only it frightened him. That house meant more than anything and every night he had it. That was what he needed but it frightened him especially when the boat lay there quietly in the willows on the canal. . . .

The Paris part came earlier and he was not frightened of it except when she had gone off with some one else and the fear that they might take the same driver twice. That was what frightened about that. Never about the front. He never dreamed about the front now any more but what frightened him so that he could not get rid of it was that long yellow house and the different width of the river. [pp. 408–9]

Superficially this is a nightmarish description of shattered nerves. The word Fossalta, however, provides an important clue; for that is the Italian river town where Hemingway himself was severely wounded in World War I. The dreamer (or rememberer) is obsessed by a yellow house, a stable, a canal, and a river wider than it should have been. He says he "needed" these images, and that "the house meant more than anything"; yet they cause him to be "more frightened than he had ever been in a bombardment" (p. 409). Clearly these associations, which recall only the place of the wounding, are screen memories.[9] Painful though they are, Nick "needs" them because they screen from consciousness the recollection of greater pain and terror: the actual wound and shock. What Nick is going through the psychiatrist might label repetition compulsion; that is, the patient is driven to go back over these memories again and again. Though by day Nick might force himself to think of other things, by night or when he rests, he returns to these memories. He must go back to them repeatedly on the chance that at least in his imagination he will gain some mastery over a peril which once made him helpless. "A Way You'll Never Be" does not explain why wounding had such an effect on the nerves and emotions of Nick Adams. We can only surmise at this point that he was preconditioned to suffer a worse trauma than many another casualty might. As to this preconditioning, however, we do have at least one hint in this story: that is, wounding is not unconnected with Nick Adams' love life. For the only other memories that come to him are about Paris and a girl there. And these recollections are colored by anxiety: anxiety that he might lose her, that she will go off with somebody else, that when they seek a Paris taxi to pet and make love they may get the same driver a second time, that is, be known and watched with disapproval. Only thus far in this story was Hemingway able to penetrate into the puzzle of the close relation he regularly makes between love and wounding.

Yet there is another curious disclosure made in "A Way You'll Never Be." As Nick more and more loses control of himself, he chatters away to an adjutant, telling the Italian that he is there "demonstrating the American uniform," and that "soon you will see untold millions wearing this uniform swarming like locusts" (pp. 410–11). Then, by a quite understandable association, the rapidly cracking Nick begins to deliver a ridiculous lecture on locusts and grasshoppers, explaining how the "medium brown" grasshopper is excellent bait for American fishermen. In other words, a desperate Nick Adams is trying to escape, to go back to his boyhood days of happier times on the streams and lakes of Michigan, to gain some possible control over his fear by concentrating on the simple and primitive rituals of fishing.[10] The narrative ends when Paravicini is called and manages to quiet Nick and send him away from the front.

The next of the stories to connect this trauma with fishing is "Big Two-Hearted River." At first glance, however, there seems little or no relation between battle wounds and this long, apparently straightforward account of how Nick Adams, all alone, hikes through the Michigan woods, makes camp, eats, sleeps, rises the next morning, and then goes trout fishing. Earlier readers must have been puzzled by it; its meanings are obscure unless we illuminate it with our knowledge of other Hemingway stories; and for most of us, the story did not seem essentially psychological until in 1945 Malcolm Cowley remarked that it had "the quality of a waking dream." [11]

One paradox is that this story consists almost exclusively of external realities, such a cumulation of sensory details as to suggest the documentary method of the naturalists. Yet the sheer abundance of the facts, a plethora which almost crowds out any introspection on the part of the hero, might make us suspect that this exact description of landscape and this exact reporting of actions are artificially brilliant, abnormally clear. Since Nick is solitary, would it not be natural for him to have at least some reveries? Only long familiarity with the story makes us realize that Nick concentrates so on outward realities because he dare not look within.

That such is the case, "Big Two-Hearted River" gives us a minimum of explicit clues. Its one obvious link with "A Way You'll Never Be" is that now Nick uses as bait the same sort of brown medium-sized grasshoppers he lectured about when he cracked up at the front. The only direct statements about what might be going on inside Nick are few and far between. Early in the story, as he begins the hike to his camping place, we read: "He felt he had left everything behind, the need for thinking,

32

the need to write, other needs" (p. 210). Superficially these remarks indicate merely a tired, stale person who hopes an outing will refresh him. A second statement, less explicit and more suggestive, comes after Nick has made camp and pitched his tent; he tells himself: "Nothing could touch him. . . . He was there, in the good place" (p. 215). The longest introspection he permits himself—it takes up scarcely one of the twenty pages of the narrative—consists of some seemingly random memories of a former fishing companion.[12] And Nick puts a swift stop to these recollections, because he does not want his mind to start working: "He knew he could choke it because he was tired enough" (p. 218).

Not until we reach the second part of the story, which deals with the fishing, do we get our first unmistakable evidence that Nick Adams' nerves are bad. When he loses his first big trout, he becomes overexcited: "The thrill had been too much. He felt, vaguely, a little sick, as though it would be better to sit down. . . . He did not want to rush his sensations any" (p. 226–27). The most explicit statement about Nick's inward being comes at the end of the story. As he wades downstream where the river deepens and quickens as it flows through a swamp, Nick becomes apprehensive. He does not want to enter that swamp; ". . . in the fast deep water, in the half light, the fishing would be tragic. In the swamp fishing was a tragic adventure" (p. 231).

So startling is the word "tragic" here that we wonder what must be the matter with Nick. We are also struck by evidence of what becomes increasingly plain throughout these stories: their creator is not, in the ordinary sense, a realist. The Hemingway method has far less in common with, say, Howells' or even James's than with those of the surrealist, fantasist, or allegorist. He is utterly clear in observing objects, a great stickler for detail, and dramatizes himself as a rule-following reporter. Yet his most "real" details have a hallucinated urgency—what is most vivid and memorable in Hemingway's pages is regularly something that has struck a psychic nerve in both reader and writer. The psychologist sees in this stance as a realist Hemingway's defensive maneuver against obsessions—those ever-recurring motifs in the fiction. Surely, this view bears on "Big Two-Hearted River," where the symbolism is unavoidable.

The easiest symbolic interpretation of the story is that Nick, whose nerves are for some undisclosed reason shaky, tries to restore himself by going back to the simplicities of the woods. So, his decision to avoid the swamp and the swift waters means merely that he is not yet ready to return to the struggles and dangers of the daily grind. Indeed, the last sentence seems to confirm this reading: "There were plenty of days coming when he could fish the swamp" (p. 232).

Yet such an interpretation leaves too many puzzles. Very little in the story suggests that Nick is really trying the romanticist prescription of back to nature. His delight in the beauties of the outdoors is always subordinated to his practical concerns with hiking, fishing, and camping. Nor does this view explain why Hemingway should pile up so many details into such a long story where almost nothing happens. Nor does it throw much light on the title, a matter about which Hemingway was regularly cunning. Usually, too, his settings are functional; never mere backdrops, they reveal and reinforce his themes, situations, central feelings.

The more fruitful approach is the one initiated by Malcolm Cowley when he remarked that this is one of those Hemingway pieces which are "nightmares at noonday, accurately described, pictured without blur, but having the nature of obsessions or hypnagogic visions between sleep and waking." [13] Look at the story as Cowley recommends, and we unravel more of its secrets. Its title becomes clear: "Big Two-Hearted River" means being of two minds—more accurately, being of two hearts; a conflict of the emotions; in modern parlance, ambivalence. So, typically, it is the outward things here which tell us all we can know about Nick Adams at this juncture of his career. Those outward things are our signs. And it is Freud, the interpreter of dreams, who provides a key to their symbolic import.

It is then easier to notice that, when Nick first arrives by train at the place where he will start his hike, he is in a ghost town in burned-over country—a setting painfully reminiscent of places destroyed by war. It is never mentioned that Nick has had acquaintance with the masculine landscape of war.[14] When he crosses the fire line, though, the landscape becomes more appealing, fertile, distinctly feminine: "a long undulating country" with "sweet fern, growing ankle-high, to walk through . . ." (p. 212). The sweet fern is a natural perfume, and Nick uses it that way: he puts its heathery sprigs under his pack straps, where the chafing crushes it and he can smell the fragrance as he walks along. Needless to say, perfume is immemorially associated with the sexually attractive. And one could point out a sufficiency of other examples where either the setting or Nick's carefully ritualized proceedings have symbolic relevancy to the sexual, to the biological, primordial survival impulses.

Insofar as this story can be said to have a climax, it comes near the end when Nick catches two big trout, rests, eats, and then decides he will not try the swamp or the deeper waters. In precisely this part of the narrative the symbols, which almost spell out Nick's ambivalence, become most plain. Going after his second trout, Nick looks for "deep holes" where he expects the fishing to be good. He finds one. Its description has certain analogies to the female organs:

A beech tree grew close beside the river, so that the branches

. . . hung down into the water. The stream went back in under the leaves. There were always trout in a place like that.

Nick did not care about fishing that hole. He was sure he would get hooked in the branches.

It looked deep though. [p. 229]

Significantly, the very next thing to attract Nick's attention is a phallic symbol: "Ahead, close to the left bank, was a big log. Nick saw it was hollow; pointing up river the current entered it smoothly. . . . It was partly in the shadow" (p. 229). With this log Nick has better luck. In fact, here he makes a quite unusual strike. Holding out his rod so that the grasshopper bait floats on the current into the hollow log, he hooks his trout. Psychologically, we can say that where the female symbol brought only apprehension and frustration, the male brings a reward—and to that extent is preferable. More comprehensively: if Nick does fear life—those deeper, swifter currents—that fear is very much involved with his fear of the female. For the swamp, with its dank overgrowth and yielding fertile softness, symbolizes femaleness; and to enter that swamp or fish there is "a tragic adventure." [15]

Whether or not we are ready to accept this interpretation of "Big Two-Hearted River," the problem now is to test it against the stories which are yet to be considered. The third story that so curiously links fishing with battle trauma is "Now I Lay Me." There Hemingway ventures much further into the wounded psyche. But in order to appreciate more fully what he has accomplished in this complex account of Nick Adams' first reaction to his wounding, we should perhaps try to understand more of what went into the making of such a hero, what predisposed him to be vulnerable in his psyche. Beyond the glimpses already provided, we want to know a little more exactly what shaped the mind and heart of Nick Adams and comparable protagonists before they underwent their ordeal by fire. My premise is that, with all of us, the foundations of the personality, the patterning of the basic impulses of hating and fearing and loving, are formed in infancy and early childhood chiefly through relations with our parents; and that these early feelings and modes of response live on as dynamic though obscure memories in our buried emotional life, largely in the unconscious. For all his devotion to external fact, Hemingway also explored this difficult terrain. The map he has sketched for us is the stories about the relationships between parents and children. To follow that map we must for a moment glance back at a few of the stories already considered.

For instance, in "The Three-Day Blow" the boys have other things to talk of besides the break-up of Nick's romance. While they talk, they are drinking; and Nick, whose father is a tee-totaler, gets high. Bill reassures him that if they do get drunk, Bill's father will not care. The subject of fathers comes up, first by way of books. Bill has been enjoying *Richard Feverel,* that tragic novel of a son whose soul is destroyed by his egoist father's systematic love. Nick says he "couldn't get into it." On the other hand, he thinks Hugh Walpole's *Fortitude* is "a real book." "That's where his old man is after him all the time" (p. 118). We surmise that a moralistic Adams, Sr., has been dogging Nick.[16] By the time they get tipsy, each boy is telling the other that his father is "all right." Of his, Bill admits, "He gets a little wild sometimes." Sadly, Nick remarks that Dr. Adams "has missed a lot." The adolescent hero can sympathize with his father; but he also resents his puritanical severity and lack of joy-in-living. It seems significant that, as the story ends, Nick seeks out Bill's father to join him in hunting.

Though less directly, similar complaints against the same father are registered by a younger Nick Adams in "Ten Indians." Again Nick prefers the ways of another father to those of his own. One reason he had such a "swell" time with the family of neighboring farmers is that theirs is a jolly, permissive attitude toward sex. Mrs. Joe Garner tells her husband, "Well, you had plenty of girls in your time" (p. 333). Then comes this ex-change:

"I'll bet Pa wouldn't ever have had a squaw for a girl."

"Don't you think it," Joe said. "You better watch out to keep Prudie, Nick."

His wife whispered to him and Joe laughed. [p. 333]

It is quite different when Nick returns home and learns from Dr. Adams that he saw Prudie and another boy together "having

37

quite a time." Adams, Sr., avoids looking into his son's face, even walks out of the room. For him, sex can never be a laughing matter.

The emotional conflicts which parents can intensify in a boy who is seeking his own identity are the subject of "The Doctor and the Doctor's Wife." A point of ethics is involved at the outset when Dr. Adams hires three Indians to cut some drift-wood logs for him. One of them, a big half-breed named Dick Boulton, flippantly suggests that the doctor has stolen the wood. Legally, the logs do belong to a lumber company which has lost them on the lake; but since Dr. Adams knows that a few logs are not worth the price of a crew to retrieve them, he feels justified. Nonetheless, his authority and moral rightness have been challenged.[17] Moreover, Boulton is spoiling for a fight. There is nothing for the doctor to do but walk away in rage. When he returns to his cottage, he tells his wife that he has just had a "row" with Boulton. She hopes her husband did not lose his temper. "Remember, that he who ruleth his spirit is greater than he who taketh a city," she pontificates (p. 101). Mrs. Adams, probably nursing a headache, is lying in a darkened room, her Bible and a copy of *Science and Health* at her bed-side. Evidently her religious persuasion is at odds with her husband's vocation. When she insists on further particulars, he explains: "Well, Dick owes me a lot of money for pulling his squaw through pneumonia and I guess he wanted a row so he wouldn't have to take it out in work" (p. 102). She cannot conceive, however, that anyone would do such a thing intentionally. As her husband leaves, she asks him to tell Nick she wants him.

The characters of the father and mother emerge plainly enough. Dr. Adams is henpecked, frustrated by a wife who fancies that the mouthing of pious apothegms can ease honest wrath. It is unlikely, too, that such a mother could ever teach a son how to manage his hostilities wisely. Dr. Adams himself has only one way to strike back at her. Coming upon Nick in the woods near by, he dutifully tells him his mother wants him. However, when the boy says, "I want to go with you," the father replies, "All right. Come on, then" (p. 103). This kind of experience can divide a boy's heart. One of the problems for little Nick Adams here is: with whom should he identify? We see him choose his father, turning away from the woman who threatens to dominate him as she dominates her husband. That the mother lies in a darkened room suggests, symbolically, the womb. Into that dark impossible security Nick will not retreat; nor will he accept another unreality from her, her denial of the existence of evil. It is not enough, though, for Nick to identify with his father. For we have seen the father defeated by a hired man, an inferior who dares to question his probity; and we have seen him browbeaten by his wife. Nick Adams is being prepared for further estrangement from his mother and for further disillusionment with his father. The story becomes more interesting now that we know the boy Ernest was present when this very incident took place between his own mother and father.[18]

How a little boy idealizes and adores his father and what it means when such an idol is smashed is the substance of one of Hemingway's most heartbreaking stories. Though he proves mastery in his own brand of pathos here, "My Old Man" cannot lay claim to great originality; it is heavily indebted to Sherwood Anderson's "I Want To Know Why." Like that story, it is about horse-racing, is told in the vernacular of a half-educated boy, and is climaxed by his disillusionment. It is also one of the very few Hemingway stories that elaborate an emotional development; and, despite all the implicit ambivalence, it is the only one in which love is given a full and free expression—something it never gets in the stories about men and women. We have, then, an atypical Hemingway piece—and perhaps with reason. For in his other accounts of boys, Hemingway does not much conceal the external facts drawn from his own experience. This time, he transforms the tall father-figure of Dr. Adams into a widowed jockey who rides at various European steeplechase courses. Behind such guises Hemingway can liberate feelings he hardly allows himself in his other fictions. The relationship between Joe and his "old man" is easy, happy, almost perfect. In several respects Butler is a superb father. But he is also a crook. So the dramatic artistry of the story—and our involvement in it—is that we soon know what the father is, though we see him only through the eyes of innocent love.

Joe admires everything his dad does. He cannot imagine why his father is forced to leave the Milan track, except that one day he gets a hint of his father's dirty dealings when he overhears a man call Butler, "You son of a bitch."

When they get to France Joe forgets the incident, and his faith in his father seems unshaken. But one day a friend, George Gardner, who is riding Kzar, the favorite, informs his father that another horse will be the winner. Profiting by the tip, Butler wins heavily on this fixed race. Afterward, he praises Gardner, telling Joe that it took "a great jock to keep that Kzar horse from winning." Joe's head is learning what his heart refuses to accept. His own thoughts surprise him: ". . . I wish I were a jockey and could have rode him instead of that son of a bitch. And that was funny, thinking of George Gardner as a son of a bitch because I'd always liked him and besides he'd given us the winner . . ." (p. 200). It is hard for the boy to call a likable man a son of a bitch, a label he has heard applied to his father. For Butler in a way is worse than Gardner: to his own son he has praised the skill with which Gardner prostituted his horsemanship.

Still the boy suppresses what he is coming to know, so keen is his need to idolize his dad. The climax comes when the father buys his own horse, begins to ride again, and to do well in steeplechases. But on one of the jumps at the Auteuil course, the horse falls and breaks a leg, and a crushed skull kills Joe's father. "I lay down beside my old man, when they carried the stretcher into the hospital room, and hung onto the stretcher and cried and cried. . . ." For once a Hemingway protagonist is permitted to cry, cry without being able to stop. But this heartache is followed by a worse pain. Joe overhears a man in the crowd say that Butler "had it coming to him on the stuff he's pulled!" Gardner's consolation, though there is truth in it, comes too late: "Don't you listen to what those bums said, Joe. Your old man was one swell guy." But the orphan sums it up this way: "But I don't know. Seems like when they get started they don't leave a guy nothing" (p. 205). From a psychologist's view, this story is interesting because through it the writer can both idolize and destroy a father-image.

If a son's feelings for his father have been expressed here with rare warmth and tenderness, in "Soldier's Home" the son's feelings toward his mother are marked by heart-chilling alienation and marrow-deep resentment. The story is based on experiences similar to Hemingway's when he returned to his parents' home to recuperate from his war wounds. For this reason, it further illuminates the use of autobiographical material in these accounts of the schooling of the heart of the Hemingway hero.[19] What torments Krebs, because it is the loss of what is precious to him, is that he finds it impossible now to be honest with other people and true to himself. Neither of his parents has any notion of what he has been through in Europe or what is wrong with him. His weak father is unimportant, out of the picture. It is the mother who forces the issue, dramatizes the living lie, and induces the real "nausea." After her son has been home only about a month, she begins to question him about whether he has found a "definite aim in life":

"God has some work for every one to do," his mother said. "There can be no idle hands in His Kingdom."
"I'm not in His Kingdom," Krebs said.
"We are all of us in His Kingdom."
Krebs felt embarrassed and resentful as always. [p. 151]

His mother goes on to tell him that she understands the

temptations men in war are exposed to; that his father will let him have the family car for dates with "nice girls"; that other boys are settling down and "on their way to being really a credit to the community."

"Is that all?" Krebs said.

"Yes. Don't you love your mother, dear boy?"

"No," Krebs said.

She starts to cry. "I don't love anybody," he tells her. At once he apologizes, knowing he cannot "make her see it." He kisses her. Mother pulls out the tremolo stop, and Hemingway offers us one of his most soul-retching vignettes:

"I'm your mother," she said. "I held you next to my heart when you were a tiny baby."

Krebs felt sick and vaguely nauseated.

"I know, Mummy," he said. "I'll try and be a good boy for you."

"Would you kneel and pray with me, Harold?" his mother asked. [pp. 151–52]

Krebs kneels but cannot pray. The sweet milk of sentimentality has gone sour. "He had felt sorry for his mother and she had made him lie" (p. 153). Against a parent who forces one into hypocrisy and who denies one's maturity, there is only one action to take: flee. Krebs escapes; and we are shown much of the world against which the Hemingway hero must rebel.

Mrs. Krebs's counterpart is the "very wholesome middle-aged lady" from New York who joins the young couple on that dreary train trip in "A Canary for One." She fusses over a canary she had bought in Italy and explains, "I'm taking him home to my little girl." The "little girl," we learn, had fallen "madly in love" with a Swiss. Because the mother clings to a notion that only an American husband could make her daughter happy, she had broken up the courtship. "That was why we left the Continent. . . . I took her away, of course" (p. 339). The rescue occurred two years ago. The wife wants to know if the girl got over it:

"I don't think so," said the American lady. "She wouldn't eat any-thing and she wouldn't sleep at all. I've tried so very hard, but she doesn't seem to take an interest in anything. She doesn't care about things. I couldn't have her marrying a foreigner." [p. 339]

She is unfeelingly self-righteous about what she has done, lacks anything like respect for the soul of her daughter. Krebs was able to escape when his mother threatened to destroy his heart. But this mother has succeeded in such destruction. The fate of the daughter is that of the caged canary which does not sing.

So far, in these stories about parents, the mothers regularly appear as domineering over their families; as destroyers, actual or potential, of their children; as champions of respectability and defenders of cruel sentimentalities and false values. Just as regu-larly, the fathers are depicted as weak; as men on whom sons dare not wholly rely. Though more attractive and sympathetic than the mothers, Hemingway fathers sooner or later bring disillusionment.

The charming little sketch "A Day's Wait" is something like an exception. The narrator is the father, who describes a sick spell of his nine-year-old boy, Schatz—German for "treasure" or "sweetheart." Schatz has influenza and a fever of 102 degrees. The father gives the boy his medicine and whiles away time by reading to him, but notices that he will not try to sleep and instead looks "very strangely" at the foot of his bed. Ascribing this to lightheadedness instead of really trying to find out what is wrong, the father goes outside for a while, with his dog and gun. The ground is so "varnished with ice," though, that the dog slips and twice the hunter falls down—characteristic Hem-ingway devices to indicate that the father is unsure of the ground he walks on. When the father returns, the son's secret finally comes out: "About what time do you think I'm going to die?" He is told that people do not die of such a fever. The boy says, "I know they do. At school in France the boys told me you can't live with forty-four degrees. I've got a hundred and two." The father then explains the difference in thermometers.

HEMINGWAY: THE INWARD TERRAIN

" 'You poor Schatz,' I said. 'Poor old Schatz. It's like miles and kilometers. You aren't going to die. That's a different thermometer' " (p. 439). Though the twist is a child's tragicomic ignorance, we still feel that somehow Schatz could and should have been spared, that somehow between him and his father the lines of communication might have been clearer.

Despite their shortcomings, these Hemingway fathers exert more obvious influence on the sons than do the mothers. So it is fitting that the final title of the collected short stories is "Fathers and Sons." Again Nick Adams is the narrator, now thirty-eight years old and driving through an autumn countryside somewhere in the South, his small son asleep beside him. Nothing happens except that Nick remembers his boyhood and talks a little when his son wakes up. The story is a poem in prose, subtle, humorous, warm, poignant, reminding us perhaps of a mood evoked by some of Tennyson's lyrics. It appears to be so close to the facts and so frankly confessional that it is hard not to take this piece as one of Hemingway's most explicit efforts to set down his feelings about his own father.

Thoughts about shooting quail in this country set Nick to reminiscing about his father, who "shot very quickly and beautifully." It is not the weak chin covered by a beard which Nick first remembers; but in images that suggest male prowess he recalls his father's wonderful eyesight and how he "saw as a big-horn ram or an eagle does, literally." Of Dr. Adams' character and final tragedy, Nick tells us that he was a nervous man and a sentimental one, that he could be cruel, that he had died in a trap "he had helped only a little to set." Nick is grateful to his father for teaching him to fish and shoot, which he loves "exactly as much as when he first had gone with his father. It was a passion that had never slackened" (p. 490).

As to another passion, Dr. Adams had been "as sound on those two things as he was unsound on sex." On that subject, Nick recalls having gotten "only two pieces of information" from Dr. Adams. Once when a squirrel bit him on the thumb,

Nick called the creature a "little bugger." His father corrected him:

"A bugger is a man who has intercourse with animals."
"Why?" Nick said.
"I don't know," his father said. "But it is a heinous crime." [p. 490]

This is followed by one of the most delicious bits of humor in all of Hemingway:

Nick's imagination was both stirred and horrified by this and he thought of various animals but none seemed attractive or practical and that was the sum total of direct sexual knowledge bequeathed him by his father except on one other subject. One morning he read in the paper that Enrico Caruso had been arrested for mashing.
"What is mashing?"
"It is one of the most heinous of crimes," his father answered. Nick's imagination pictured the great tenor doing something strange, bizarre, and heinous with a potato masher to a beautiful lady who looked like the pictures of Anna Held on the inside of cigar boxes. He resolved, with considerable horror, that when he was old enough he would try mashing at least once. [pp. 490–91]

For the rest, Nick Adams' father had been no more enlightened than the average middle-class Victorian paterfamilias:

His father had summed up the whole matter by stating that masturbation produced blindness, insanity, and death, while a man who went with prostitutes would contract hideous venereal diseases and that the thing to do was to keep your hands off of people. [p. 491]

The conclusion, then, is an injunction against tenderness; the kindly gesture or touch can pave the way to hell. "On the other hand his father had the finest pair of eyes he had ever seen and Nick had loved him very much and for a long time" (p. 491).

These remembrances of things past bring pain, though; and how Nick meant to manage that pain he tells us briefly: "If he wrote it he could get rid of it. He had gotten rid of many things by writing them. But it was still too early for that" (p. 491).

Hemingway is, then, conscious of using his art as therapy. But apparently it was little help in handling his feelings about his father. This story is the last chapter on the education of Nick Adams which his creator has left us. Any reconciliation with the memory of his father was not to come for many, many years, and then it was in a form quite different from the Nick Adams stories. As to why this reconciliation is "still too early," we understand better when we follow Nick's reverie. His thoughts turn to his father's suicide:

He had complimented the undertaker. . . . But it was not the undertaker that had given him that last face. The undertaker had only made certain dashingly executed repairs of doubtful artistic merit. The face had been making itself and being made for a long time. It had modelled fast in the last three years. [p. 491]

These cryptic references are to the illness, financial bad luck, and despair of Hemingway, Sr., and to the shot that had ruined his face and ended his miseries—a tragedy the son will brood on with shame and guilt for long years.

The sad thoughts are interrupted by more pleasant ones, the reminiscence of Nick's sexual initiation, a matter we have earlier considered. As dusk falls, the recollections go back to Dr. Adams, and in a lovely paragraph his image is linked in Nick's mind with the beauties of nature. But the paragraph ends in a minor key: "The towns he lived in were not towns his father knew. After he was fifteen he had shared nothing with him" (p. 496). Just how father and son became alienated we are not told, except for one crisis which is both comical and morbid.

Nick tells us that his active father sweated much in hot weather, and, though Nick loved him, he hated the smell of him. On one occasion Nick was forced to wear a suit of his father's laundered underwear. Such was his revulsion against intimacy, against touch and smell, that "it made him feel sick" (p. 496). So, the boy hid the underwear and, when he returned from fishing, told his father he had lost it. Nick was whipped for lying. The punishment so insulted his soul that afterward he sat in the woodshed, watching his father on the porch of their cottage, Nick with his shotgun loaded and cocked, and thinking: "I can blow him to hell. I can kill him" (p. 496). The ancient Oedipal urge to kill the father scarcely needs further comment. But when it goes so far that the son actually has a readied murder weapon in his hand, we gain a little more insight as to why the father's suicide, as a fulfillment of an old obscure wish, might induce greater guilt than was normal.

What in Nick Adams' secret heart his father and mother meant to him we learn in "Now I Lay Me." That is the story toward which our extensive survey seems inevitably to lead us. Concentrated on the shock that resulted from Nick's—and his creator's—death-threatening wound at Fossalta, it affords us our most penetrating insight into the mind and heart of the Hemingway hero. As such, it is a key to most of these stories, and a not inconsiderable help in understanding the novels. In fact, Hemingway never wrote a more obviously psychological study, in the sense that we have here an explicit and rather elaborate search into the depths of a tormented psyche. And nowhere else has he provided so cogent an account of how a heart comes to be schooled less in love than in fearful fascination with destruction.

As we approach this story, we are at once confronted with a paradox. Though during his Paris years, especially through his friendship with Joyce, Hemingway probably heard talk of Freud and Jung, his contempt for modern depth psychology is well known.[20] On the other hand, whether or not Hemingway was ever consciously influenced by Freudianism or merely stumbled on it and intuitively made an artist's use of it, the amazing fact is that "Now I Lay Me" bears unmistakable analogies to what occurs in psychoanalysis. Without some awareness of Freud's therapeutic methods, the meanings of the story and even its structure must remain problematic indeed. For the inward

ramblings of the traumatized hero are set down—yes, with art
—but also in the manner of free association.

The title itself is our first clue. We are being reminded of the
child's prayer:

> Now I lay me down to sleep;
> I pray the Lord my soul to keep.
> If I should die before I wake,
> I pray the Lord my soul to take.

The longing is to return to the nursery, to the imagined security
of infancy—to regress. To the adult mind, the prayer also suggests the fear that death might come during the night's sleep.
Such connotations accrete around the title when we know that
Hemingway suffered from insomnia, as do several of his heroes.
The implications multiply when Nick tells us how he felt
when the mortar shell hit him. Here is Nick Adams' report—
and its very phrasing is close to the language Hemingway used
when he told a friend what it was like when he himself was
hit:[21]

I myself did not want to sleep because I had been living for a long
time with the knowledge that if I ever shut my eyes in the dark and
let myself go, my soul would go out of my body. I had been that
way for a long time, ever since I had been blown up at night and
felt it go out of me and go off and then come back. I tried never to
think about it, but it had started to go since, in the nights, just at
the moment of going off to sleep, and I could only stop it by a very
great effort. [p. 363]

These memories are entertained at night in a makeshift hospital behind the Italian lines. The first half of "Now I Lay Me"
is comprised of Nick's ruminations as he tries to stay awake and
yet not think back on the horror that shattered his nerves. The
rest of the story is chiefly dialogue between the insomniac lieutenant and John, his orderly. John, we may recall, is sure that if
only Nick would marry it would "fix up everything." And the
link between Nick's rejection of the idea of marriage and his

wounding is undeniable. The ruminations that follow his memory of the murderous explosion appear chaotic until we recognize that Nick is pouring out thoughts and images and memories in much the same way that a patient in analysis does. Nick's associations look chaotic, but they have their own emotional logic. And they point to half-forgotten events and old, deep-lying feelings which the surface ramblings disguise but do not totally conceal.

A patient in analysis might begin with an observation of some trivial external fact, say, a crack in the ceiling. Similarly, Nick first notices a sound, the sound made by the silkworms as all night long they gnaw on the nearby mulberry leaves. Those silkworms cause him to think back on other worms, on the time when as a boy he used worms as bait for fishing. Then come recollections and fantasies about fishing. These are precise, detailed, and elaborate. They serve two functions. Practically, they help Nick while away the hours of sleeplessness. Psychologically, they help to blot out, to screen away from awareness, the painful contents of Nick's psyche. The tenacity with which Nick clings to and expatiates upon these fantasies symptomatizes something compulsive:

Sometimes I would fish four or five different streams in the night; starting as near as I could get to their source and fishing them down stream. When I had finished too quickly and the time did not go, I would fish the stream over again. . . . Some nights too I made up streams, and some of them were very exciting, and it was like being awake and dreaming. Some of those streams I still remember and think that I have fished in them, and they are confused with streams I really know. [p. 364]

If, with this perspective, we glance back at "Big Two-Hearted River," we begin to understand the import fishing has in Hemingway's fiction and in his own life. Of course, it is therapy and escape, and yet not of the sort enjoyed by the Izaak Waltons of our acquaintance. We want to know what emotions are bound to this fishing. Nick Adams tells us.

"But some nights I could not fish, and on those nights I was cold awake" (pp. 364–65). Such impeding of the fishing fantasies is analogous to what the psychoanalyst calls "resistance." Ordinarily, "resistance" (the checking of the flow of words and recollections and associations) indicates that some unrevealed part of the psyche, though blocked by conflicting currents of feeling, is pushing toward consciousness. Then the struggle is with memories and feelings that lie deeper and are harder to dig up. So it is with Nick's halting recollections:

But some nights I could not fish, and on those nights I was cold-awake and said my prayers over and over and tried to pray for all the people I had ever known. That took up a great amount of time, for if you try to remember all the people you have ever known. . . . [pp. 364–65]

The praying does not directly help Nick, though it does afford him a link to stir still earlier memories. The free associations begin to flow again, and Nick tells us he is "going back to the earliest thing" he remembers. With him it is:

. . . the attic of the house where I was born and my mother and father's wedding-cake in a tin box hanging from one of the rafters, and, in the attic, jars of snakes and other specimens that my father had collected as a boy and preserved in alcohol, the alcohol sunken in the jars so that the backs of some of the snakes and specimens were exposed and had turned white—if you thought back that far, you remembered a great many people. [p. 365]

Of all the possible "earliest" things a boy might remember, these attic souvenirs are rather remarkable. Obviously, these memories are centered on the father and mother. To the Freudian, the images are unmistakable: the tin box symbolizes the female genitals—emphatically so when it contains the wedding-cake; the snakes symbolize the male organ—emphatically so, for a Caucasian, when their whiteness is recollected.

Try as he will, Nick can remember no further back than "to that attic in my grandfather's house. Then I would start there and remember this way again, until I reached the war" (p. 365). In other words, Nick's earliest memory is here directly related to the war, specifically, the war wound. It is the battlefield trauma which drives him into a self-analysis that takes him so far back into time and brings back a forgotten trauma of childhood. For, as Nick pushes further his *recherche du temps perdu,* we learn more about her who owned the tin box and about him who owned the whited snakes:

I remember, after my grandfather died we moved away from that house and to a new house designed and built by my mother. Many things that were not to be moved were burned in the back yard and I remember those jars from the attic being thrown in the fire, and how they popped in the heat and the fire flamed up from the alcohol. I remember the snakes burning in that fire in the back yard. But there were no people in that, only things. [p. 365]

There is fearsome fascination in this image of phallic snakes being destroyed in flames. Since there were "no people in that," and since Nick also tells us he "could not remember who burned the things," we infer that the memory is blocked because it is too painful. And yet we do learn that the destruction occurred in connection with moving to a new home and that in this affair the dominating figure was the mother. The next recollection that comes to Nick is of another similar burning and tells us plainly enough who was the destroyer:

About the new house I remember how my mother was always cleaning things out and making a good clearance. One time when my father was away on a hunting trip she made a good thorough cleaning out in the basement and burned everything that should not have been there. [pp. 365–66]

When Nick's father returned and saw the fire still burning, he was upset. Then carefully he raked out his prized Indian relics: "stone axes and stone skinning knives and tools for making arrow-heads and pieces of pottery and many arrow-heads." His only comment was, "The best arrow-heads went all to pieces" (p. 366). Some of these relics might be considered phallic symbols; all of them except the pottery are representative of masculine authority and prowess.

The immediate significance of these recollections is that Nick's mother is remembered as the destroyer. She destroyed possessions important to his father. In particular, when she burned the white snakes, she symbolically destroyed the male organ. Here, then, is the very image, the prototype, of Nick Adams' first "wound"—the child's fear of emasculation. This long-established and buried trauma has been revived with terrible power through the physical battle wound. That somehow this is the earliest memory, dredged up through so much pain, indicates that in Nick Adams the fear of castration is stronger than in most men. It is the mother who intensifies that fear.

So we begin to see that the formal unity of "Now I Lay Me" derives from an organic unity. It is not merely a two-part story whose first half records the insomniac rambling of a casualty and whose second half informs us that Nick Adams takes no hopeful view of marriage. In a very real emotional sense the same "wound" operates in both parts of the story: a wound that cripples the ability to love.

The Freudian view of "Now I Lay Me" affords an insight as to why Hemingway himself was so deeply and so long affected by his own wounding. With him, evidently, the emotional connections between his battle wound and his childhood fear of castration were more direct and stronger than with most men. In time the wound was to become essential to his personality as man and as artist. "Now I Lay Me" clarifies why wounding was to become an obsessive theme in Hemingway's writings, and why that wounding was so often eroticized.

The story also gives us other clues that bear on other persistent features in Hemingway's fiction. It is by fire that the mother destroys, symbolically, the male organ. It is also by fire that most of the Hemingway protagonists are wounded or destroyed. It is the woman, then, who is the threatening figure and must be guarded against. If the mother could so unman the father as she does here, so might a woman in a love affair emasculate her man. Thus, if a man cannot keep away from women, he does well at least to keep them in their place. In the Hemingway world, full of danger though it is, men are usually safer without women.

However pain-ridden and limited his view of men and women, in these stories Hemingway proved himself an artist of unquestionable power and originality. In form and technique he had developed a new kind of short story, and he had mastered a style absolutely his own and perfectly adapted to the effects he aimed at. He had also found the vehicle to express his own response to the terrors and tensions of the interwar years. For better or worse, it seemed, no short-story writer coming after him could escape the Hemingway influence. He also had accomplished all this in a brief span of years. His first appearance as a fictionist in his own country came in 1925 with *In Our Time*. Five years later he had won an international reputation not only as a short-story writer but also as a novelist.

Chapter II

The Defeat of Love:
Novels of the Twenties

The 1920's were Hemingway's best decade, for at least two reasons. Whatever his struggles in getting established, he was then most secure in himself and in his art. He had found his métier, and it was exactly right for him. Beyond the satisfactions of his own conscience, the proof was his popular success and the critics' acclaim. Second, this was his most prolific decade. Besides publishing nearly two thirds of all the short stories he was to write during his lifetime, he gave us two novels destined to become modern classics: *The Sun Also Rises* (1926) and *A Farewell to Arms* (1929). To these he added in 1926 a minor fiction, *The Torrents of Spring*. By the time he was thirty Hemingway was recognized on both sides of the Atlantic as an outstanding spokesman for his generation.

Of the historical and cultural import of these two novels—their general place in the history of letters, their sureness in capturing the malaise of an era—not much more needs to be said. It goes without saying, too, that each of them is a love story. If we come to them after being immersed in the short stories, our first impression is that Hemingway's treatment of the erotic is pretty much what we might expect; Eros seems always the companion of wounds or death. Yet the handling of

54

the love relationships in these novels reveals an intention quite distinct from that in the stories. The short-story writer had all but convinced us of the impossibility of love. The novelist tries to work his way toward an affirmation of love. In fact, Hemingway now develops a conception of love, of romantic love, which will regularly dominate his novels for more than twenty years. To trace that development in the early novels and to inquire whether his conception of love makes for a valid affirmation is the purpose of this chapter.

The first of these novels is *The Sun Also Rises*. But before that book appeared—in fact for relaxation between its first draft and the final version—Hemingway dashed off, in little more than a week, *The Torrents of Spring*. Though this is the least of his writings to appear between hard covers, it nonetheless belongs in the record—as much as *Shamela Andrews* does in Fielding's. For the author, its publication cleared the way to a lifelong alliance with Charles Scribner's Sons. More important, it also amounted to his public declaration of independence from the mentorship of Gertrude Stein and Sherwood Anderson. In form something like a novel, *The Torrents of Spring* is a parody of Anderson. In his *Memoirs* that writer described it as "a parodistic book which might have been humorous had Max Beerbohm condensed it to twelve pages." Hemingway was no Beerbohm, and time has pretty well substantiated Anderson's judgment. Though some reviewers found the book amusing— Allen Tate was one—it has had fewer readers than any of Hemingway's other fiction.[1] It is slapdash in manner, slapstick in its humor; zany is probably the best adjective for it. To readers with a taste for such clowning, an acquaintance with Anderson, and some recollections of the cultural currents of the 1920's, *The Torrents of Spring* will provide a sufficiency of belly laughs—and perhaps something more. For though this book is *sui generis,* it is typically Hemingway. It is also a ludicrous but in no way misleading curtain raiser for the love dramas in the novels to follow, even to 1950.

These torrents happen to be the springtime winds that blow in the Michigan of Hemingway's youth. They stir in his heroes —the tale supplies us with two protagonists—a vague, dumb Andersonian yearning toward Eros. The one hero is Scripps O'Neil, a Harvard man who has published a few stories. The other is an ex-doughboy named Yogi Johnson. Somehow these two meet as workers in a pump factory in Petoskey. Deserted by his wife, Scripps starts out for Chicago, but en route he falls in love with and marries the elderly waitress of Brown's Beanery. For all the charms of her English Lake Country background and for all her desperate expertise in literary gossip, Diana loses Scripps to a younger waitress, Mandy, who has a richer and readier store of literary anecdote. Yet Mandy herself pales before Scripps's dreams of the Indian woman who, one chilly night, presents herself naked in Brown's Beanery.

Upon Yogi Johnson, this squaw exerts a stronger pull. The spring wind worries Yogi because it does not make him want a woman—not the local librarian, nor a waitress, nor any of the high school girls. Wandering aimlessly about, he is joined by a couple of woods Indians. When they develop a thirst after a round of pool, the Indians lead Yogi to a private club, whose membership is exclusively town Indians. But when Yogi is discovered to be a white man, he is ejected at gunpoint, and the two woods Indians follow him—violently. They go to the Beanery. When the squaw enters—"She was clad only in a pair of worn moccasins. On her back was a papoose" (p. 77)—Yogi has his epiphany. At once his black thoughts vanish, he unburdens himself by recounting the love-disillusionment that has darkened his past, and he follows the squaw out into the cold night. As they stride along, Yogi throws off his garments one by one. Following the lovers come the two Indians, who retrieve Yogi's clothes and intend to sell them to the Salvation Army.

What makes the story hilarious is not the plot but the mad juxtapositions. For instance, when Red Dog conducts the visitors into the committee room of the Indian club, Yogi sees this:

On the walls were framed autographed photographs of Chief Bender, Francis Parkman, D. H. Lawrence, Chief Meyers, Stewart Edward White, Mary Austin, Jim Thorpe, General Custer, Glenn Warner, Mable Dodge, and a full-length oil painting of Henry Wadsworth Longfellow. [p. 69]

One of the best of Mandy's literary anecdotes informs us of how a great expatriate novelist received the Order of Merit:

"Professors Gosse and Saintsbury came with the man who brought the decoration. Henry James was lying on his deathbed, and his eyes were shut. There was a single candle on a table beside the bed. The nurse allowed them to come near the bed, and they put the ribbon of the decoration around James's neck, and the decoration lay on the sheet over Henry James's chest. Professors Gosse and Saintsbury leaned forward and smoothed the ribbon of the decoration. Henry James never opened his eyes. The nurse told them they all must go out of the room, and they all went out of the room. When they were all gone, Henry James spoke to the nurse. He never opened his eyes. 'Nurse,' Henry James said, 'put out the candle, nurse, and spare my blushes.' Those were the last words he ever spoke." [p. 51]

Surely, only pedantry would approach this book with a solemn face. Yet there is in *The Torrents of Spring* one passage which is deadly serious. Scorning Willa Cather's notions of war (in her *One of Ours*) and ridiculing Sherwood Anderson's sentimentality about it, Hemingway tells us what battlefield killing was really like:

Most of the men he had known had been excited as hell when they had first killed. The trouble was to keep them from killing too much. It was hard to get prisoners back to the people who wanted them for identification. . . . They would give the prisoner a poke in the seat of the pants with a bayonet, and when the prisoner jumped they would say, "You would run, you son of a bitch," and let their gun go off in the back of his head. They wanted to be sure they had killed. . . . All this sweetness and truth. Not if you were in there two years. [p. 62]

This passage is recognizably Hemingway, the writer on war. But it has nothing to do directly with the story and is quite out of harmony with its goofy tone and subject matter. It is as if Hemingway's grimness about war and killing cannot help breaking through even in this holiday book.

Another thing also breaks through here, though it is supposed to be part of the comedy. That is, Hemingway's preoccupation with wounds. The little Indian, one of the two redmen who are Yogi's companions—both are decorated heroes of World War I—is a quadruple amputee. We could laugh this off as in the tradition of some of Mark Twain's earlier, gorier clowning. But Hemingway fails to make it truly funny. When they play pool and Yogi compliments the little Indian on his skill, he replies, "Me not shoot so good since the war." Hemingway notes carefully that the artificial arms are of "brown leather and . . . both buckled on at the elbow." When the three companions climb a ladder as they make their way into the private club, we hear "the metal hinges of his artificial limbs squeaking." Inside, the Indians play pool again: "They had removed their coats, and the light above the pool-table glinted on the metal joints in the little woods Indian's artificial arms." When they are expelled from the club, Yogi "in the starlight, saw that he had lost one of his artificial arms" (pp. 65–70).

" 'Me no play pool no more,' the little Indian sobbed." Yogi tries to cheer him up: "I'll buy you a new arm" (p. 71). There is even a touch of bitterness in the treatment of wistful, mistful brotherhood: "All three of them striding on together. The arms of those that had arms linked through each other's arms. Red men and white men walking together" (p. 75). I count about eight references to amputation, as if Hemingway were obsessed with it.

It would seem that, even in a book like *The Torrents of Spring*, Hemingway cannot resist linking affection and love with wounds. For example, we learn near the end of the story that the naked squaw who means so much to the two heroes happens to be the squaw of the same little Indian amputee. Love maimed also figures crucially in the problems of Yogi. When he first lays eyes on the naked squaw, his black mood vanishes: "He had been on the verge of suicide. Self destruction. Killing himself. Here in this beanery. What a mistake that would have been. He knew now. . . . Let spring come. He was ready for it" (p. 78). Thereupon he tells his Indian companions what happened to him to poison the springs of his affections. When he was on leave in Paris, one day on the Boulevard Malesherbes a beautiful woman called him from a passing car. She took him to an ancient mansion, where "a very beautiful thing happened" to him. Then she dismissed him, telling him she could never see him again. But the lovelorn Yogi was desperate to find her once more. By accident he did. A Paris guide took him to "a real place." There through slits in a wall one could watch a sex show, performed by a young officer and a beautiful woman. Alas, Yogi recognized her as none other than "the lady whom I had been with when the beautiful thing happened to me." Looking at his plate of beans, Yogi explains that ever since then he has never wanted a woman. "How I have suffered I cannot tell. But I've suffered, boys, I've suffered. . . . Now I am cured . . ." (p. 79).

In the light of our American mythos it is plain that we have here a turning away from the corruptions of Europe to the innocence of a lost America, from the refined voluptuousness of Paris to the primitivism of the Western Wilderness. Yogi is cured of his trauma by running off into the woods with the naked squaw. Scripps, too, prefers her to the Old World cultivation of his waitress loves.

All this, to be sure, is uproarious. Yet if we are trying to penetrate Hemingway's state of mind at this point of his career —while he is at work on *The Sun Also Rises* and absorbed in the woes of the sexually maimed Jake Barnes—we can hardly help remarking how curious it is that Yogi's ludicrous tale of love disillusionment should hinge on a rather gross example of voyeurism commercialized. This is funny, yes. But it is not exactly Aristophanic that the source of the funny business lies in sexual pathology. Eros is sick here—as Eros had been sick, hurt, or destroyed in the short stories.

Granted, *The Torrents of Spring* is only a jest of a book. And yet, no matter how zany are its ingredients or how crazily they are juxtaposed, through all the clowning the pain is unmistakable. We have not only the preoccupation with wounds but also the linking of that preoccupation with the love life. These now look like two constants in the Hemingway universe, the wounded lover and the love that is denied him or lost. They are comically present in *The Torrents of Spring*; they are to be fused, painfully or tragically, in the careers of the Hemingway protagonists to come.

The first full-length portrait of the wounded lover is Jake Barnes, narrator of *The Sun Also Rises*. He is Nick Adams grown up, and he heads a list of heroes that includes Frederic Henry, Robert Jordan, Harry Morgan, and Colonel Cantwell. The dramatic conflicts in this novel all develop from a love affair which at the outset is "begotten by Despair upon Impossibility." For, whatever else we want to make of *The Sun Also Rises*, the central fact of the story is that the love between hero and heroine can never be consummated. Jake has been so injured in the war as to emerge physically incapable of sexual love.

He has been compared with T. S. Eliot's Fisher King in *The Wasteland*. Rightly, we have made much of Jake's "unreasonable wound" as a symbol of the frustration and sterility of those of his generation whose spirit had been shattered by the war. Jake's disability, we have come to feel, signifies that, in Hemingway's ruined world, love too has been destroyed. Such we might call the orthodox interpretation of this novel.[2]

But the treatment of the love life here is not quite such a simple matter as some of our clichés would persuade us. For one thing, Hemingway is less bent on recording the destruction of love than on debating whether love can possibly exist. In technique, in psychology, and in moral values, *The Sun Also Rises* provides a more penetrating and more comprehensive view of human nature than it has usually been credited with. That is, Hemingway has given us more complex characters and, with a steady hand, worked out among them more complicated love relationships than have been generally appreciated.

The least of these complexities is the heroine. In Brett Ashley, Hemingway has afforded us one of the only two women characters in all his fiction who are autonomous and fully developed —the other being Pilar of *For Whom the Bell Tolls*. Brett herself is an emotional casualty. Her first love had died of dysentery in the war. The husband she now seeks to divorce came back from the front a psychiatric case; he has threatened to kill Brett, and regularly sleeps with a loaded service revolver. Like Pilar, Brett has some masculinity in her character. Sometimes she calls herself a "chap," she has boyishly bobbed hair, and she affects mannish hats. Whether or not emancipated, she has broken with all nineteenth-century respectabilities. She drinks heavily and is frankly promiscuous. Uprooted by the war, Brett, like her expatriate companions, has no function, no place in life. With her, sex is forever cut off from enduring love. If she could form a lasting relationship, the only man for her would evidently be Jake Barnes. And their impossible love is summed up in this exchange:

> "Couldn't we live together, Brett? Couldn't we just live together?"
> "I don't think so. I'd just *tromper* [cheat on] you with everybody. You couldn't stand it."
> "I stand it now."
> "That would be different. It's my fault, Jake. It's the way I'm made." [p. 55]

We can hardly call this real love on Brett's part. True, she does confide in Jake, but she trusts her heart so completely to him because there can be no sexual entanglements with him. For all her promiscuity, Brett is as incomplete a woman as Jake is incomplete as a man. They are a fit pair: Brett too hurt in her emotions ever to love, Jake deprived of his maleness.

So she can make only trouble for the two men with whom she has affairs during the weeks covered by the narrative. Restless whim sends her off with Robert Cohn, who becomes so involved that he annoys everybody by hanging around like a lovesick schoolboy. "I hate his damned suffering," she tells Jake (p. 182). Cohn bothers her, really, because he takes love seriously. "You know I do know how he feels," she says. "He can't believe it didn't mean anything" (p. 181).

Her nerves raw from the jealousies of both Cohn and her sottish fiancé, Mike Campbell, Brett's next diversion is to fall for Romero. When she lays eyes on the young matador, she tells Jake she is "a goner." "I'm in love with him, I think" (p. 183). Jake's dissuasion has no effect on her nervous eroticism. The upshot is that she rids herself of Cohn—though not until he beats up the young Spaniard and then goes off in sheepish disgrace. Brett has her thrill running away to Madrid with Romero, and then she gives him up. At her call, Jake goes to her rescue. Brett explains why she has dismissed the nineteen-year-old Romero. "I'm thirty-four, you know. I'm not going to be one of these bitches that ruins children" (p. 243). Then, after a good cry and two martinis, she tells Jake: "You know it makes one feel rather good deciding not to be a bitch." However odd or twisted, Brett's sense of honor is still there. "It's sort of what we have instead of God," she adds (p. 245). Yet she must go on being destructive and self-destructive. She will return to Mike. "He's so damned nice and he's so awful. He's my sort of thing" (p. 243).

The witness and recorder of these sad and messy loves is Jake Barnes. His wound we are never allowed to forget. The exact nature of that injury Hemingway spelled out for us in an interview published in the Spring, 1958, issue of the *Paris Review*:

Who ever said Jake was "emasculated precisely as is the steer"? Actually he had been wounded in quite a different way and his testicles were intact and not damaged. Thus he was capable of all normal feelings as a *man* but incapable of consummating them. The important distinction is that his wound was physical and not psychological, and that he was not emasculated.

This looks plain enough. If Hemingway expects us to infer, though, that the physical hurt entailed no psychological wound, we can only be amazed at his naïveté. For, barring blindness, paralysis, or severe facial disfiguration, Jake's wound is perhaps the one most dreaded by men. No matter how stoic or brave, a man with such a disability must *feel* he is less of a man. Though an amputation like Jake's may not reduce the sex urge, it kills the most exquisite and primordial of pleasures, puts an end to the sharing with another the joys of physical union, and makes the satisfactions of parenthood forever impossible. In sum, common sense tells us that Jake Barnes could not possibly be in a normal state of mind about one of the fundamentals of human existence.

What is admirable about Jake is that he manages so well as he does, makes so little fuss, and is generally so fair-minded in his response to others and in his judgment of them. Nonetheless, when we have a man thus disabled tell a story about himself and his cronies and his loves and their loves, we must make allowances. No matter how good-hearted or disciplined, a man in Jake's plight cannot help feeling in his deeper heart resentment toward other human beings to whom sex is not impossible. Since we must see *The Sun Also Rises* through Jake's eyes, we need to adjust our own perspective. When he tries to tell us how it really was about the woman he loved and the men who are his rivals in that love, he is bound to give us something less than the gospel truth. Jake, in fact, is the most problematic of all the Hemingway narrators. Whatever Hemingway's intentions, Jake as chronicler is not wholly trustworthy.

But he is supremely persuasive. Such is Hemingway's art that Jake at once wins and holds our confidence and sympathy. We can be sure he is telling us how it really was when he describes Paris or the Spanish landscape, the fishing at Burguete, the festivities and the bullfighting at Pamplona. His very wound gives him a sort of despairing detachment so that we find him solid in his understanding of Brett. He is, however, far less reliable when he deals with his three rivals, Mike Campbell, Romero, and Robert Cohn. His responses, especially to Cohn and the matador, are colored by feelings of which Jake can hardly be sufficiently aware. He cannot help being inwardly hostile toward any other man who goes to bed with Brett. What can soften that hostility is Jake's recognition that the rival might also be in a bad way. Mike Campbell fits this category. Jake never much resents Mike, though Mike is to marry Brett. For Mike is the sort who does not really count. Since Mike's life is far more of a mess than Jake's, Jake can feel a secret contempt for him. He is only an alcoholic playboy, a parasite on his family's wealth.

The characterizations of Romero and Cohn are far more complicated for two reasons: first, Jake's feelings toward these two men are definitely mixed; and, second, Hemingway himself is expressing through these characters, and through Jake's reactions to them, his own internal debate over romantic love. We have only to glance ahead for a moment at the lover-heroes in the later novels to be reminded that throughout his career Hemingway was fascinated with, and in a way believed in, romantic love. What, then, is his present argument over such love?

In *The Sun Also Rises* our first reaction is that, if anyone is romantic about love, it is Robert Cohn. At first Hemingway seems to regard him—and to wish us to regard him—as an ass: a perfect example of shoddy ideals, false values, and clumsy manners. Cohn does not live by the code accepted by Jake's group. He does things that are "not done." He spoils the fun at

Pamplona by his insistent mooniness. He won't go away when Brett discourages him. He uses his fists in defense of his lady-love. After he beats up Romero, he wants, in prep-school fashion, to shake hands. Cohn makes the mistake, too, of letting his feelings show, of even allowing other persons to see him crying. In the generally accepted view, Cohn is the sentimental knight whose puny romantic pretensions send him off in the right sort of puppy-dog defeat.

By contrast, Romero is usually regarded as embodying an ideal of manhood. He is handsome, courageous, successful, and unspoiled. He has breath-taking skill in the bull ring; as a matador, "Romero had the old thing, the holding of his purity of line through the maximum of exposure . . ." (p. 168). Seen against the misfits and the ne'er-do-wells of the Paris cafés, Romero looms upward as a model of conduct, both morally and esthetically. He takes from the raging Cohn a terrific beating, not knowing how to box, yet never staying down. As a lover performing before Brett in the bull ring, he never once looked up to her: "He made it stronger that way, and did it for himself, too, as well as for her. Because he did not look up to ask if it pleased he did it all for himself inside, and it strengthened him, and yet he did it for her, too. But he did not do it for her at any loss to himself" (p. 216). The language, of course, is Jake's, who is watching Romero in the bull ring with the almost adoring eyes of a high-schooler cheering for his football hero. And the majority of readers have taken Jake at his word: that Romero embodies untarnished heroism.

But this response to *The Sun Also Rises* greatly oversimplifies and undervalues what Hemingway has done here. Cohn is not so black nor Romero so white as at our first acquaintance. To begin with—as Robert Stallman has pointed out—Romero in fact violates the code and the traditions of the young simon-pure matador.[3] He should stay with his own people and should not even speak English, let alone run off with a thirty-four-year-old Englishwoman. The *aficionado* Montoya is pained that Romero should be led, so young, toward corruption. Furthermore, if Cohn is romantic, Romero is even more so. To be sure, he is a simpler romantic, even an archaic one, because he is the creature of an old and tradition-bound culture. When he slays the bull for Brett and gives her the ear, he is behaving straight out of the chivalric tradition—like a knight in the lists for his lady.

Attractive as he makes Romero, Hemingway himself is scarcely so impressed by him as some commentators seem to be. Romero is not so great a matador as he appears in Jake's eyes. He has never undergone the matador's crucial test: to be severely gored and then to try to resume his career. Hemingway was to make much of this test in *Death in the Afternoon*. (In actual historical fact, Romero was modeled on the matador Niño de la Palma, whose great period came to an end after he suffered a series of bad wounds.[4]) Plainly, Jake idealizes Romero beyond what the young Spaniard deserves.

If Jake overvalues Romero, the other side of this admiration is his degradation of himself. Toward Romero, Jake feels altogether too inferior. He is even willing, for Romero and Brett, to punish himself. I refer to his pimping for Brett. Such a service is at once masochistic and sadistic. That deed intensifies Jake's erotic frustrations. It also tortures his conscience. In fact, Jake is so ashamed of having gone against the code of the *aficionado* that he cannot look Montoya in the face. Psychologically, this action is doubled-edged: if Jake hurts himself by it, he also manages, whether consciously or not, to strike back at his idol and rival. Jake leads the way toward getting a fine youngster into a mess. Whatever harm Cohn had done to Romero physically, Jake paves the way to doing even more harm to Romero spiritually.

The case of Robert Cohn is still more complicated. Explicitly, he is the most fully revealed character in the novel. Jake is more involved in him than in any of the other male figures, and his attitude toward Cohn is plainly mixed. In fact, the marvelous first two chapters contain not nearly so much satire as careful realism in disclosing the narrator's ambivalence toward Cohn. Outwardly Jake is less nasty to Cohn than Mike and Bill Gorton are. Almost never does he express the anti-Semitism shown by them and Brett. Jake is far more perceptive, more understanding, and more fair-minded toward Cohn than any of the rest are. Everyone recognizes that Cohn is an outsider; but so is Jake because of his wound. On this score there is a bond of sympathy between the two men. Yet Jake never defends Cohn against others' attacks.

Jake has excellent reasons to be jealous of Cohn. Cohn is reasonably attractive to women. He can and does go to bed with Brett. He can and does fight over her, even if foolishly; there could never be any point in Jake's fighting over any woman. Yes, Cohn is guilty of forcing situations, but at least he is capable of taking action. "I try and play it along and just not make trouble for people," Jake tells us in one of his insomniac ruminations (p. 31). Jake is so passive, in fact, that through the course of the narrative he does only three things: (1) expresses his love for Brett, mostly verbally, and serves as her confidant; (2) pimps for her; and (3) goes to Madrid when she asks him to rescue her.

What by no means simplifies this is that Hemingway seems so much identified with his narrator. Many of Hemingway's own attitudes, values, qualities, and experiences have been projected into Jake Barnes. In the conversations between Jake and Robert Cohn in those first two chapters, it is at least in part because we know Hemingway himself that we begin to take clues from the narrator. For instance, we know that Hemingway preferred being an expatriate, that he loved Paris and bullfighting and Africa; because Cohn does not care for these, we tally it up as four points against Cohn. We know Hemingway prided himself on being a connoisseur of wine and a good drinker; when we learn that a few drinks put Cohn to sleep, we score another point against him.

Still, this is in no sense the full account of Jake's reaction to

Robert Cohn—or of Hemingway's attitude toward Cohn. Cohn's capacity to disturb the other characters, and to disturb his creator, too, cannot be dismissed as merely an instance of gauche manners or a failure to shape his life by the "code." If there is much of Hemingway in the characterization of Jake Barnes, there is more than a little of him in Robert Cohn.

Cohn is not a mere loafer or playboy. To be sure, we cannot much respect him for the arty little magazine he finances because "he liked the authority of editing" more than the real thing (p. 5). But he has published a novel, and it is not exactly a disgrace that a writer's first novel does not amount to much. We sometimes wonder if Jake does not a little envy Cohn for having at least started novel writing. In fact, on one occasion Jake's pal, Bill Gorton, remarks to him: "And you claim you want to be a writer, too. You're only a newspaper man . . ." (p. 114). More significantly, Cohn is a pretty fair athlete, a good tennis player, and no sore loser. When Jake tells us Cohn had "a good body" and kept in shape, and when we know Jake respects Cohn as an amateur boxer, we can be pretty sure that Hemingway also approves.

About the most damning thing Jake can report about Cohn is the romanticism that made him read and reread W. H. Hudson's *The Purple Land*:

"The Purple Land" is a very sinister book if read too late in life. It recounts splendid imaginary amorous adventures of a perfect English gentleman in an intensely romantic land, the scenery of which is very well described. For a man to take it at thirty-four as a guidebook to what life holds is about as safe as it would be for a man of the same age to enter Wall Street direct from a French convent, equipped with a complete set of the more practical Alger books. [p. 9]

In its shy leery skepticism, its wariness about books, this passage is pure Hemingway. Of course it makes Cohn look like a bookish booby. Yet we catch in the phrasing overtones of pride in Jake's having outgrown such pubescent literary illusionism.

(And we wonder if Hemingway himself might not have been through the same kind of literary love affair as Cohn's?)

More to the point, Cohn is made ridiculous for falling so hard, so romantically, for Brett. Of Hemingway's own love life his friend Malcolm Cowley has told us:

He is romantic by nature and he falls in love like a big hemlock tree crashing down through the underbrush; also he has a puritanical streak that keeps him from being a cocktail-party flirt. When he falls in love he wants to get married, and stay married, and he regards the end of a marriage as a personal defeat.[5]

About Robert Cohn's previous love life Jake informs us that, after his lonely college years, his inferiority feelings caused him to be "married by the first girl who was nice to him" (p. 4). Then after four years Cohn "hardened into a rather unattractive mould under domestic unhappiness with a rich wife" (p. 4). Divorced and on the rebound, Cohn had next been captured by Frances Clyne, so forceful and possessive that "Cohn never had a chance of not being taken in hand" (p. 5). Though he is amused by Cohn's ineptitude with the women in his life, Jake is certainly not unsympathetic to Cohn as a victim of bitch-women. One of the most rasping scenes in the novel occurs when Jake listens to Frances' tongue-lashing of Cohn. (It compares favorably with Strindberg; and one sees what gifts Hemingway had for this sort of thing, had he ever chosen such subject matter.) Jake is astounded by Cohn's masochistic ability to absorb punishment.

The point is that Hemingway is both subtle and scrupulous in his characterization of Cohn. Early in the novel, Jake lays his cards on the table:

Somehow I feel I have not shown Robert Cohn clearly. . . . Externally he had been formed at Princeton. Internally he had been moulded by the two women who had trained him. He had a nice, boyish sort of cheerfulness that had never been trained out of him, and I probably have not brought it out. [p. 45]

In other words, might we not say that Cohn is the sort of boy-man, victimized by the American bitch, who earns his short happy life—later in the story about Francis Macomber?

As to Princeton, the important thing is the scars Cohn received there. About these Jake could not be more explicit. Cohn had been treated there as an outsider: "He was a nice boy, a friendly boy, and very shy, and it made him very bitter" (p. 4). In other words—and this has been the most common oversight of readers of *The Sun Also Rises*—Cohn, like the rest of Jake's friends, has been hurt, too. So, "painfully and thoroughly" he learned boxing—a sport he disliked—"to counteract the feeling of inferiority and shyness he had felt on being treated as a Jew at Princeton" (p. 3). He became a collegiate champion, was overmatched by his coach, and got his nose "permanently flattened."

Symbol searchers, one might note wryly, have paid too little attention to Robert Cohn's nose. For, like Jake, Cohn does not suffer only in spirit; he has a very specific physical wound, too: his broken nose. This accident, Jake informs us, gave Cohn "a certain satisfaction of some strange sort, and it certainly improved his nose" (p. 3). Jake's ambivalence is curiously focused on that nose. As a gentile, he might feel some distaste for the Jewish nose; but the break "improved" Cohn's looks. That is, Jake likes the hurt nose better. He feels more kindly to a fellow sufferer. And Hemingway himself was familiar with that "strange sort" of masochistic satisfaction one gets out of being hurt.

It is not at all certain that Hemingway intends us to regard Cohn as one of the lost and damned. Besides, there are at least two things to be said for Cohn, however he blunders and annoys people: first, though he may not have the most knowing principles and enlightened values, he never violates them—which is more than we can say of Jake and Romero; second, however bumbling as a lover, Cohn at least does not separate his sexuality from his heart. On the contrary, in some respects

Cohn appears to be a less rigid personality, possibly more capable of development, than Jake and his pals. To be sure, the drunken, wisecracking Harvey Stone tells Cohn to his face: "You're not a moron. You're only a case of arrested development" (p. 44). In a way this is true. Cohn does represent a kind of romanticism which most people lose sooner or later— perhaps sooner than Cohn. In hating Cohn, Jake is hating a part of himself, that part of himself which Hemingway, too, is embarrassed by and wishes to discard. On the other hand, Jake's idealization of Romero reveals Hemingway's search for a hero —the sort to which he will devote his informal treatise, *Death in the Afternoon.*

Between Romero and Cohn, Jake stands in loveless misery. His only happiness is the fishing holiday at Burguete. There no female shadow crosses the sunshine. There in jolly, joshing, masculine company the heart can take its ease. There the affection of male for male brings jokes but few blushes. Bill tells Jake:

"And you're a hell of a good guy. Anybody ever tell you you were a good guy?"

"I'm not a good guy."

"Listen. You're a hell of a good guy, and I'm fonder of you than anybody on earth. I couldn't tell you that in New York. It'd mean I was a faggot. That was what the Civil War was about. Abraham Lincoln was a faggot. He was in love with General Grant. . . ."

"Old Bill," I said.

"You bum!" [p. 116]

Those who wish to, might draw homoerotic inferences from the whole Burguete outing. My present point is somewhat different. That is, if Cohn is to be laughed at for his sentimentality over a woman, we are evidently supposed not to snicker but to be touched by the sentimental note on which this pastoral closes. A clubby Londoner, Harris, who has joined the companions, insists on treating them to drinks when the time for parting comes. Harris, who gets "a little tight," insists, repeatedly, "You don't know what this all means to me" (p. 129). When the Americans board their bus, Harris hands to each of them a farewell valentine—an envelope. "I opened mine, and there were a dozen flies in it. Harris had tied them himself. He tied all his own flies" (p. 130).

In creating the two opposing figures, Cohn and Romero, Hemingway as artist lays bare something of his own inner conflict. He wants to turn away from the Robert Cohns of this world. He prefers the Romeros. There is no question about which type is the more glamorous. But if, with Jake, we scorn the sort of lover Cohn is, Hemingway as a moralist is too honest to damn Cohn completely. He is also too knowing to offer us in Romero a satisfying model of heroic conduct. In sum, Hemingway has not yet found his way—not yet made up his mind about love and manliness.

For these reasons it is somewhat misleading to call *The Sun Also Rises* a parable on the death of love. True enough, in the postwar world as he sees it, Hemingway finds that love can scarcely exist. For Brett and Jake love is out of the question from the start. The relation between Brett and Mike Campbell is based on mutual tolerance of each other's destructive tendencies. What went on between Brett and Romero might be called infatuation or, less kindly, lust. Despite the illusions in it, the closest we come to love is Robert Cohn's feeling for Brett; and Hemingway almost—but not quite—wants us to despise that. To be sure, no one in *The Sun Also Rises* finds a satisfying and enduring love; but at least no one has been destroyed by its lack.

Evidently, Brett and Mike will go on, for a while anyway; Romero returns to the bull ring, presumably wiser for his experience; Robert Cohn might possibly have a chance to find love. Not every door to love is shut. There are questions still unanswered. None of the characters has found that life is not worth living. Even Jake, who has most reasons for despair, is far from wrecked. He may have given up his desire to figure out the world, but he has not given up the world. He tells us: "I did not care what it was all about. All I wanted to know was how to live in it. Maybe if you found out how to live in it you learned from that what it was all about" (p. 148). Jake Barnes as pragmatist has not yet resigned to despair; he is still asking questions.

Discouraging as *The Sun Also Rises* is in the matter of love, Hemingway is not yet ready to conduct the obsequies for Eros. On the contrary, his next novel will be his greatest effort to affirm the value of love. In fact, he referred to it as his *Romeo and Juliet*. In *A Farewell to Arms*, Hemingway went back in time to reassess his experience—to tell us how his hero was wounded and how he learned to love.

The most obvious connection between love and war here is that each makes for a part of the education of the hero. It is not war, however, which destroys Frederic Henry and his sweetheart. War is merely the situation in which their star-crossed love exists. The war serves as a gigantic metaphor of the indifference and cruelty of the universe. We might say that Hemingway is putting as a question what for Matthew Arnold was an assertion sixty years before: "Ah, love, let us be true to one another"; for the world is but "a darkling plain . . ./Where ignorant armies clash by night." In *A Farewell to Arms* Hemingway asks: is there any real value in lovers' being true to one another in such a world? Toward understanding Hemingway's answer, I suggest that we look closely at this love affair. To trace its development to its final destruction may lead us toward the center of Hemingway's vision of life.

Like most soldiers, Lieutenant Henry is familiar with the standard opiates for dulling the pangs and boredom of war: heavy drinking and raw sex. Yet in the officers' mess he is not quite at one with his fellows. They enjoy baiting their young chaplain, and they urge the lieutenant to spend his leave in the cities where "he should have fine girls" (p. 8). In the midst of the tipsy uproar the priest recommends that Lieutenant Henry

73

go instead to his home country, the Abruzzi. "There is good hunting," he adds. "You would like the people and though it is cold it is clear and dry" (p. 9). But that evening the lieutenant visits the officers' brothel, and on his leave he goes in for wine and women. Afterwards, he tries to explain to the chaplain— Lieutenant Henry is no Catholic but somehow it eases him to talk with a father confessor—"how we did not do the things we wanted to do; we never did such things" (p. 9).

When it comes to the love life, Frederic Henry swings between two extremes. On the one hand is his longing for the clear, cold and dry Abruzzi, a place traditionally renowned for the piety of its peasants. There, when the young men serenade they are forbidden to play the flute because, so we are informed, "it was bad for the girls to hear the flute at night" (p. 73). This touch of folk custom reminds us of Nick Adams' youth in the wilds of Michigan where sex could be simple and primitive. Later the priest says to Henry: "What you tell me about in the nights. That is not love. That is only passion and lust. When you love you wish to do things for. You wish to sacrifice for. You wish to serve" (p. 72). To the young American the chaplain represents one side of love. And it is interesting that through this teacher figure Hemingway links sexual purity with the satisfactions of hunting and killing animals.

On the other hand, we have brawling, drunken eroticism. Lieutenant Henry's best friend, the surgeon Rinaldi (who functions as the Mercutio of *A Farewell to Arms*), represents for him this view of love. Rinaldi is a sweet-tempered, good-hearted cynic, earthy and obscene, and a habitué of the bordello. For Frederic Henry neither Rinaldi nor the priest is enough as a guide. If Rinaldi lacks idealism, the priest has had no experience of women. Between these two extremes, the hero—creature of nineteenth-century, middle-class, American Protestantism— seems aware of no other course. Such has been Frederic Henry's education-in-love before he meets the English nurse, Catherine Barkley.

74

The account of how these two become lovers is convincing enough. Catherine's heart has already been hurt; her fiancé has been killed in the Somme and she blames herself for not having married him or at least slept with him. Love being an escape from grief, she falls in love with Frederic before he does with her. When she tells him she loves him, he lies to her that her love is returned. Yet Catherine is undeceived: "You don't have to pretend you love me," she tells him (p. 31).

A little later we follow Frederic's private thoughts about this new adventure. They are not so much dreams of love as sophomoric fantasies: he would take Catherine to a hotel in Milan where the boy coming up with *capri bianca* and a silver bucket full of ice would be asked to set his things down outside the door because the lovers would be naked, and "we would both love each other all night in the hot night in Milan. That was how it ought to be" (p. 38).

Not until after he is wounded and Catherine appears in his hospital room is Frederic able to report: "When I saw her, I was in love with her. Everything turned over inside of me" (p. 91). In a matter of minutes they are in bed together despite his wounded leg. When she leaves, he admits to himself: "God knows I had not wanted to fall in love with her. I had not wanted to fall in love with any one. But God knows I had . . ." (p. 93). Why, we might ask, had there been this reluctance to fall in love—with anybody? At any rate, it might be said that love comes to him only after the wound eases his conscience: this puritan libertine has paid the proper sacrifice now to enjoy love. In a way, his love promptly gets the blessing Frederic might want from another sort of father figure. The bouncing, laughing surgeon who is to operate on the lieutenant's shattered knee is appropriately named Dr. Valentini. He bubbles over when he sees Catherine and delights in their love affair.

The next episode, which describes the love-making of Catherine and Frederic the night before he undergoes surgery, is more revealing than perhaps Hemingway intended. Not only does the novelist's technique falter here; this chapter also intimates that the love may not be so splendid and true as the narrator-hero would have us think. Instead of trying to convey what lovers might feel toward each other, Hemingway, as is his usual practice, concentrates on certain external facts. But these do not comprise an objective correlative. As Isaac Rosenfeld has pointed out, the particular facts Hemingway chose this time communicate to his readers impressions and emotions which rather lessen the substance of the love-making. In the darkness of their room the couple are so aware of seeing lights and hearing sounds made by other human beings outside that their mood suggests that of the uneasy child taking comfort from knowing there are grown-ups around him. Then, too, the attention focused on the bat which enters and flies around the room can be taken as epitomizing castration anxiety, an anxiety physically centered on the wounded leg. (The old superstition is that bats get into the hair and can be removed only by cutting off the hair.) Besides, Catherine reassures and comforts Frederic less as a lover and mistress than as one who re-enters the room and brings food in the night—as a mother might to a wakeful child.[6]

Questions about this problematic love scene nag us for more obvious reasons. When Catherine asks Frederic about other girls—the professionals—he has slept with and wants to know if that sort of girl "says just what he wants her to," he replies, "Not always." Catherine responds: "But I will. I'll say just what you wish and I'll do what you wish and then you will never want any other girls, will you?" (p. 105). No doubt, love should make a woman want to serve and please her man. But in her amusing pathos Catherine is becoming the passively adoring creature who exists only in the narcissistic fantasies of the male. That there might be something seriously lacking in their love comes out as this chapter ends. "I want what you want. There isn't any me any more," Catherine declares (p. 106). Such a disvaluing by Catherine of her own self, such a need to flee the normal burdens of selfhood, indicates that her love is feverish in its dependency. Trying in this way to escape her own insecurities, she puts too great a burden on a love relationship.

In his different way her lover does the same. During his stay in the hospital he exploits their love to relieve the ennui of convalescence. Catherine takes on night duty "indefinitely"; that relieves the other nurses and allows her to be in Frederic's room often. But it takes their nurse-friend Ferguson to penetrate Frederic's selfishness. She points out that Catherine is really "getting very tired" and asks Frederic to "give her just a little rest" (p. 109). We begin to see the sadistic tendencies in him and the masochistic in Catherine.

"We had a lovely time that summer," the hero tells us (p. 112). (Indeed, how many wounded officers have ever had such a blessed hospital experience?) He adores her physical beauty, makes almost a fetish of her blonde hair. They think about getting married, but Henry's feelings are muddled: "I wanted us to be married really because I worried about having a child if I thought about it, but we pretended to ourselves we were married and did not worry much and I suppose I enjoyed not being married, really" (p. 115). It is interesting that the word "really" appears twice, each instance contradicting the sense of the other. In their discussion Catherine tells her lover: "There's no way to be married except by church or state. We are married privately. You see, darling, it would mean everything to me if I had any religion. But I haven't any religion. . . . You're my religion" (pp. 115–16). To make a religion out of such love is quite compelling in romance, though it may be a risky business in the world of actuality. And evidently to that world of actuality Hemingway intends to pay careful allegiance.

More questions about Catherine's self-abnegating religion of love are stirred as soon as Hemingway allows reality to penetrate this dream. The first important bit of reality to intrude is the natural result of love-making: pregnancy. Such true love as theirs, one would suppose, ought to have made these lovers able to trust each other. Instead, Catherine must now face Frederic in fear and anxiety. Not until she is a third of the way through her pregnancy, and then with great reluctance, does she inform her lover:

"I'm going to have a baby, darling. It's almost three months along. You're not worried, are you? Please, please don't. You mustn't worry."
"All right." [pp. 137–38]

The Hemingway cunning in dialogue is in full operation here. The rhythm, the very length of Catherine's speech, her repeated pleas to her lover not to worry, his brief "All right"—all these are clues enough as to what she must have read in his face. She goes on:

"Is it all right?"
"Of course."
"I did everything. I took everything but it didn't make any difference."
"I'm not worried." [p. 138]

And a moment later:

". . . But you mustn't mind, darling. I'll try and not make trouble for you. I know I've made trouble now. But haven't I been a good girl until now? You never knew it, did you?"
"No." [p. 138]

From any common-sense and manly point of view, Frederic is failing Catherine in this crisis. When she makes her big announcement and then confesses that she tried to induce a miscarriage, he makes practically no response. The lover-hero at this point reveals a startling lack of awareness, an unpleasing absorption in himself. Thereupon Catherine takes on herself all the blame for "making trouble"—and he allows her to do exactly that! Granting the certainty that a baby in their circumstances will create enormous difficulties, one would think that at least

78

the lovers might be drawn closer together at such a moment. Instead, we read:

We were quiet a while and did not talk. Catherine was sitting on the bed and I was looking at her but we did not touch each other. We were apart as when some one comes into a room and people are self-conscious. She put out her hand and took mine. [p. 138]

So it is Catherine, the one who must go through childbirth, who does the comforting. A depth of pathos—or of downright absurdity—is reached toward the end of the scene when both lovers concern themselves with whether the pregnancy makes *Frederic* feel trapped:

"You aren't angry are you, darling?"
"No."
"And you don't feel trapped?"
"Maybe a little. But not by you."
"I didn't mean by me. You mustn't be stupid. I meant trapped at all."
"You always feel trapped biologically."
" 'Always' isn't a pretty word."
"I'm sorry." [p. 139]

When he had been wounded, Lieutenant Henry had been brave and self-forgetful. But now he lacks some element of ordinary manhood. He has been given no mysterious foreknowledge that he will encounter tragedy. He knows only that he is facing fatherhood; and it scares him—too much. Then he brightens: "And I'm very brave when I've had a drink" (p. 140). Whereupon he downs a third of a glass full of cognac. The episode concludes with the expectant father having another such drink.

When Frederic returns to the front, the lovers' parting on that sad, rainy night leads us into further ambiguities. When they walk past a cathedral and Frederic suggests that they go in, Catherine does not want to enter. They feel like outcasts, maybe ill at ease that their love is not sanctioned by the church. They find shelter instead in a second-rate hotel, where Catherine is miserable. "I never felt like a whore before," she tells her lover (p. 152). After they have eaten they try to convince themselves that the room is "like our own home," but Catherine cannot quite talk herself into it: " 'Vice is a wonderful thing,' Catherine said. 'The people who go in for it seem to have good taste about it. The red plush is really fine. It's just the thing. And the mirrors are very attractive' " (p. 153). Frederic is troubled, too, and grateful to be drinking. For a moment they touch on the subject of their parents; each lover seems pleased that he will never have to meet the other's father. Then Catherine flees into her love-dream: "I don't take any interest in anything else any more. I'm so very happy married to you" (p. 154).

Returned to the front, Lieutenant Henry encounters the war weariness and gloom of his old comrades. Rinaldi has lost his zest. Working on so many casualties has made him a skillful surgeon. Yet now he can only operate; he no longer dares to think. At the officers' mess, to make it look like old times, Rinaldi tries to tease the chaplain: " 'That Saint Paul,' Rinaldi said. 'He was a rounder and a chaser and then when he was no longer hot he said it was no good. When he was finished he made the rules for us who are still hot . . .' " (p. 173). But Rinaldi, sensitive, humanitarian, no cynic at heart, is beginning to crack under the strain. When he gets drunk he blurts out what is really tormenting him: he believes he has syphilis. And this is the last we see of that lively and affectionate sinner. Has this Mercutio served his purpose by demonstrating to the hero that the wages of sin is death?

The chaplain, at any rate, seems to be enduring the war better than Rinaldi. To Lieutenant Henry, he appears "surer of himself now than when I had gone away" (pp. 177-78). The Italians have been losing; but as defeatism gains among the officers and soldiers, a new gentleness sways them. The priest sees this. Henry remarks wisely: "It is in defeat that we become Christian." Yet, if Rinaldi represents profane love and the chaplain divine love, Henry is not yet ready for the latter. For he adds: "But I don't believe in defeat" (pp. 178–79).

He soon learns all he needs to know about defeat when he is caught in the retreat of the Italians after they have been routed at Caporetto. What makes him decide to pull out of the conflict and make his "separate peace" is not the horror or in-humanity of war, but his face-to-face confrontation with its sheer unreason. In the chaos of the retreat—and what can be added to the praise already given to this part of *A Farewell to Arms?*—the panic-stricken Italians are shooting their own men. So, when Lieutenant Henry is held for interrogation by the *carabinièri* and battle police, he sees the reality:

I was obviously a German in Italian uniform. I saw how their minds worked; if they had minds and if they worked. They were all young men and they were saving their country. . . . We stood in the rain and were taken out one at a time to be questioned and shot. So far they had shot every one they had questioned. The questioners had that beautiful detachment and devotion to stern justice of men deal-ing in death without being in any danger of it. [pp. 224–25]

In the dark he manages to break from his captors and dive into the river. It is not an act of self-regarding desertion but an act of common sense. As he hides in a flatcar bound for Milan, Lieutenant Henry no longer feels any anger nor any obligation. It is not his show now. He wishes his old comrades luck, but expects never to see them again and will not trouble his brain with complicated thoughts. And so, with a clear, cool head the hero chooses to alienate himself from society. He has decided to make his journey from war to love—to love alone.

He rejoins Catherine in Stresa. Of the near-perfection of their love at this time, he tells us: "Often a man wishes to be alone and a girl wishes to be alone too and if they love each other they are jealous of that in each other, but I can truly say we never felt that." In the next sentence, though, we are tempted to reconsider such perfection: "We could feel alone when we were together, alone against the others" (p. 249). To be sure, the privacies of love should be sacred; and all lovers deserve, at least sometimes, to feel alone and *away* from "the others." But why, even in a threatening world, *"against* the others"?

Frederic Henry insists that when he and Catherine were together they were "never lonely and never afraid." But at the conclusion of this very paragraph about the lovers' unafraid togetherness, Hemingway, with egregious disregard for the logic of the situation, makes one of his most memorable and gloomiest pronouncements:

If people bring so much courage to this world the world has to kill them to break them, so of course it kills them. The world breaks every one and afterward many are strong at the broken places. But those that will not break it kills. It kills the very good and the very gentle and the very brave impartially. If you are none of these you can be sure it will kill you too but there will be no special hurry. [p. 249]

Soon enough we learn why gloom and anxiety mar their loving togetherness. It is not merely worry about having deserted. Catherine is aware of Frederic's deeper malaise:

"What's the matter, darling?"
"I don't know."
"I know. You haven't anything to do. All you have is me and I go away."
"That's true."
"I'm sorry, darling. I know it must be a dreadful feeling to have nothing at all suddenly."
"My life used to be full of everything," I said. "Now if you aren't with me I haven't a thing in the world. . . . I'm just so in love with you that there isn't anything else." [p. 257]

This is a strange love if the obverse side of it is, admittedly, nothing.

The empty feeling is a little mollified when Frederic talks

with the ninety-four-year-old Count Greffi, who has seen history and known love since the time of Metternich. Once again the young lover is, so to speak, turning to a father figure, looking for advice and consolation from someone he wants to believe is wiser than he. Momentarily Frederic seems reassured when the count tells him: "Then too you are in love. Do not forget that is a religious feeling" (p. 263).

What puts a temporary check on these anxieties and misgivings is the plunge into action and physical adventure. The lovers escape by night, fleeing in a rowboat across the stormy waters of Lake Maggiore to the safety of Switzerland. Chapters xxxvi and xxxvii are among the most enchanting of all Hemingway's fictions. Our hearts are won by the stuff of high romance—an escapade in which we willingly suspend all disbelief, our critical alertness conquered by the painstaking realism of the narration. Thus Hemingway transports us to the final and climactic section of his novel. Book Five might well be titled *Liebestod*.

Secure in Switzerland, with the comforts and conveniences of a well-ordered society, the lovers escape the war and the world's unreason. They achieve a *solitude à deux*—almost a universe for two alone. So begins their Alpine idyl.

Affectionately Hemingway describes the simplicity of their quarters, their way of living, and the serene beauties of the countryside. They settle in "a brown wooden house in the pine trees on the side of the mountain" (p. 289). They go for walks, read books and magazines, and are pleased with their landlady. "The war seemed as far away as the football games of someone else's college" (p. 291).

Worries spoil the idyl somewhat. Both lovers now regret that they did not marry, but Catherine says she would be too embarrassed to go through a wedding now so obviously pregnant. The other worry is that her physician says Catherine's hips are narrow and that she must eat carefully to keep the fetus small. Near Christmas the first big snow falls. The lovers' isolation—

83

their being thrown in upon each other so exclusively—begins to pall a little. Catherine thinks maybe Frederic ought to go away for a little while and be with other people—"so you won't be tired of me." He says no. Then playfully she suggests he grow a beard:

> "All right. I'll grow one. I'll start this minute. It's a good idea. It will give me something to do."
> "Are you worried because you haven't anything to do?"
> "No. I like it. I have a fine life. Don't you?" [p. 298]

The lovers are lying to each other, and now we hear more and more false notes. When Catherine remarks about Frederic's restlessness, he admits he sometimes does think about the front and the people he knew. Repeatedly, though, he insists he does not think "about anything much" (p. 298).

There is a sort of paradox here as to Hemingway's technique. Intentionally or not, he succeeds in conveying to us the malaise and emptiness and insincerities which are gnawing their way into the lovers' Eden. At the same time, he occasionally bumbles in the dialogue. For instance, when the question whether Rinaldi has syphilis comes up, we have this:

> ". . . Did you ever have anything like that?"
> "I had gonorrhea."
> "I don't want to hear about it. Was it very painful, darling?"
> "Very."
> "I wish I had it."
> "No you don't."
> "I do. I wish I'd had it to be like you. . . ." [p. 299]

When any woman, let alone a nurse like Catherine, says a thing like this, it is bathos, and we snicker. If Hemingway intends to show us how terribly in love Catherine is, he has failed. What he has revealed is a kind of desperate silliness.

> "I want us to be all mixed up. . . . Why, darling, I don't live at all when I'm not with you."

"I won't ever go away," I said. "I'm no good when you're not there. I haven't any life at all any more." [p. 300]

Already we hear the duet, the love-death song. For if one hasn't "any life at all," then one must have no-life: or death. The love Hemingway is celebrating is not the opposite of nothingness or the antagonist of death. It begins to look like the ally of nothingness and of death. So, for something to do—boredom, too, is a kind of death—Frederic will go on growing his beard; they will play chess; after that they will make love. When love-making must be used in desperation to escape ennui and worse, it can become compulsive.

We encounter now another paradox in the art of *A Farewell to Arms*. Often the deadest chapters are those that concern the life of love, and the livelier chapters are those that concern war or death. Anyhow, as the winter of Catherine's pregnancy wears on, their conversations wear thinner; the little jokes become flatter. "It was a fine country," we are told, "and every time that we went out it was fun" (p. 303). But there is nothing in these final chapters to make us feel any of the fun. Catherine remarks: "We live in a country where nothing makes any difference. Isn't it grand how we never see any one? You don't want to see people do you, darling?" She must know she is lying. When Frederic answers "No," he must know he is lying (p. 303). Their next exchange, a dismal one, is about becoming parents. Catherine asks, "She won't come between us, will she? The little brat." "No. We won't let her" (p. 304). Then more about the beard and more of Catherine's worry that her pregnant appearance makes her unattractive to him:

"Hell," I said, "I love you enough now. What do you want to do? Ruin me?"
"Yes, I want to ruin you."
"Good," I said, "that's what I want too." [p. 305]

Of course, it is just about inexcusable to pull a long face at little jokes about the erotic. Yet lovers' jokes can hide meanings.

In this context, "ruin" as a synonym for sexual love has connotations somewhat ominous.

By early spring come the first thaws and the rains. With the baby due in April, the lovers leave their retreat for Lausanne, where a hospital will be available. Only now does Catherine think of buying baby clothes and things—another indication of her anxieties about becoming a mother. Against her frequent fretting that she is no longer attractive, Frederic tries to reassure her, though he cannot help letting her know how "nice" his whisky is. The second-last chapter ends with this summary of contradictions: "When there was a good day we had a splendid time and we never had a bad time. We knew the baby was very close now and it gave us both a feeling as though something were hurrying us and we could not lose any time together" (p. 311).

From a strictly esthetic point of view, we can call this foreshadowing. If for the moment, though, we overlook what everybody knows is to be Catherine's fate, we are tempted to blurt out: Did any other writer ever make of pregnancy a matter of such relentless anxiety? We have indeed been informed of Catherine's narrow pelvis. But it is not so much a difficult delivery these parents dread as it is the mere fact of giving birth to new life at all.

The old romancers who spun out the Tristan and Isolde story had an advantage over Hemingway. They were unfettered by anything like modern realism. So, however much sleeping together Tristan and Isolde do, they are miraculously sterile. Yet those old romancers also understood, however dimly, that the consequences of such soaring love were somehow premature death. For all his outward realism, Hemingway, consciously or not, is reworking the Tristan and Isolde legend.[7] He has in effect pushed it to an extreme. He has given us a case of romantic love which is, so to speak, chemically pure. That is, he has isolated his lovers almost completely. They have not only pulled out of the Great War; they are also cut off from their own families and all friends, and during their six months in a snowy fairyland they have practically no contact with any other human being. They exist exclusively in and for their love. Catherine Barkley and Frederic Henry are not rebels against society; they have simply withdrawn from the world. They have no idea, purpose, plan; they never consider returning to the world to live in it in any role. They are not trying to learn or understand or grow. To cut oneself off from life in this way—or to keep only such a tenuous connection with life—means to drift toward not-life.

It is a nice question to ask at precisely what point these lovers began to die of their love. It was not when Lieutenant Henry escaped by diving into the river. But, as we have traced the consequences of his "separate peace," we see it turn into a flight into an almost absolute solitude, where two people live and love for themselves alone. Each can gaze only into the other's eyes. Each finds there the beloved reflection of his own self-image. When they look elsewhere, it is all nothing, *nada*. When they look at each other, it is narcissism twinned—and thus self-defeating. As to the logic of the emotions, the love affair of Catherine and Frederic was bound to end in sterility or premature death. Thus the rightness of Hemingway's conclusion: that Catherine dies, and the baby is born dead.[8]

With no loss of tragic qualities, however, Catherine might have died in any number of ways. But Hemingway chose childbirth, the natural result of loving and love-making. Somehow, in his anguished reading of the human situation, love must punish itself. He sees in sexual love only brief joys; the seeds it sows are not of new life but of death. However lyrical is the affair in this novel, the love impulses in it are fettered by sadism and death wishes.

Esthetically, however, this mixture of negatives is fortunate. Hemingway's art subdues and makes a tragic harmony out of these discords. In his final chapter, where Catherine dies in childbirth, we have the most powerful and the most successful part of the novel. Hemingway is fascinated by love; but what really grips his emotions and what he really understands is dying. And what most inspires him is the death of love.

Doubtless certain external events colored Hemingway's mood during the composition of *A Farewell to Arms*. He has told us that while he was writing it his second son was delivered by Caesarean section, and that during the rewriting his own father committed suicide. Yet these facts hardly explain why *A Farewell to Arms* is his blackest, most despairing novel. What gives this book its peculiar, almost unbearable darkness, is not so much our awareness of a God-abandoned universe as it is that in such a universe the only view of love which Hemingway can realize is a fearsomely limited kind. The gloom and despair come from his excessively bleak view of human sexual love.

For instance, when at the hospital Frederic worries during Catherine's labor, he utters the same word he used when Catherine first announced her pregnancy: "trap." Even before anything has been said about a Caesarean operation, Frederic is already sure:

> Poor, poor dear Cat. And this was the price you paid for sleeping together. This was the end of the trap. This was what people got for loving each other. . . . So now they got her in the end. . . . But what if she should die? She can't die. . . . What reason is there for her to die? There's just a child that has to be born, the by-product of good nights in Milan. [p. 320]

Such torment and dread and guilt ring true. Yet to call the baby merely the "by-product" of love-making betrays a little why Frederic thinks of love as a trap.

Catherine of course does die, of an accident: the narrow pelvis, the Caesarean, the hemorrhage. Her tragedy, though, in no sense necessarily develops out of the love-in-wartime predicament. She dies, it would seem, to dramatize Hemingway's theme —or rather to put the question this story raises: what values are there in a love experience?

As to Catherine, she has gained at least some wisdom out of it. She dies bravely, calmly, unselfishly, with no sourness. When she knows she is going to die, she tells her lover:

"You won't do our things with another girl, or say the same things, will you?"
"Never."
"I want you to have girls, though."
"I don't want them." [p. 331]

And later: "Don't worry, darling," Catherine said. "I'm not a bit afraid. It's just a dirty trick" (p. 331). She is able to die in such a spirit because she has risked more and given more to love than Frederic has. Here at the end, at least, she has gone beyond self-concern.

By comparison, what does Frederic learn from his experiences of love—and of war? He has learned that both of these alienate and destroy. He found in love passing pleasures and transient ecstasies. In the times between love's high moments, he knew only a restless, boring emptiness. His reflections at the novel's end indicate that he regrets having loved. When he learns that the baby has been born dead, his thoughts take these turns: "Now Catherine would die. That was what you did. You died. You did not know what it was about. You never had time to learn. They threw you in and told you the rules and the first time they caught you off base they killed you" (p. 327). These lines catch perfectly the agony he would feel at such a moment. Yet they do more than cry out against the heartlessness of the world. They also rage against some power in nature which allows, even drives, men to destroy. That power, in Frederic Henry's experience, appears to be Eros. Still, most people have usually regarded love as a force in nature and in human nature that can oppose hate and destruction and be at least a temporary stay against, and possibly a consolation for, death. Then why are we given here a lover-hero who is so totally pessimistic about love?

Because Frederic Henry wants to be sure of something, needs a kind of absolute security not possible through human love. To love is to risk: to take a chance on having—and on losing. If one sees the universe as predominantly evil and ever threatening—in the words of the old prayer, a place of "mourning and weeping in this valley of tears"—then it may be best to renounce the world and try to live, as might the rigorously orthodox Christian or the mystic, for that better world of heaven and eternity. T. S. Eliot took this step. Hemingway does not. For Eliot, any human love relationship which is not based on the supernatural is an impossibility built on sand: you cannot love another human being unless you love God first of all. Hence Eliot has no pragmatic approach to love, no interest in human love as a discipline or an experience out of which could come insight or growth in spirituality. With Hemingway in this novel it is about the same. Through his love the hero is battered but in no sense disciplined, takes not one step further toward wisdom. Having loved Catherine, Frederic Henry "placed himself in a position to lose"; having lost her, he lost everything; and *nada* will conquer more and more of his life. He has given up Jake Barnes's quest: to learn "how to live in it."

But the hero of *A Farewell to Arms* emerges with such a hopeless view of love because he has never learned how to love. He has had a strangely limited experience of love. That is because his creator holds to a very romanticized and inadequate conception of it. Hemingway has loaded the dice against Eros. His hero's love is the sort that never allows him to get beyond his own self; so it is narcissistic and ultimately self-destroying. Unlike the great masters, Hemingway fails to show us how love operates in the actual world. After all, his story of Frederic Henry and Catherine Barkley is a picture of love on a holiday—a holiday that ends in a tragic accident.

If the hero has learned that one cannot count on love, there are left only two things one can count on: faith in God, or death. Plainly, this novel ends with no hint about a faith in

God. Rather, the drift is toward death. At this juncture in Hemingway's career, it seems quite logical that his next book should be *Death in the Afternoon*. Craving certitude, finding in Eros only the proof of nihilism, what is left for Hemingway now but to make of Death the only true god in his pantheon?

Chapter III

The Triumph of Death:
Writings of the Depression Years

In the 1920's Hemingway met with uncommon triumph; in his next period he flirts with disaster. Both of these impostors come to be a trial to his peace of mind and to his art. Virtually in mid-career, he seems now to lose his way. The grim finale of *A Farewell to Arms* presages his entry into years of confusion and uncertainties. The world of course changed with the advent of the Great Depression, and fame was evidently changing Hemingway. At any rate, throughout the 1930's he is not so productive as he had been, and little of what he does publish compares in excellence with the earlier work.

His last book of stories appeared in 1933; and though in *Winner Take Nothing* there is no diminution of his powers—in fact it includes three or four of his finer short fictions—there is no appreciable progress beyond the mastery he had won in the 1920's. The year before, came *Death in the Afternoon*, his study of bullfighting; and in 1935, his account of a safari, *Green Hills of Africa*. These two are the only nonfiction books to come out during his lifetime.

Both of them had a mixed critical reception. In fact, now that so many of his fellow expatriates were returning to their troubled homeland, it was not exclusively critics of the Left who wondered why Hemingway showed so little social consciousness. Another complaint was the emergence into his writings of the well-publicized Hemingway, that creature of the "legend," whom Edmund Wilson called "the worst invented character to be found in the author's work." [1] Whatever might be impeding his creation of fiction, at this point of his career Hemingway evidently felt the need to explain himself. That meant public self-questioning and, too often, self-justification. The malaise is laid bare in his extremism. The controlled lyricism now gives way to sensationalism. And, having come to distrust all values, he becomes ever more obsessed with death. Desperate in his nihilism, he searches for a kind of absolute heroism as a way out. For Hemingway, the quest takes the form of a neurotic concern with integrity and a sometimes ludicrous anxiety over virility. For these reasons, *Death in the Afternoon,* whatever our reservations about it, is an indispensable book for anyone who wants to understand Hemingway the man, the moralist, and the fictionist. Here, most plainly, we see him make the passage from his victories of the twenties into the bafflements and defeats of his most problematic decade.

Ostensibly about bullfighting, *Death in the Afternoon* is in reality a work of many facets. In it the writer pushes further his meditations on the certainty of death and on the possibility of heroism. The subject also afforded Hemingway, always so chary of the self-deceiving pedantries of the intellect, a means of discoursing on the principles and practices of his own art in the jargon and images of the bull ring. The result is one of the most curious books in the history of American letters and perhaps one of the most revealing.

How he happened to write *Death in the Afternoon,* Hemingway tells us in his opening pages. Although familiarity has dulled our response, to quote this passage again seems justified in hope of a fresh scrutiny. In these paragraphs we learn something about Hemingway's apprenticeship, how his aim in writing was to know "what you really felt" and to set down "the actual

things . . . which produced the emotion that you experienced."
Since the wars were over, he adds, "the only place where you
could see life and death" was in the Spanish bull rings.

I was trying to learn to write, commencing with the simplest things,
and one of the simplest things of all and the most fundamental is
violent death . . . and if these very simple things were to be made
permanent, as say, Goya tried to make them in *Los Desastros de la
Guerra,* it could not be done with any shutting of the eyes. . . . I
had never been able to study them as a man might, for instance,
study the death of his father or the hanging of some one. . . . [pp.
2–3]

Certain things are noteworthy here. We are told that for one
who wants to learn to write, "violent death" is the best subject
because it is the "simplest" and "most fundamental." This prescription is even more specialized than Poe's notion that the
most poetic of subjects is the death of a beautiful woman. One
might suppose that to depict a man eating or carrying a load
of wood could be still simpler for the novice and no less fundamental. But the spectacle of violent death is specified as the
means to get at one's real feelings. It is also interesting that
Hemingway wants to watch and describe such deaths without
"any shutting of the eyes," as one might "study the death of his
father or the hanging of someone." This sequence of images and
comparisons looks casual, but their close association indicates that
in Hemingway's heart they are all linked—and saturated with
both pain and pleasure. For he adds that, though he found death
in the bull ring by no means simple, he liked what he saw
there and got from it "the feeling of life and death I was working for" (p. 3).

Among other statements about his art is a passage in response
to Aldous Huxley's charge that Hemingway appeared bashful
about any frank expression of delight in culture. Though Hemingway does not take up the larger question of his seeming anti-
intellectualism, he does set forth his aims as a novelist. For one
thing, he will never, to please his "egotism," spoil a piece by

any trope or phrase that is not functional. As to style: "Prose is architecture, not interior decoration." For another thing, he will eschew "characters," which for him means caricatures. Rather, he tries to "create living people." If he can make them live, "it is possible that his book will remain as a whole; as an entity; as a novel." His ideal Hemingway puts in these terms: "People in a novel, not skillfully constructed *characters*, must be projected from the writer's assimilated experience, from his knowledge, from his head, from his heart and from all there is of him" (p. 191). In the short stories our interest is naturally not in Hemingway's personalities but in the emotions generated by their situation. As to his novels, though, he has provided us here with a standard for measuring their success or failure.

A more inclusive principle for judging art and artists emerges when, in comparing Spain's three greatest painters, Hemingway declares: "You can only judge a painter by the way he paints the things he believes in or cares for and the things he hates . . ." (p. 203). "Velasquez," he says, "believed in painting in costume, in dogs, in dwarfs, and in painting again" (pp. 204–5). But it is Goya who grips Hemingway. Behind his appreciation is no doubt Hemingway's knowledge of that painter's tempestuous career:

Goya did not believe in costume but he did believe in blacks and in grays, in dust and in light, in high places rising from the plains, in the country around Madrid, in movement, in his own cojones, in painting, in etching, and in what he had seen, felt, touched, handled, smelled, enjoyed, drunk, mounted, suffered, spewed up, lain-with, suspected, observed, loved, hated, lusted, feared, detested, admired, loathed, and destroyed. [p. 205]

Hard living, sensuously experiencing, bodily adventuring, lusting and loathing, violence—this stuff of the Goya legend sums up the kind of artist's life Hemingway can wholly respect. What he admires about Goya is that he was physically daring and, for one dedicated to art, reassuringly hard in his maleness. When it comes to El Greco, Hemingway grants him the honors he merits; then assigns him his proper place in Purgatory. Admittedly, El Greco believed in Toledo and in some of its citizens, and in "blues, greys, greens and yellows, in reds, in the holy ghost, in the communion and fellowship of saints, in painting, in life after death and death after life and in fairies." What Hemingway takes to be homosexual features in El Greco's canvases leads him into this pulpit thumping:

If he was one he should redeem, for the tribe, the prissy exhibitionistic, aunt-like, withered old maid moral arrogance of a Gide; the lazy, conceited debauchery of a Wilde who betrayed a generation; the nasty, sentimental pawing of humanity of a Whitman and all the mincing gentry. [p. 205]

That a homosexual might conceivably have his own brand of courage and that in the arts he might, with genius, triumph and endure—such a possibility Hemingway can contemplate only with deep malaise. His last hurrah for such unfortunates is "Viva El Greco El Rey de los Maricones." (*Maricon* denotes both coward and homosexual.)

Plainly, the Hemingway logic goes this way: a great artist can be effeminate; as such he must be cowardly; hence his works are suspect; therefore greatness in art is no proof of manhood. For among great artists, the guaranteed masculine heroism of a Goya is all too rare. Where do we find the indubitably male hero? Only in the great matadors.

That Hemingway thrilled to the heroism of the bullfighter we know from his story "The Undefeated" and from Jake Barnes's idealized portrait of Romero in *The Sun Also Rises*. Like the soldier under fire, the matador always faces the probability of serious wounding or death. He needs all the physical courage of the man on the battlefield plus all the skill and coordination of the champion athlete, for he often undergoes harder tests of courage, skill, and honor. If he goes through his ordeal with grace and skill and integrity, his mere conduct, even though he may be hurt or killed, saves something of truth and goodness and beauty. Out of the common doom—that we all must die—the matador, in Hemingway's view, wins something that is denied even to true lovers. The moment of his greatest danger is, usually, the moment he goes in for the kill. Through tricks which go undetected by the majority of his public, the matador can kill in relative safety. Only when his integrity makes him scorn such cheats can he, at greater risk to himself, kill the bull properly.

For Hemingway the supreme exemplar here is Manuel Garcia, Maera, whose valor was "absolute." In his last year of fighting Maera knew he was dying of tuberculosis. Though during that year he was twice badly gored, each time he fought immediately afterward, his fresh wounds still bandaged. "He was a long way beyond pain," we are told. His most amazing feat—the fictional version is "The Undefeated"—occurred when, in stabbing his bull, he hit one of the animal's vertebrae and so dislocated his wrist, the wrist so indispensable in the work of cape, muleta, and sword. Five more times, with that nearly useless wrist, he stabbed and hit bone. When urged to go to the infirmary, " 'Let me alone,' " he said, " 'and go f⎯⎯k yourselves' " (p. 81). On the sixth try he got the sword in. Maera was a man after Hemingway's own heart:

I thought that year he hoped for death in the ring but he would not cheat by looking for it. . . . Era muy hombre. . . . He was generous, humorous, proud, bitter, foul-mouthed and a great drinker. He neither sucked after intellectuals nor married money. . . . He knew he had tuberculosis and took absolutely no care of himself; having no fear of death he preferred to burn out, not as an act of bravado, but from choice. [pp. 82–83]

Such courage stirs the heart—and so does the masochism. Note also the gratuitous compliment paid Maera for avoiding two equated evils: intellectuals and marrying wealth.

As to the many different kinds of courage, Hemingway informs us that the common element is the ability to ignore, if not despise, the consequences. *Death in the Afternoon* provides a generous catalogue of the consequences—accounts of gorings and sufferings and dyings full enough to satisfy any curiosity and sear any nervous system. Sooner or later all matadors are severely gored—a necessary test and more important than the test of wounding for the soldier. For after a bad goring (*cornada*), the matador may be too fearful to perform at all. Or he may become braver. Or he may still have all his courage and yet, "by his nerves, be unable to face that danger coldly" (p. 167). Imagination, especially when it has been fostered by a *cornada*, can undermine the matador's cool courage; and imagination frequently goes with intelligence. So we have another reason for the supremacy of Maera: ". . . of the naturally brave ones, he was most intelligent" (p. 94).

We may now begin to see what exceptional values Hemingway finds in bullfighting. Those of us who are neither Latins nor *aficionados* have erroneously supposed that bullfighting is a gory, sensational spectator sport, its origins reaching back to the gladiatorial shows of the ancient Cretans. Hemingway teaches us that bullfighting is not a sport but an art—a genuine art! "But it is an impermanent art as singing and the dance are, one of those that Leonardo advised men to avoid. . . . If it were permanent it could be one of the major arts . . ." (p. 99). So, for Hemingway, the matador is not like the trapeze performer, an athlete skilled in a dangerous specialty; he is an artist. And the great bullfighter he labels an artistic "genius."

Such is the beauty of this art that Hemingway asserts: "I know no modern sculpture, except Brancusi's, that is in any way the equal of the sculpture of the modern bullfight" (p. 99). So he lauds the loveliness of the cape work and the terpsichorean grace of the matador's motions. It is all an ordered art; for the bullfighter has to know its rules, rules ritualized through long tradition and experience, and know exactly how to apply them, which is technique. The highest perfection of this art is in killing the right way: ". . . the beauty of the moment of killing is that flash when man and bull form one figure as the sword goes all the way in, the man leaning after it, death uniting the two figures in the emotional, aesthetic, and artistic climax of the fight" (p. 247).

When Hemingway sketches for us the more recent evolution of bullfighting, he might be sketching the history of any other art. We learn, for instance, that in the old days, when the bulls were usually bigger, the emphasis was on the form of the killing, "the final sword thrust, the actual encounter between the man and the animal, what the Spanish call the moment of truth . . ." (p. 68). The emphasis has shifted, so that now the matador must "try to pass the points of the horn as mathematically close to his body as possible without moving his feet" (p. 68). Smaller bulls have made this sort of bullfighting possible— and also decadent. "It is a decadent art in every way and like most decadent things it reaches its fullest flower at its rottenest point, which is the present" (p. 68). What Hemingway means by the decadence of bullfighting is "the decay of a complete art through a magnification of certain of its aspects" (p. 70). He also labels it "this malady of specialization."

The critics of bullfighting, too, can do as much mischief as critics in other arts. And if it comes before the matador has truly proved himself, too much publicity, whether harsh or overindulgent, can mar if not wreck a matador's career. To flourish, bullfighting needs the right sort of public and the right sort of critical attitude toward that art. The genuine *aficionado* is as indispensable to bullfighters as are *cognoscenti* to other artists.

It is interesting to see how many connections Hemingway can draw between bullfighting and the arts. What is fascinating, though, is how badly the arts begin to fare in the comparison:

Bullfighting is the only art in which the artist is in danger of death and in which the degree of brilliance in the performance is left to the fighter's honor. In Spain, honor is a very real thing. Called pundonor, it means honor, probity, courage, self-respect and pride in one word. [p. 91]

By implication no other art can be so honorable. The artist is less than the bullfighter, for this reason: his blunders and failures do not bring him pain or death, may well go undetected by most critics, and may even bring to the second-rater nice rewards.

For all his devotion to writing, Hemingway seems seldom to have been content with being an artist. Somehow his deepest impulses were not enough stirred or satisfied by the practice of his art. Carlyle's insight that there can be no great artist without a heroic soul was beyond him. Only that which demanded physical courage could win and hold Hemingway's respect. By heroism he means the bravery which risks bodily pain and death. Since the practice of art does not make this immediate demand, it is, in Hemingway's view, neither heroic nor fully manly. In fact, a virile fellow might even be ashamed of his dedication to art. That Hemingway felt such shame we have a hint as far back as *The Sun Also Rises*. In an episode where Jake Barnes and his friends are doing "a lot of drunken talking" (p. 175), we encounter this bit of dialogue: "Tell him [Romero] I think writing is lousy," Bill said. "Go on, tell him. Tell him I'm ashamed of being a writer" (p. 175). This may not be exclusively a stroke of fiction. Its bearing on the oddness of Hemingway's own self-appraisal is indicated when his friend Morley Callaghan quotes him on a related subject: "But my writing is nothing. My boxing is everything!" [2] At any rate, in his need to find an artist-as-hero, Hemingway will seek only among the great matadors.

All this we might smile away as harmless enough. It looks like the problem of, say, any American high-school boy who enjoys contributing to the school magazine but all the while is disappointed with himself because he knows the real heroes are those manly chaps getting bruised out there on the football field. It is easy enough to remark here that Hemingway, like Scott Fitzgerald, never outgrew the wish to be a star on the playing field. In *Death in the Afternoon*, however, the mature Hemingway carries this puerility to some startling extremes. For in this book he tries to convince us that the bullfight, in both its esthetic and its ethic, is nothing less than a tragedy.

The question is not about the parallels Hemingway draws between the ritualized drama of the bullfight and the tragic drama. These he makes persuasive enough in matters of structure and style.[3] The question is, rather, why Hemingway claims for the emotions of the bullfight such ethical, even spiritual, significance. For when an *aficionado* sees a great matador perform, we are told he participates in something "that takes a man out of himself and makes him feel immortal while it is proceeding, that gives him an ecstasy, that is, while momentary, as profound as any religious ecstasy . . ." (p. 206). Into the mysteries of this "religious ecstasy" Hemingway probes further:

Now the essence of the greatest emotional appeal of bullfighting is the feeling of immortality that the bullfighter feels in the middle of a great faena [total performance] and that he gives to the spectators. He is performing a work of art and he is playing with death, bringing it closer, closer, closer, to himself. . . . He gives the feeling of his immortality, and, as you watch it, it becomes yours. Then when it belongs to both of you, he proves it with the sword. [p. 213]

One would suppose that in responding to, or surely in creating, a great work of art, one might possibly have similar, even better, intimations of immortality. For Hemingway, though, the surest way to these intimations is through watching a great matador kill bulls.[4] And his explanation as to just why such a bullfighter can attain an "immortality" which both he and his spectators feel "belongs" to them is wondrous indeed. It is not a matter of desperate artistry with cape and muleta. It is in the manner of killing:

A great killer must love to kill; unless he feels it is the best thing he can do, unless he is conscious of its dignity and feels that it is its own reward, he will be incapable of the abnegation that is necessary in real killing. The truly great killer must have a sense of honor and a sense of glory far beyond that of the ordinary bullfighter. . . . Also he must take pleasure in it, not simply as a trick of wrist, eye,

and managing of his left hand that he does better than other men
. . . but he must have a spiritual enjoyment of the moment of
killing. [p. 232]

What we are to make of this spiritual revelation Hemingway
tells in plain enough language: "Killing cleanly and in a way
which gives you aesthetic pleasure and pride has always been
one of the greatest enjoyments of a part of the human race" (p.
232). No one can deny, alas, how correct Hemingway is about
a certain part of our species. And yet—even if we take a Swiftian
view of our fellow-Yahoos—we might boggle at the argument
Hemingway advances to defend the killer branch of humanity.
For he reminds us that the rest of the human race has "always
been the more articulate" and has had "most of the good writers"
(p. 232). In brief, the killers have always lacked a good "press."
Hemingway offers to give them one. He does so by directly connecting the pleasure of killing with the feeling of immortality.
The news is that, when you kill, you somehow triumph over
death:

Once you accept the rule of death thou shalt not kill is an easily
and a naturally obeyed commandment. But when a man is still in
rebellion against death he has pleasure in taking to himself one of
the Godlike attributes; that of giving it. This is one of the most
profound feelings in those men who enjoy killing. These things are
done in pride and pride, of course, is a Christian sin, and a pagan
virtue. But it is pride which makes the bullfight and true enjoyment
of killing which makes the great matador. [p. 233]

It is perhaps impertinent to remark here that, not merely
among Christians and Jews, but also among the pagan Greeks,
pride or *hubris* was a sin. What is surely relevant at this point,
however, is to recall a fragment from one of those amusing
dialogues between the "Author" and the "Old Lady" which
Hemingway inserts here and there in his book. The subject of
courage had come up:

Old lady: Sir I do not know.

Author: Madame, neither do I and it may well be that we are talking horseshit.

Old lady: That is an odd term and one I did not encounter in my youth.

Author: Madame, we apply the term now to describe unsoundness in an abstract conversation or, indeed, any over-metaphysical tendency in speech.

Old lady: I must learn to use these terms correctly. [p. 95]

If a stench assails our nostrils as we read Hemingway's immortality-through-killing discourses, it is because he has indulged himself in an "over-metaphysical tendency." His "unsoundness," though, is worse than ridiculous. It is downright sick. For what the Hemingway idol has come to be here is, to put it plainly, a man who gets perverted satisfaction from killing because at the moment of the kill he feels like a god in his power to destroy life. This is not heroism. This is criminal pathology. And if such sickness lies near the heart of the Hemingway hero, we do right to defend ourselves against him. For any twisted personality, any sadist, can get this same "Godlike" satisfaction when he murders—though only assassins of kings and presidents can be reasonably sure of immortality. Hemingway has thus not merely indulged in abstraction. With the cunning and power of his art he has nearly won us over to accepting as an epiphany from on high what in reality is an expression of his own morbidity.

In *Death in the Afternoon,* though, he has not merely tried to persuade us that the matador is a heroic artist in a tragic art. He has also, in his desperate need for certainty, sought to make an affirmation out of death itself. He has developed nothing less than a mystique out of the facts of killing and being killed. Nor is this comparable to anything like a medieval Catholic meditation on death, or to the ruminations on that finality by some of the seventeenth-century writers. Hemingway has gone in for a phony mysticism.

The irony is that he set the trap for himself. In one of the more amusing passages of *Death in the Afternoon* he scores the jargon and highfalutin rhetoric of Waldo Frank's *Virgin Spain*, labeling Frank's style and thought "bedside mysticism" (p. 53). What he most scorns is Frank's interpretation of the bullfight. "It is a searching symbol of the sexual act," Frank had asserted.[5] To anyone aware that the mind often uses analogies, to anyone enough acquainted with Freudian psychology to understand how in its depths the psyche is a kind of poetry-making organ, Frank's statement is not entirely nonsense. No one has ever denied that the bull is primordially representative of maleness. Nor is it sheer fantasy to see in the maneuvers of the matador an almost feminine gracefulness: a sort of dance that seduces the bull to his death. When, in the moment of truth, bull and man become one figure with the thrust of the sword, there is a certain similarity to the sexual act. Normally of course the phallic thrust is accompanied by pleasure, and its biological aim is to bring new life. The matador's sword thrust brings the threat of pain or death to the man and the certainty of it to the animal. That Waldo Frank called attention to these analogies goaded Hemingway into satire. "The whole thing," he tells us, "is what, to make a belated entry into the pseudo-scientific field, I call erectile writing" (p. 53). Such writing is the product of "the slight distortion of vision that unrelieved turgidness presents"—in other words of sexual frustration. Hemingway is amused that we have had in America "a school of writers" who afforded us "an interesting mechanical experiment while it lasted, and full of pretty phallic images drawn in the manner of sentimental valentines" (p. 53). And he wonders what *Virgin Spain* might have been like "if written after a few good pieces of that sovereign specific for making a man see clearly" (p. 54).

This is red-blooded high-school boy fun of the locker-room variety, and it might be thoroughly entertaining if it were not undermined by the whole purport of *Death in the Afternoon*. No doubt Waldo Frank could not see the bullfight whole; his view may have been falsified by erotic impulses which he did not recognize in himself. But whatever the bedside mystic may have to answer for, at least he has not made a fetish of pain, nor worshiped death as the one true god. At least he is not so driven by unconscious sadistic and destructive impulses as to become rigidly, agonizingly preoccupied with the satisfactions of killing.

Hemingway would persuade us that the great truth which the less heroic branch of the human race seeks to dodge is the fact that mankind are killers. We can, of course, admire him because he did have the courage to face these dark impulses of our common humanity. And we can be grateful to his art that he made this confrontation so compelling for us. We can also agree that no rational conduct of life can even be philosophized about without a frank cognizance of our hidden destructive urges. But Hemingway here has created a mystique of death.

Hemingway's fascination with death accounts for his inserting into *Death in the Afternoon* a longish narrative which he later republished in his next book of stories. "A Natural History of the Dead," though not about bullfighting, is perfectly appropriate in this book.[6] For the story, one of Hemingway's most revolting and agonizing, dramatizes, nakedly, his obsession.

In the first of its three parts, the narrator, taking the stance of an objective recorder of natural phenomena, satirizes some old-time naturalists who found in their study of "natural history" evidence for their religious beliefs. With cold fury he slashes down long-forgotten figures like the Reverend Gilbert White and Bishop Stanley and Mungo Park. To "see what inspiration we may derive from the dead" (p. 134), he next proceeds to set down in grotesque and horrific detail his recollections of violent death in wartime: the fragmented remains of women killed in a munitions plant explosion outside Milan; the battlefield dead after the Austrian offensive in Italy in June of 1918—the precise hues and textures of the carcasses and how wondrously they change and swell if left long enough in the heat, all described with tortured loving care. In delight he forces us to look at these horrors. It is a powerful lecture.

In the second part of the story the New Humanists of the late 1920's come in for their punishment. Against those academic champions of decorum Hemingway fires this salvo:

So now I want to see the death of any self-called Humanist. . . . In my musings as a naturalist it has occurred to me that while decorum is an excellent thing some must be indecorous if the race is to be carried on since the position prescribed for procreation is indecorous, highly indecorous, and it occurred to me that perhaps that is what these people are, or were; the children of decorous cohabitation. But regardless of how they started I hope to see the finish of a few, and speculate how worms will try that long preserved sterility; with their quaint pamphlets gone to bust and into foot-notes all their lust. [p. 139]

The wit and style carry off this blast at the Genteel Tradition. But they should not obscure the Hemingway premise: that only those who can face unflinchingly the facts of dying and killing—and relish these facts whenever a writer depicts them with sufficient violence—will be healthy and honest about their lust.

In the third part of the story, an anecdote, this hysterical sensationalism is brought under a desperate control. In a dressing station a quarrel breaks out between a harassed doctor and a wounded artillery officer over what is to be done about the helpless agony of a dying soldier. Nothing can be done; and both men are near the breaking point. When the lieutenant, hurling obscenities at the doctor, starts toward him, the doctor throws a saucer of iodine into his eyes, then trips and disarms the temporarily blinded man. As he turns to work on the man he has just subdued, instructing his aids to wash the man's eyes with alcohol and water, word comes that the soldier has died. "See my poor lieutenant? We dispute about nothing. In time of war we dispute about nothing." The lieutenant screams.

" 'Hold him tight,' said the doctor. 'He is in much pain. Hold him very tight' " (p. 144). Such, in sum, is the Hemingway prescription. If we are to suffer—or merely contemplate in print —such concentrated anguish, we have one recourse only: an iron-rigid exertion of the will.

To blast the simple pieties of another generation, to pummel the New Humanists—all this is whipping a dead horse. Yet the icy rage with which Hemingway lashes seemingly everyone beyond the pale of his own nihilism is saturated, as is so much of *Death in the Afternoon,* by displaced eroticism. The charge he leveled against Waldo Frank we can in fairness turn upon Hemingway himself. If Frank's brain was befuddled by the soft and pleasureful impulses of Eros, in Hemingway those same impulses are translated into a hard and painful lusting after death. But so compelling is his art that he almost forces us to believe there never was, is not, and never can be any other world than his own sadistic and masochistic nightmare. It is obvious that in "The Natural History of the Dead" we are supposed to wallow in pain. Equally obvious is the drear repetition of the soldier's omnibus word, the blunt term for sexual intercourse. What is interesting to the psychologist is that not until the maddened lieutenant cries, "F——k yourself. F——k your mother. F——k your sister," does the physician quell him by blinding him (p. 143). So in the frenzy of his incestuous guilt did Oedipus quell his own torments. In *Death in the Afternoon* the other side of Hemingway's mystique of Thanatos is his view of Eros. The two are inseparable with him. And one can be understood only in terms of the other.

Toward unraveling this puzzle, we might reconsider the reasons that impelled Hemingway, after two classic novels and some immortal short stories, to turn to bullfighting as the subject of his next book. To be sure, he had been harrowed on the battlefield, where sudden death is routine. And for the artist who seeks intensity it is undeniable that, compared to warfare, all other violent enterprises, all other games and sports, however dangerous, are insipid—the only exception being what happens in the bull ring. But Hemingway afforded us an equally significant clue when he said, as we noted, that he went to the bullfights to observe violent death as "a man might, for instance, study the death of his father . . ." (p. 3). And, from one point of view, the bullfight is a ritualized acting out of the universal Oedipal struggle. The bull (a totem animal, as it were) represents the powerful father; the matador is the son who challenges. That they fight for the possession of a woman is suggested in that, when particularly successful, the matador presents the severed ears of the dead bull to the woman of his choice—the trophies of a symbolic castration.[7] That the mortal struggle between matador and bull was not unconnected, in Hemingway's emotions, with the death of his own father is indicated also by an "odd" story he includes in this book, an account of a strange revenge taken on a killer bull. This particular bull had, in amateur bull baiting held in village squares, killed sixteen men and boys and injured more than sixty. One of his victims was a fourteen-year-old gypsy boy. For two years, the boy's sister and brother followed that bull wherever it was used in bull baiting. When finally it was sent to the slaughterhouse, the boy got permission to do the killing. He proceeded by "digging out both the bull's eyes while the bull was in his cage, and spitting carefully into the sockets . . ." (p. 25). After he killed the bull, "he asked permission to cut off the bull's testicles, which being granted, he and his sister built a small fire at the edge of the dusty street outside the slaughter-house and roasted the two glands on sticks and when they were done, ate them" (p. 25).

This bit of local color might turn some stomachs. As an item for the anthropologist, however, this story of gypsies' revenge hearkens back to some primordial ritual: the destruction of the animal god and the eating of his sacrificial parts to gain some of his powers. Our concern here, though, is not with Hemingway's primitivism, but with his view of masculinity. Male genitality is central in *Death in the Afternoon,* and not merely for the bulls in the Spanish rings. *Cojones,* the Spanish word for testicles, is, so we learn from Hemingway's "Explanatory Glossary," part of the jargon of bullfighting: "A valorous bullfighter is said to be plentifully equipped with these. In a cowardly bullfighter they are said to be absent." The American equivalent is "guts." For Hemingway there is a curious rightness about the Spanish version, because he somehow seems to regard the male genitals more as instruments of fighting and destroying than of loving and creating. Whatever he has to say about sexual love in this book is regularly associated with sickness, pain, or death—as so often in the short stories. Only now this linking is made to seem heroic.

He informs us, for example, that "the two occupational diseases of the matador" are tuberculosis and syphilis (p. 100). The connection between heroism and syphilis is that "it is a disease of all people who lead lives in which a disregard of consequences dominates" (p. 101). To the Old Lady he explains that bullfighters contract this disease "as all men do who go with women thinking only of the woman and not of their future health" (p. 103).[8] When the Old Lady concludes, "It must be most dangerous then to be a man," she is answered: "It is indeed, madame, and but few survive it. 'Tis a hard trade and the grave is at the end of it" (p. 103). The intention is light-hearted enough; but why, we ask, does Hemingway make self-destructiveness the concomitant of virility?

Of the futility of love Hemingway is almost as certain as he is about the finality of death:

Especially do all stories of monogamy end in death, and your man who is monogamous while he often lives most happily, dies in the most lonely fashion. There is no lonelier man in death, except the suicide, than that man who has lived many years with a good wife and then outlived her. If two people love each other there can be no happy end to it. [p. 122]

Death in the Afternoon is a strange case from beginning to end. One of its most curious aspects is the way Hemingway concludes it. He tells us—or tells himself?—that "the great thing is to last and get your work done and see and hear and learn and understand. . . ." Unquestionably that is the only possible prescription for the artist. Yet throughout *Death in the Afternoon* Hemingway has tried to convince us that the great matador is superior to the artist—superior because he has more physical courage, damns the consequences, and is indifferent to "lasting." But Hemingway wanted to last as a writer, even against the forces of history. *Death in the Afternoon* was published in 1932—for Americans, the nadir of the Great Depression. In his final page, Hemingway had declared: "Let those who want to save the world if you can get to see it clear and whole. Then any part you make will represent the whole if it's truly made." Yet something else drove him to be as much like a matador as possible: seeking life-and-death adventures, testing his manhood, pitting his nerve against bodily danger. To expose oneself to such risks is to make a drama out of oneself—and excellent copy for the journalists. For the artist, though, it can also be a distraction, if not at times a desertion, from his true calling.

Neither writing fiction nor studying and reporting the feats of the bullfighters was enough for Hemingway. In *Death in the Afternoon* he remarks, "It is a strange feeling to have an animal come toward you consciously seeking to kill you, his eyes looking at you, and see the oncoming lowered horn that he intends to kill you with" (p. 24). In search of that "strange feeling," he went to Africa in the winter and early spring of 1933–34 to hunt big game. For us, the result is *Green Hills of Africa* (1935).

The work has some obvious similarities to the discourse on bullfighting. Again, Hemingway is the central figure and the narrator; though his chip-on-the-shoulder exhibitionism begins to irk us, we do have here a more relaxed Hemingway who can more often laugh at himself. The setting is even more exotic than that of Spain; in fact, now that we can no longer think of

the Dark Continent as a hunting ground for well-heeled sports-
men, *Green Hills of Africa* reads almost like a period piece. And
again, the killing of big animals is life's most intense pleasure.
In another way, too, this book is like its predecessor: Hemingway still feels the need to explain himself; at intervals he affords us provocative comments on life and art, his own in particular.

For the rest, *Green Hills of Africa* has little of the dark intensity of *Death in the Afternoon*. It describes the rigors rather
than the heroics of hunting, and danger or the threat of death
are not much emphasized. Only once, after stalking a lion, does
Hemingway talk about fear. In actual fact, what most harrowed
him in Africa was a bout with amebic dysentery, severe enough
for him to be flown to Nairobi for medical care—an experience
he mentions only briefly.

In a short Foreword Hemingway sets down his aim: "The
writer has attempted to write an absolutely true book to see
whether the shape of a country and the pattern of a month's
action can, if truly presented, compete with a work of the
imagination." He proves they cannot. There is no drama in
Green Hills of Africa. The only real conflict in it is within
Hemingway's own mind; and, since that conflict is never realized
concretely, we can infer it only. Whatever kind things might
be said about the structure of the narrative or about the style, it
is a bore to learn how many animals Hemingway can kill and
whether they are bigger than those bagged by his fellow hunter,
Karl. And the great issue—will he or will he not finally shoot
a kudu—is something to yawn over.

Nor do the persons in the story engage us. Karl, Mrs. Hemingway, and Pop, the white hunter, are only the supporting cast.
If Karl sticks in our memory, that is because Hemingway is so
conscious of him in their puerile rivalry. The natives in the
party are also two-dimensional. M'Cola's odd sense of humor
might pique us, and as the hunt proceeds we note how suspicion
between this old gun bearer and Hemingway yields to respect

and companionship. More eye-catching is "David Garrick," so dubbed because of his costumes and his theatrical posturing—and his irksome uselessness on the hunt. For the most part, we see these Negroes only as *bwana* Hemingway's servants. Of the tribes he encounters Hemingway likes the Masai. In their playfulness and handsomeness and good will, he evidently finds his Noble Savage. In general, however, the African people stir no curiosity in Hemingway.

Green Hills of Africa is a minor piece that does not deserve to last. We read it today only because Hemingway wrote it and because we can glean from it a few insights into his state of mind. Why, we ask, did Hemingway in the mid-1930's flee even further from the life most of us know? *Green Hills of Africa* is a holiday book. Yet, as Philip Young has pointed out, nine times in its first seventy-two pages Hemingway so insists that he is happy and doing what he most enjoys that we cannot help asking what is wrong.[9] As to what was troubling Hemingway, it is hard to avoid making at least two inferences here. First, his increasing fascination with danger suggests that he is seeking distraction, trying to flee something—something within. Second, the writer who had made his "separate peace" back in the twenties is now more and more pulled between an ideal of solitary dedication to his art and the call to action, especially to commitment on the great social issues of the era. The anxieties which in the preceding decade he had transmuted into successful art have become a source of distraction rather than of creativity. During the years when Hemingway had struggled to perfect his art and had fought for recognition, he probably had little chance to doubt that he was doing a man's work in the world. Those battles over, where and how would he direct his aggressive energies? In *Death in the Afternoon* we saw them drive him to idealize as artists the killers of bulls. Now they impel him to go in for the strenuous life and to satisfy his needs by hunting down dangerous animals. With Hemingway, the conflict is intensified because concern about his integrity as an artist is bound up with concern about his very manhood. His pursuit of violence and his preoccupation with artistic probity look like two aspects of the same inward drive. And the state of the world further complicates for him these private troubles.

One of the passages that throws some light on this tangle comes in the first chapter. A truck stalled near Hemingway's camp brings Kandisky, an Austrian who has read Hemingway's early contributions to *Querschnitt* and wants to talk about literature. The conversation allows Hemingway to express himself about writing and about American writers. He seems here to scorn the literary life, especially coteries in big cities, adding that writers who join them "are afraid to be alone in their beliefs and no woman would love any of them enough so that they could kill their lonesomeness in that woman . . ." (p. 22). Our "good writers," according to Hemingway, are only three: Henry James, Stephen Crane, and Mark Twain. And of course it is here that we come upon the famous dictum: "All modern American literature comes from one book by Mark Twain called Huckleberry Finn" (p. 22).

When Hemingway looks for reasons why the careers of so many American writers are aborted, we might detect his own worries. He specifies women and money:

They make money . . . increase their standard of living and they are caught. They have to write to keep up their establishment, their wives, and so on, and they write slop . . . not slop on purpose but because it is hurried. . . . Then, once they have betrayed themselves, they justify it and you get more slop. [p. 23]

Other enemies of writers are the critics: "If they believe the critics when they say they are great then they must believe them when they say they are rotten and they lose confidence . . ." (p. 23). And partisan involvement in society's problems makes for still another threat to the integrity of writers: "they get frightened and join organizations that do their thinking for them" (p. 24). In contrast, what attracts Hemingway, he announces pretentiously, is the possibility of getting "a fourth and fifth dimension" out of prose (p. 27).

It is the fear of becoming *engagé* that seems to trouble him most. Three more times in *Green Hills of Africa* he returns to the conflict of individualism against social solidarity. After a country and its people are gone, he remarks, the only ones of any importance are those who practiced the arts: "A thousand years makes economics silly and a work of art endures forever, but it is very difficult to do and now it is not fashionable" (p. 109). Again he protests his proud isolation:

If you serve time for society, democracy, and the other things quite young, and declining any further enlistment make yourself responsible only to yourself, you exchange the pleasant, comforting stench of comrades for something you can never feel in any other way than by yourself. [p. 148]

That "something" is writing in a way which satisfies the artist's conscience. We might admire such devotion to art if it were not soured by uncalled-for misanthropy and unattractive narcissism. The curdling shows up, for instance, in the memorable passage about the Gulf Stream, a current that flowed long before man appeared and will flow after "all systems of government" are gone. Five times daily

. . . a high-piled scow of garbage . . . spills off its load into the blue water . . . and in ten miles along the coast it is as clear and blue and unimpressed as it was ever before . . . and the palm fronds of our victories, the worn light bulbs of our discoveries and the empty condoms of our great loves float with no significance against one single, lasting thing—the stream. [pp. 149–50]

As if this rejection of mankind, its works, and its history were not enough, Hemingway adds his reasons for renouncing America. Ours is a country which is "finished" (p. 284). "It had been a good country and we had made a bloody mess of it. . . . Our people had seen it at its best and fought for it when it was well worth fighting for. Now I would go somewhere else" (p.

285). All of America of the Great Depression and the New Deal is dismissed in this exchange:

> "What's going on in America?" [Pop asks Hemingway.]
> "Damned if I know! Some sort of Y.M.C.A. show. Starry eyed bastards spending money that somebody will have to pay. Everybody in our town quit work to go on relief. Fishermen all turned carpenters. Reverse of the Bible." [p. 191]

We can endorse Hemingway's rage at the way Americans have ruined the wilderness. But the dream he indulges of remaining in his African playground as long as he wants to is childish: he would live there and hunt every day, "sometimes laying off and writing for a week, or writing half the day, or every other day," and so on (p. 282). He assures us that he loved Africa "so that I was happy as you are after you have been with a woman that you really love" (p. 72). Such declarations fail to convince because the bulk of the book tells us plainly enough what most attracted Hemingway to Africa: the animals. And these appeal to him exclusively as moving targets.[10]

Again and again we are invited to share the feelings of the hunt and the kill: to be amused at "that comic slap of the bullet and the hyena's agitated surprise to find death inside of him" (p. 37); to thrill to the tactile sensations as Hemingway searches for the heart of a wounded reedbuck: "I could feel it hot and rubbery against my fingers, and feel the knife push it, but I felt around and cut the big artery and the blood came hot against my fingers" (p. 53); to share the suspense as he aims at a rhinoceros, "stopping the excitement as you close a valve, going into that impersonal state you shoot from" (p. 76). What he wants is not only the actual feel of the killing but also the sensation of being himself a possible target of violence. As he waits for a wounded buffalo to charge, he thinks of himself as prize fighter and matador as well as hunter:

This was different, this was no rapid fire, no pouring it on him as he comes groggy into the open. . . . He will have to put the head down to hook, like any bull, and that will uncover the old place the boys wet their knuckles on and I will get one in there . . . (p. 115).[11]

While waiting, he experiences "the best elation of all, of certain action, action . . . in which you can kill and come out of it . . ." (p. 116). The kill is successful; and afterward Hemingway's mood is marked by self-absorption: "You cannot live on a plane of the sort of elation I had felt in the reeds and having killed, even when it is only a buffalo, you feel a little quiet inside. Killing is not a feeling that you share . . ." (p. 120).

Structurally the climax of the narrative, as well as the culmination of the hunter's passion, is the pursuit and killing of a kudu. Hemingway gloats over the carcass:

I looked at him, big, long-legged, a smooth gray with the white stripes and the great, curling, sweeping horns, brown as walnut meats, and ivory pointed, at the big ears and the great, lovely heavy-maned neck the white chevron between his eyes and the white of his muzzle and I stooped over and touched him to try to believe it. He was lying on the side where the bullet had gone in and there was not a mark on him and he smelled sweet and lovely like the breath of cattle and the odor of thyme after rain. [p. 231]

A pastoral simile at this fragrant conclusion! The amorous colorations are unmistakable—and rather sickly; this is killing eroticized. And the fact is, none of the living human characters in the book stirs in him emotions of such depth and happy intensity.

The question is not why any man, or any writer, would choose hunting as a favorite sport or go on a safari. Rather, it is why in such a world a major writer should give so much of himself to the killing of animals. As if anticipating our query, Hemingway prepares an answer in the talk with Kandisky. At least three times the Austrian asks him why he wants to hunt big game. At first Hemingway is evasive; then finally we have this exchange:

"You really like to do this, what you do now, this silliness of kudu?"

"Just as much as I like to be in the Prado."

"One is not better than the other?"

"One is as necessary as the other. There are other things, too." [p. 25]

A year after *Green Hills of Africa* was published, Hemingway explained much more satisfactorily why hunting was "necessary" to him. In a belligerent sketch which he contributed to a book of portraits of contemporary writers, he made this statement about himself: "Since he was a young boy he has cared greatly for fishing and shooting. If he had not spent so much time at them . . . he might have written much more. On the other hand, he might have shot himself." [12] The implications of this declaration are obvious: it carries a note of self-justification for not being as productive in fiction as he should have been; it exposes further the conflict between his avowed aim of being a hard-working writer—"last and get your work done"— and spending so much of himself in strenuous and violent pastimes; and, finally, it is a frank display of a pathological state of mind, this public admission of suicidal tendencies. Now that we know Hemingway so often exposed himself to danger and injury —was manifestly accident prone, and did kill himself with a hunting gun—we cannot help seeing *Death in the Afternoon* and *Green Hills of Africa* as the writings of a sick spirit.

In this period of his career, Hemingway can no longer manage his neurotic impulses, as he had been able to do in the earlier fiction. The symptoms are plain in what he writes now: the loss of perspective, the extremism, the melancholy and bloating egoism. Writing stories and novels no longer provides the needed release, nor does all his empathy with the bullfighter. He himself must face and kill dangerous animals in pursuit of a violence that is "necessary," compulsive. He can preserve his integrity as artist-hero, he can assert his manhood, only by conquering big beasts.

At whatever cost, he must flee the monsters that throng the nightmares of childhood. The oedipal fury of Nick Adams—disgusted at having to put on his father's underclothes, insulted by the whipping he got when he lied about hiding them, sitting with a shotgun in his hand and with rage enough to kill his father—that long-standing fury is still flaming here. In a boy's jealous fantasies the father often appears as a gigantic and threatening figure, to be hated and feared; and in dreams he takes the shape of a huge and terrible animal. Surely, Freud's seems the most cogent explanation why Hemingway, who might have been busy about other things, must again and again slaughter fierce animals.

That Hemingway's own father committed suicide while the son was writing *A Farewell to Arms*—the father's great "failure" coming when the son makes his greatest bid for success—only intensified the unconscious guilt and resentment Hemingway must have been feeling. Such torments might well inhibit the creation of fiction. They might also force the kind of self-examination, and self-justification, we find in both *Death in the Afternoon* and *Green Hills of Africa*. Besides, since to the boy the father stands for the greater world, for the authority and power of society at large, the Freudian view helps us to see why in his book on Africa Hemingway is still at war with his fatherland and society—and why he is so touchy toward those who question his right to have a good time on a sportsman's holiday while the nations are rushing toward war. He has other dragons to slay, and he knows he must slay them.

The triumph over killing the kudu is undercut by a piece of poor luck which concludes *Green Hills of Africa*. In going after the last trophy he hopes for, sable antelope, Hemingway succeeds only in gut-shooting one of these handsome creatures. After long, hard trailing, he cannot find the animal to deliver the *coup de grâce*. The failure troubles his sportsman's conscience:

I was thinking about the bull and wishing to God I had never hit him. . . . Tonight he would die and the hyenas would eat him, or, worse, they would get him before he died, hamstringing him and pulling his guts out while he was alive. . . . I did not mind killing anything, any animal, if I killed it cleanly. . . . But I felt rotten sick over this sable bull. . . . It was my own lousy fault. [pp. 271–72]

So, at the ending of the narrative the issue is left in doubt. The sable bull is, psychologically considered, another symbolic target.[13] Hunting him, though, brings no joyful release as does the kudu kill. Instead the hunter reproaches himself; guilt about what he has done makes him feel "rotten sick."

Such troubling of the Hemingway heart and conscience becomes more nearly objectified in the fiction that comes at this juncture of his career. It is regrettable that, after proving himself a world master in the genre, Hemingway wrote very few short stories during the rest of his lifetime. But three superb examples do come the next year. All of them were published in 1936, and all are tragic. In each the protagonist meets death in a way that is accidentally-on-purpose. All three stories are concerned with integrity, with a reaching toward heroic manhood. And in all of them are essentially the same conflicts we saw in the two nonfiction books.

Because it deals with the slaughter of an innocent, the most pitiful of these is "The Capital of the World." [14] The capital is Madrid, the setting the Pension Luarca, a lodging place that attracts second-rate bullfighters. Here, one evening after the guests have left the dining room, Paco, the youngest waiter, performs a mock bullfight with Enrique, the dishwasher. Tying two butcher knives onto the legs of a chair, the older boy acts the part of the bull. In his fantasies Paco is the brave matador. But then as Enrique rushes in, Paco moves "his left foot two inches too far forward" (p. 49), and the knife severs a femoral artery. Before a doctor can arrive, Paco's life drains out of him "as dirty water empties from a bathtub when the plug is drawn." "He died," the narrator comments, "as the Spanish phrase has it, full of illusions" (p. 51).

This time, of course, the killer is not a bull, but an improvised minotaur, an older boy with makeshift horns. What touches us is Paco's rare innocence. An inexperienced boy from a primitive village, he thinks Madrid "an unbelievable place" and his job "romantically beautiful." Though he has two sisters who are chambermaids at the Luarca, Paco is evidently an orphan. There is no mention of his mother. As to his father, Hemingway opens his story this way:

Madrid is full of boys named Paco, which is the diminutive of the name Francisco, and there is a Madrid joke about a father who came to Madrid and inserted an advertisement in the personal columns of *El Liberal* which said: PACO MEET ME AT HOTEL MONTANA NOON TUESDAY ALL IS FORGIVEN PAPA and how a squadron of Guardia Civil had to be called out to disperse the eight hundred young men who answered the advertisement. But this Paco . . . had no father to forgive him, nor anything for the father to forgive. [p. 38]

At the outset, then, Hemingway provides us with a hero who is different from all other sons. If the oedipal struggle is crucial in the education of every heart, then we understand why Paco, who has somehow been spared this conflict, is unique in being without fear and still "full of illusions." He has never felt a boy's jealous rivalry with the father for possession of the mother, nor suffered the consequent fear, guilt, and anxiety. He has never had to face the fact that his rival is bigger than he and stronger and that his fantasies are impossible to carry out. In short, he has never been brought up against reality; and so the normal reactions of fear and guilt simply do not operate. In his romantic dream of being a matador, Paco is unable even to imagine the danger of the bull's horns.

The agent who does bring reality to him—too late, and in the form of death—is Enrique. Though only three years older than Paco, Enrique is "very cynical and bitter"; and insofar as he initiates the boy into the real world, he functions somewhat as a father figure. The motives for his actions are not simple. In part, no doubt, he really does want to demonstrate the danger, as one might teach a stubborn child. In part, also, he resents Paco's ignorant confidence, since it makes Enrique more aware of his own fear. But when Paco accepts his suggestion about the knives and the chair, Enrique, "suddenly not bitter," does not want to go through with it. Twice he says, "Don't do it," and after the accident he cries, "All I wanted was to show the danger" (p. 49).

Hemingway has not concentrated merely on a freakish accident. That he is implying broader significances we realize from the attention he gives to the minor characters, more of them here than in any other Hemingway story. At one's first reading, these people seem to represent only the indifference of the world to tragedy in its midst. But each of them throws a light or a shadow on Paco's dream and death; each underlines the uniqueness of Paco. The men have been hurt or warped or worn down by their experience in the bull ring or by their conflicts with power and authority. The women have become hardened or tainted or otherwise inadequate. All, in contrast with Paco, are disillusioned.

Most obvious are the cases of the five bullfighters living at the Luarca. One matador had been very brave and skillful until "a peculiarly atrocious horn wound in the lower abdomen" deprived him of his courage; now women, even prostitutes, spurn him. A second is hiding from the world the fact that he is dying of tuberculosis. The third has "courage and a calm capability," but because of his "old-fashioned" style he has "never succeeded in imposing himself on the public's fancy" (p. 40). Of the two picadors, one is losing his ability through dissipation. The other is "too headstrong and quarrelsome to stay with any matador more than a single season" (p. 40). The middle-aged *banderil-lero* will have good enough legs only for the present season; after that "when his speed of foot would be gone he would always be frightened . . ." (p. 41).

The four other male figures do not fight bulls, but each has been or is about to be broken by power and authority. The fifty-year-old waiter at the Luarca has long ago accepted the treadmill of his existence; he is grateful to have a job and looks forward only to working all his life. His fellow-waiter, who attends anarcho-syndicalist meetings, entertains dreams of a revolution. In his dogmatic naïveté he, too, will be disillusioned, for he lives in pre-Civil War Spain. "There are the two curses of Spain, the bulls and the priests," he says. His ideological cocksureness is amusing, and the two enemies he singles out indicate an almost childish rebellion against paternal authority.

For the priests themselves, life looks no more hopeful. Two of them staying at the Luarca have come to Madrid seeking help from a hierarch of Mother Church. Their conversation takes this turn:

> "It is ten days since I have been here waiting to see him and all day I sit in the ante-chamber and he will not receive me."
> "What is there to do?"
> "Nothing. What can one do? One cannot go against authority."
> "I have been here for two weeks and nothing. I wait and they will not see me. . . . If they would simply see one and refuse."
> "No. You must be broken and worn out by waiting." [pp. 44–45]

But Paco, who is thrilled by the idea of being "a good catholic, a revolutionary, and . . . at the same time, being a bullfighter," is unaware of what reality has done to the men about him. Nor, as he acts out the ritual of the bullfight, has he lost his illusions about the women he knows. Though he adores his sisters, they hardly deserve his esteem; we suspect that for them the step from chambermaid to prostitute might be easy. Two of the other women at the Luarca are already whores, and "very houseworn-looking." Although the proprietress is a kindly and maternal person, she is too far away to protect Paco. She is quite religious and has never "ceased to miss or pray daily for her husband, dead now twenty years." When the accident occurs, she is asleep in her bed, "big, fat, honest, clean, easy-going" (p. 48).

As a sort of overarching representative of the woman who fails one or betrays or is tainted, Hemingway makes ironic use of the movie star, Greta Garbo. When the mock bullfight is in process, Paco's sisters are watching the film *Anna Christie,* and they are terribly disappointed because it showed "the great star in miserable low surroundings when they had been accustomed to see her surrounded by great luxury and brilliance. The audience disliked the film thoroughly and were protesting by whistling and stamping their feet." We can sense why the Madrid audience, so involved in the bullfight, did not want to see their ideal of womanhood debased. But Paco is spared even this, for the last sentence tells us, "He had not even had time to be disappointed in the Garbo picture which disappointed all Madrid for a week" (pp. 50–51).

In his earlier stories Hemingway had, in effect, asked how a man could have satisfying love. His answer was that it might be had through innocence, that is, if it were simple, primitive, and "without consequences." In "The Capital of the World," he asks how a man can have courage. His answer is the same. Paco's triumph is that, through his innocence, he already has what the Hemingway hero aspires to: an absolute fearlessness in the face of danger and death. Paco's tragedy, and the irony, is that he dies at the moment when reality would have replaced illusion and when he might have achieved a fuller manhood.

In more than one way the hero of "The Short Happy Life of Francis Macomber" resembles Paco. He has the same first name, and he, too, is something of an innocent killed almost at the moment he proves his manhood. But where Paco is brave because he has never known fear, Macomber achieves his courage through fear, humiliation, and anger. His trouble at the start is that he has not quite grown up. Trying to figure him out, the professional hunter Wilson reflects: "It's that some of them stay little boys so long. . . . The great American boy-men" (p. 33). Then, too, like Robert Cohn, Macomber is victimized by a bitch-woman. His marriage is unhappy, even though it has a "sound basis": "Margot was too beautiful for Macomber to di-

123

vorce her and Macomber had too much money for Margot ever to leave him" (p. 22).

For physical adventure, this is one of Hemingway's most exciting tales; the action is perfectly structured for suspense until the final sentence. And in a seemingly uncomplicated way we respond to the hero, the cowardly underdog who in one brave act wipes out his shame. But exactly how Macomber casts off his fear is no simple matter. Only a superficial view sees him as transformed in one moment of intense action from coward to hero.[15]

In fact, the label "coward" perhaps should not be applied to Macomber at all. He does one terror-ridden thing: he runs the first time he is rushed by a wounded lion, and we cannot admire him when he worries that the news of his bolting might be broadcast at the Mathaiga Club. On the other hand, he is honest with himself and unpretentious. What had happened is this: Macomber had gut-shot the lion; then wants to dodge the danger of going after and finishing off the beast—something the sportsman's code and simple humaneness demand. When Wilson spells out the necessity, Macomber says, twice, he will go in with him despite the fear he admits. He does that, and it takes courage. The lion charges, Macomber runs, and the professional is left to do the killing. Afterward, Macomber surprises Wilson by making no excuses and wanting to wipe out the shame.

Macomber's essential weakness is not cowardice but a timidity whose mark is lack of self-assertion. We are not told what made him this way, but we certainly see its effect on his love life. His wife scorns him, is unfaithful to him, never worries that he will retaliate in kind, and regards his "great tolerance" as "the nicest thing about him." Whatever is wrong with him, Margot worsens it, relentlessly undermining his confidence at every opportunity. When the hunters return from the lion hunt to the car, where she has seen it all, Margot punishes her husband again: Macomber reaches for her hand; she withdraws it and kisses Wilson on the mouth.

During the bad night that follows for Macomber, Margot administers further punishment, and Macomber undergoes his change. Waking from a dream of a bloody lion standing over him,[16] he realizes that his wife is not with him. Two hours later she returns—from Wilson's cot. Coolly she taunts him, and it looks as if there is nothing for Macomber to do but swallow one more humiliation. During the silence of the night, though, something happens in his heart.[17] We can be sure of it the next morning:

> At breakfast they were all three at table before daylight and Francis Macomber found that, of all the many men that he had hated, he hated Robert Wilson the most.
> "Sleep well?" Wilson asked in his throaty voice, filling a pipe.
> "Did you?"
> "Topping," the white hunter told him.
> You bastard, thought Macomber, you insolent bastard. [p. 23]

From this moment Macomber begins to assert his manhood. He is bitter and sarcastic with Wilson, and he tells Margot, "I hate that red-faced swine. . . . I loathe the sight of him" (p. 25). On the buffalo hunt Macomber has "no fear, only hatred of Wilson." In that state of mind he shoots well. Having wounded a buffalo, this time he is eager to go after it.

Wilson is puzzled and pleased by Macomber's metamorphosis:

> Damned if this isn't a strange one, he thought. Yesterday he's scared sick and today he's a ruddy fire eater . . . he had seen men come of age before and it always moved him. . . . Probably meant the end of cuckoldry too. . . . Well, that would be a damned good thing. . . . Beggar had probably been afraid all his life. Don't know what started it. But over now. Hadn't had time to be afraid with the buff. That and being angry too. . . . [pp. 31–33]

Wilson sees rather far and almost deeply enough: the relations between Macomber's long-standing timidity, its disappearance

125

in anger, his emergence as a man, and the implications for his love life. Macomber's fear has been driven out by rage, but not simply by the jealous rage of a husband in the standard triangle. Because Wilson is the older and more experienced man, the braver and better hunter, and the guide on safari, he unconsciously represents for Macomber a surrogate father. When Macomber is able to recognize in himself the full power of his anger toward a man of such import, and able to express that anger and rebel against that man and assert his independence from him, then he gains his own manhood, wins his integrity, and throws off his long-standing timidity. In this way, too, he comes at last to escape the tyranny of Margot, who has ruled him like a domineering mother and kept him a boy.

More an enemy than Wilson ever was, and a far greater danger than any charging lion or buffalo, is Macomber's wife. In Hemingway's world it is no news that the female of the species is more deadly than the male. But for Margot it is a necessity of life that she have power over others, particularly over her husband. The change in Macomber makes her "ill" with fear that she has lost it. And what she cannot dominate, she must destroy. Seizing the gun they have left behind (appropriately, it is a Mannlicher, German for "manly"), she puts a bullet into her husband's brain just as the buffalo seems about to gore him. It looks like an accident and would pass for one in a court of law. But Wilson rightly reads her motives. "Why didn't you poison him?" he asks. "That's what they do in England" (p. 37).

If this nearly perfect story has a flaw, it can be argued that it lies with the extremism in the characterization of Margot. She is a Goneril-Regan in her bitchhood, more monster than woman. In *Green Hills of Africa* Pop repeatedly expresses unflattering opinions of American womanhood. Wilson is harsher and more articulate about them: "They are, he thought, the hardest in the world; the hardest, the cruelest, the most predatory and the most attractive and their men have softened or gone to pieces nervously as they have hardened" (p. 8). Wilson's views on American women seem more accurate for Margot Macomber than they do for Helen, another American wife on safari. The role of this woman, loving but still dangerous, is considered in "The Snows of Kilimanjaro."

This one might be subtitled, "Self-Portrait of the Artist in Mid-Career." In none of his other short stories has Hemingway drawn between himself and the protagonist so many, so extensive, and even such specific parallels. It has been often anthologized and commented on, not so much for its art—it lacks the taut structure and incisive drama of Hemingway at his best —as for its self-revelations. Recording the last few hours of a writer dying of gangrene in the African wilderness, the narrative is virtually without action; its central conflict is a psychological one, Harry's bitter fight with himself.

Again we have a wounded hero, the gangrenous leg suggesting the long-standing castration anxiety, its stench the decay of Harry's moral nature. He admits that for years he has been "obsessed" by death. He has, in fact, been steadily destroying himself. That he neglected the thorn scratch which turns out to be fatal points to Harry's unconscious wish to die. What makes the story painful, however, is not his dying, but the bitterness and self-disgust that accompany it. For he turns upon himself a conscience which is now allied with all his destructive urges. In a mood of savage honesty, Harry condemns himself for having thrown away his integrity as a writer and as a man.

For Hemingway the story must have been an effort to purge himself of long-accumulated guilts. No one, of course, would suggest that he has given us a full self-portrait here; it is more of a sketch drawn in a black mood. Yet in 1936 Hemingway had reasons to be dissatisfied with himself. For seven years he had given the world no novel. After *Winner Take Nothing* (1933), he had published only three short stories. These are the years when the broad-jowled grin flashes from too many news photos and the publicity makers are busy inflating the image of the brawny sportsman and *bon vivant*. Hemingway had been playing about in Africa and Europe and the Carribean, drinking too much and cavorting with the rich. And he was being censured by critics on the Left and criticized for cashing in on his talents with articles to well-paying magazines. He had been through one divorce; and within four years his second marriage, to wealthy Pauline Pfeiffer, was to break up. The man who in his two most recent books had declared that the main thing for a writer was to last and get his work done appeared to be neither really lasting nor working.[18]

At least a dozen times in this story Harry lashes himself for neglecting or betraying his art or regrets that it is too late to make stories out of the experiences his memory now teems with:

He had destroyed his talent by not using it, by betrayals of himself and what he believed in, by drinking so much that he blunted the edge of his perceptions, by laziness, by sloth, and by snobbery, by pride and by prejudice, by hook and by crook. . . . It was a talent all right but instead of using it, he had traded on it. . . . He had sold vitality, in one form or another, all his life. . . . [pp. 60–61]

When the burden of guilt gets too heavy, we tend to put at least some of it on others. Harry does this with a vengeance. Just as in *Green Hills of Africa* Hemingway blamed money and women for wrecking American writers, so now Harry turns on Helen, for him the personification of both evils. Our pain in reading the story comes not only from contemplating a man die in spiritual wretchedness, but also because we see him use his last hours to torture his wife. With the Macombers, Margot had been the sadist and her husband the masochist. Now the roles are reversed; it is Harry who acts the bitch. He tells Helen he has never loved her. "Love is a dunghill," said Harry. "And I'm the cock that gets on it to crow" (p. 57).

Once when his nastiness makes her cry, Harry says, "Listen. . . . Do you think that it is fun to do this? I don't know why I'm doing it. It's trying to kill to keep yourself alive, I imagine"

(p. 58). That admission makes some sense out of Harry's cruelty. And his insight into himself is sound: if his aggressions cannot be used up in his work and in killing animals, then they may be turned upon other people; that failing, they can be turned against himself.

But Helen deserves something better than this brutal treatment. She has had troubles and sorrows enough of her own. Widowed when fairly young, she has seen her children "embarrassed" by her devotion to them, known lovers and drinking and one child killed in an accident, and then no more lovers but more loneliness. She has been a loving and devoted wife to Harry. And she pleads with him: "You don't have to destroy me. Do you? I'm only a middle-aged woman who loves you and wants to do what you want to do. I've been destroyed two or three times already" (p. 63). Once even Harry wonders why he is so hard on "this rich bitch, this kindly caretaker and destroyer of his talent. Nonsense. He had destroyed his talent himself. Why should he blame this woman because she kept him well?" (p. 60).

He can blame her precisely because as one who takes care of him she is a maternal figure—and the Hemingway hero is regularly threatened by the mother. Part of Harry's sickness of soul comes from the fact that the life he has lived with Helen has been a lie. In this he is like Krebs, who felt such "nausea" when his mother forced him to be false to himself. But in Harry's case the woman is not to blame. Still, he resents it that when they married "she had built herself a new life and he had traded away what remained of his old life. He had traded it for security, for comfort too . . ." (p. 62). He can be kind to her now only by an effort of will, only by using the old, comfortable lies.

But we wonder if Harry has ever been able to love, except at a distance—love remembered. His reminiscences include one sorry entanglement. He had quarreled with his first wife in Paris before being sent to Constantinople. Alone there,

He had whored the whole time and then, when that was over, and he had failed to kill his loneliness, but only made it worse, he had written her, the first one, the one who left him, a letter telling her how he had never been able to kill it. . . . [p. 64]

And "hollow sick inside" from missing her so much, he had fought with a British subaltern over a "hot Armenian slut, that swung her belly against him so it almost scalded"; then, escaping the M.P.'s, he took her to bed.

Lust and violence mingle. For Harry, tenderness comes with the erotic only when distance makes it enchanting or impossible. Sham has evidently worked at the core of Harry's love life: "After he no longer meant what he said, his lies were more successful with women than when he had told them the truth" (p. 59). So, in love and work—two fundamentals in any man's life—Harry has made a botch of it. He suffers not only because he has betrayed his art but also because he recognizes that he does not love Helen, that he cannot love any woman. His loss of integrity as a writer is the counterpart of his lack of integrity as a lover.

Death is the only way out. As Harry dies, he dreams that an airplane has arrived to rescue him; that it climbs over the flatlands and the hills, goes through a storm, and then, "there, ahead, all he could see, as wide as all the world, great, high, and unbelievably white in the sun, was the square top of Kilimanjaro. And then he knew that there was where he was going" (p. 76). Using symbols more explicitly than is his custom, Hemingway has informed us in an epigraph that the Masai name for the western summit of Africa's highest mountain is "The House of God." He adds: *"Close to the western summit there is the dried and frozen carcass of a leopard. No one has explained what the leopard was seeking at that altitude"* (p. 52).

Various interpretations of the symbolism are possible and valid. In simplest terms we might say that Harry finally gets peace through death; literally, the dream of flying to Kilimanjaro eases his passing. The irony is that a dumb beast has surpassed him. However absurd or enigmatic is the frozen and enduring presence of the leopard on that pinnacle, it presents a contrast with Harry, who stopped seeking and who sold out his chance to scale similar heights. His flight to "The House of God" is only an illusion. The last scene takes us back to the camp where, drawn by the stench of his gangrene, the vultures and hyenas have gathered.

In "The Snows of Kilimanjaro" Hemingway had seemingly driven to their ultimate the obsessions and anxious self-questions that had absorbed him for half a decade. The story marks a dead end. With the demise of Harry, it is as if Hemingway meant to bury the sort of man he himself was determined never to become. The way out, for one of Hemingway's temperament, might be a plunge into action, preferably action that would call for courage, yet could satisfy his conscience more than hunting big game.

The outbreak of the civil war in Spain provided the opportunity. About the time the stories of Harry's death and Macomber's short happy life got into print, Hemingway was raising forty thousand dollars to help the Loyalists with ambulances and medical supplies. Early in 1937 he sailed for Spain. For the next two years he was either in Spain—on four different occasions he spent time at the front—or working for the Loyalists elsewhere or writing about their struggle.[19] His "separate peace" was over. Hemingway had joined up in another war for democracy.

And then in the fall of 1937 the man who, while relaxing on safari, had dismissed his country's efforts to climb out of the Great Depression as "some sort of Y.M.C.A. show" gave us a novel whose very title, *To Have and Have Not*, suggested the class struggle. Critics on the Left rejoiced. The book had a "message," easily found in the hero's last words as he dies in depression-ridden Key West: "No matter how a man alone ain't got no bloody fucking chance." As if to make no mistake about it, the author underscored Harry Morgan's epiphany when he added: "It had taken him a long time to get it out and it had taken him all his life to learn it" (p. 225). It all looked like a great and sudden change of heart in Hemingway.

Actually, his running off to Spain was not such a revolutionary move. Getting close to dangerous action, or into it, was of course irresistible to him. Besides, though Hemingway was never politically doctrinaire, he had been on record as an enemy of fascism since shortly after Mussolini came to power. Our aim, though, is to assess Hemingway not as a political activist but as a fictionist. And the fact is that the one novel which is most explicitly devoted to social protest happens to be the least coherent he ever wrote. Hemingway himself was not satisfied with it and thought it was not "a real novel."[20] Certainly, the motivations in it and the structure raise questions; and nothing in it prepares us for understanding how or why Harry Morgan arrived at his big revelation.

There are several explanations why *To Have and Have Not* is muddled. Hemingway had finished it at a time when he was rushed by his commitments to the Spanish cause. Second, the novel has a peculiar history of composition and publication. Its first two parts, titled "Harry Morgan (Spring)" and "Harry Morgan (Fall)," had appeared in magazines as long short stories, the first as far back as April, 1934, the second in February of 1936. In July of that year, Hemingway decided to develop the Morgan stories into a novel by recounting the last adventure of his hero and enlarging upon the milieu where he is defeated.[21] The problems arose with introducing here a subplot about a writer named Richard Gordon whose spiritual shoddiness is intended as a contrast to the heroism of Morgan. But the doings of Gordon and the other visitors at Key West are pasted onto the main action rather than made integral with it. Such obvious flaws by a novelist so painstaking in his craft make *To Have and Have Not* a second-rate product. Yet, despite its shortcomings, it is never a bore; even the unfocused third part is interesting and often gripping. The taut narrative of Morgan moves at a furious pace, its intensity a relentless attack upon the reader's nerves.

Exactly here in this matter of intensity we approach another and, I think, the most cogent reason why *To Have and Have Not* falls apart; and why Harry Morgan's courageous battle against a world in chaos never makes for any convincing social protest. A close look at the protagonist, at his heroism, and at what went into his making should take us far toward understanding why the novel fails in its purpose.

He is Hemingway's toughest hero. An ex-policeman from Miami, a sometime rum-runner, Harry Morgan manages to support his family during the Depression by taking the well-to-do deep-sea fishing off the Florida Keys. When one of his clients goes off without paying the $825 he owes, Harry returns to law-breaking. He makes a deal to transport a dozen Chinese coolies from Cuba to Florida. On this venture Morgan collects his $1,200, then kills Mr. Sing, the go-between, and dumps the coolies back on Cuban soil. Harry has more than recouped his loss, but in the next episode, several months later, he is still outside the law, having gone back to smuggling liquor. On this trip he loses his right arm in a gun battle and his boat to the United States Customs. Deeper in desperation, Harry next pilots the escape boat for four Cuban revolutionaries who are making their getaway after robbing a Key West bank. When he realizes they intend to kill him, Harry manages to kill them all, in the process receiving his own death wound. Such is the career of Harry Morgan.

His skills and virtues are those of the guerrilla fighter; his natural element is war; he is at his best in a kill-or-be-killed predicament. As to his ancestry, we can regard Morgan as piratical like his namesake or as an offspring of the hard-bitten frontiersman who responded to injustice by taking the law into his own hands. His seems a native American sort of violence. And from his loins have come the parade of tough guys who clutter the movies, television, cheap fiction, and the comics. He is also the most naturalistic hero in all the Hemingway novels: he is the most brutal and primitive, is more than once likened to an animal, works on a survival of the fittest basis, and lives by the two basic instincts, sex and fighting.[22]

No Hemingway hero is more sadistic. He dispatches Mr. Sing in cold blood. As Sing hands over the money, Harry grabs his wrist with one hand and his throat with the other. He promptly breaks Sing's arm. And then: "I got him forward onto his knees and had both thumbs well in behind his talk-box, and I bent the whole thing back until she cracked. Don't think you can't hear it crack either" (pp. 53–54). Thereupon he counts the money carefully, with quiet efficiency ties weights to the corpse, drops it into the sea like fish bait, and proceeds neatly to scrub the blood off his deck. Though Harry doublecrosses Sing because the Chinese might have done the same to him, afterward he thinks it over: "Some Mr. Sing. He certainly wasn't much of a business man. Maybe he was. Maybe he just trusted me. I tell you I couldn't figure him" (p. 60).

Morgan also intends to kill his alcoholic companion who had stowed away on the boat. Though a pitiful wreck of a man, Eddy has been a solid help on this trip. But Morgan is worried that when the rummy gets drunk, he might talk. Later he reconsiders the problem of doing away with Eddy: "When everything had come out so nice I didn't have the heart. But looking at him lying there it certainly was a temptation" (p. 60).

This near-murder and the actual murder put the hero in a mellow mood. Heading for home waters, he thinks to himself: "I tell you I felt pretty good steering, and it was a pretty night to cross" (p. 61). Part One ends on a scene of domestic peace. Harry is in his living room with his wife, and he is "smoking a cigar and drinking a whiskey and water and listening to Gracie Allen on the radio" (p. 64).

To be sure, there was no way out when Morgan found himself in the boat with the bank robbers who had already killed several men, but his sadism is useful in slaughtering the four.

One of his tactics is to pretend to listen sympathetically to the youngest and most nearly decent of the Cubans as the idealistic youngster talks of his country's woes and his hopes for the revolution, meanwhile setting him up as a nice target. Of Harry's joy when he has shot all four, Hemingway writes: "All the cold was gone from around his heart now and he had the old hollow, singing feeling . . ." (p. 171).

It is hard to sympathize with such a hero. In *Macbeth* Shakespeare had solved the problem of the criminal as tragic hero by frequently reminding us of Macbeth's better past, of the finer nature in him, now ruined. Of Harry Morgan's past, we know only that he had been a cop who went in later for violence and law-breaking. All that is good in him we see in the novel: his resourcefulness and icy bravery, his skill with boats and weapons, his absolute steadiness against the worst possible odds, his enduring the agony of dying in a drifting boat laden with corpses and awash with blood and water and gasoline.

We can feel the terror of his fate, but we cannot pity him as a victim of society. Nothing in his story demonstrates that conditions in America forced Harry Morgan to use his abilities destructively. For instance, out of the dirty business with the coolies, Harry more than makes up what he had been cheated out of; but once he has returned to crime, he simply stays in it. It is not enough to be told that he refuses to work at starvation wages digging sewers for the government. If we are to feel that a sick economy has forced a man into law-breaking in order to survive, then we need to watch how step by step he is ground down to such extremes. Hemingway skips all this; naturally, it is not his forte, and it does not interest him. The rationalization that he fights and risks so much for his wife and family is a thing of mere words. What Morgan's deeds accomplish is to deprive him of an arm and thus reduce his capacity as a breadwinner. Then, by inviting further wounds and finally death itself, he deprives them of a husband and father. What Hemingway does prove is that his hero is driven far less by a hostile society than by an ungovernable inward violence. In a novel that does catch something of the mood and the shattered morale of the Depression years—and the only novel Hemingway wrote about his own country—the esthetic blunder is the choice of a protagonist who relishes violence and killing for their own sake.

Wherever Morgan figures centrally, the social protest does not ring true. Consider how clumsily and sentimentally it is handled in Part Two. Harry and his Negro helper have both been wounded as they smuggled liquor out of Cuba, and the cargo is still aboard. The first boat to approach them is piloted by a friend, Captain Willie Adams; but he has with him one Frederick Harrison, a vacationer who is exhilarated by the idea of catching a smuggler. Though Harrison sees enough so that later he can swear out an affidavit against Morgan, Captain Willie refuses to get any closer to Morgan's boat and shouts a warning to him:

> "Thanks, brother," came the voice of Harry.
> "That chap your brother?" asked Frederick Harrison. . . .
> "No, sir," said Captain Willie. "Most everybody goes in boats calls each other brother." [p. 83]

This brotherhood among the have-nots might move us if we did not soon discover that Morgan can prey on his own brothers also.

Far more credible as a victim of the Depression is Albert Tracy. Like Morgan he has a family of four; unlike him Albert tries to support them by digging sewers at $7.50 a week. He is desperate enough to do something outside the law; but he makes it clear to Harry that he wants to avoid any real trouble. The one-armed Harry needs such a dependable mate and takes Albert on. Then he has just about decided against using anyone else when Albert shows up and again asks for a job because his relief work has just been cut to three days a week. Morgan offers him five dollars a day and completely conceals from him the Cubans' planned bank robbery. So, when the four desperadoes dash to the boat, Albert blurts out: "Wait a minute. . . . Don't start her. These are the bank robbers" (p. 152). He is cut down with a burst from the Thompson gun. Morgan avenges his death, but it is he who has betrayed Albert.

Part Three, twice as long as the first two sections of *To Have and Have Not*, is the most obviously incoherent. Though its main action is the final adventure and death of the hero, Morgan no longer monopolizes our attention. Many new characters are now crowded in. These, providing a cross section of society, range the economic gamut from those who stand at zero, the desperate and degraded veterans of the A.E.F., to the millionaire vacationers. Hemingway experiments now with rapidly shifting points of view, but he cannot bring his subject under control. Though a sympathetic reader might argue that this shifting and this uncertainty of structure mirror the disintegration of a world adrift, Hemingway lacks anything like the unifying view which, say, a Dos Passos might bring to such materials.

Freddy's bar provides one external device to get the diversity of characters into contact with one another. Morgan is a regular customer; and Freddy's is also patronized by the veterans, the tourists, and the lamentable Richard Gordon. If there is any really unifying motif for Part Three, we might call it Eros. Though love is excluded from the earlier episodes, now it figures crucially. And it is in his depiction of and commentary on the love lives of the haves and the have-nots that we get the core of Hemingway's social criticism. At least he makes unmistakable which characters he blesses and which he regards as the damned.

Most heartily admired as a lover is Harry Morgan. We are left in no doubt about this hero's sexual prowess or the high value his wife puts on it. Interestingly, Morgan is also monogamous; once, when a woman flirts with him in Freddy's bar, he takes pleasure in insulting her. By his own lights he is also a good family man. When he gets his death wound, he thinks at once of his wife, wishing he could "do something about Marie."

It is characteristic of Hemingway that he presents the bedroom scene after Harry has lost his arm—in one sense a castrative wound; and in this respect we are reminded of the hospital love-making scene in *A Farewell to Arms*. Hemingway's obsession is palpable in the eroticizing of Harry's amputation:

> "Listen, do you mind the arm? Don't it make you feel funny?"
> "You're silly. I like it. Any that's you I like. Put it across there. Put it along there. Go on. I like it, true."
> "It's like a flipper on a loggerhead."
> "You ain't no loggerhead. Do they really do it three days? Coot for three days?" [p. 113]

This loving pair are a hoodlum and an ex-whore, Marie's former profession having given her enough experience to judge that Harry is the best bed-mate she ever had. Are we to conclude that the only good lover is the man who also loves to kill? Marie herself is not the type to appeal to most men; she is a large woman, forty-five years old, broad-hipped and big-bosomed and blousy. She is an earth-mother type, the uncomplicated, readily available woman—as such somewhat like Nick Adams' Indian girl. At any rate, Marie and Harry are the only couple in all the Hemingway novels who find happiness in a marriage that works.

At the opposite pole is the love life of Richard Gordon, for whom Hemingway has only disgust and contempt. Gordon is unfaithful to his lovely young wife, Helen, not because uncontrollable lust drives him into promiscuity but because he fancies the experience will be beneficial to his development as a writer. When we first meet the Gordons, the subject of his affair with socially eminent Mrs. Bradley comes up:

> "I like her, you know," said Richard Gordon. "She interests me both as a woman and as a social phenomenon. . . ."
> "Do people go to bed with a social phenomenon?" asked Helen Gordon, looking out the door. . . .
> "A writer has to know about everything," Richard Gordon said. "He can't restrict his experience to conform to Bourgeois standards."
> "Oh," said Helen Gordon. "And what does a writer's wife do?" [p. 140]

But in the scene in Mrs. Bradley's boudoir where Gordon is compiling his novelistic data, he is inept and laughable. After this debacle, Gordon returns to his wife for a showdown. They quarrel cruelly; and for the heartsickness of love turned sour, chapter xxi is among Hemingway's best. It ends on the cold, bleak realization of affection destroyed and a marriage ruined. The climax comes with Helen telling off her husband—in the bitterest statement Hemingway ever made about the sickness of Eros in our world:

Love was the greatest thing, wasn't it? Love was what we had that no one else had or could ever have? And you were a genius and I was your whole life. . . . Slop. Love is just another dirty lie. Love is ergoapiol pills to make me come around because you were afraid to have a baby. . . . Love is that dirty aborting horror that you took me to. Love is my insides all messed up. It's half catheters and half whirling douches. I know about love. Love always hangs up behind the bathroom door. It smells like lysol. To hell with love. . . . Love is all the dirty little tricks you taught me that you probably got out of some book. All right. I'm through with you and I'm through with love. Your kind of picknose love. You writer. [pp. 185–86]

Even this, Helen thinks she might stand if she could only respect Gordon as a writer. "But I've seen you bitter, jealous, changing your politics to suit the fashion . . ." (p. 186). A failure in the bedroom, Gordon also lacks integrity in his work. His novels of social protest are cliché-ridden, false, and aimed at cashing in on the fads of the moment. After these blows to his ego, Gordon goes out to a bar, where he is scarcely encouraged to have his books praised by a well-to-do psychotic. Three absinthes and one whisky likewise fail to do him any good. "Whatever he had now he had, and it was from now on, and if he drank himself unconscious when he woke up it would be there" (p. 195).

Gordon's harsh awakening to the ugliness within himself proceeds now in a setting of equal ugliness. He next heads for

Freddy's bar, where he becomes involved in the sickly mayhem of the veterans who come up from the Keys on payday. Their degradation, their violence, turn the place into a hell on earth. (Hemingway knew firsthand the historical facts here. These were the ex-doughboys of the bonus army who had been driven out of the Capital and sent to work camps in the Keys, where hundreds of them died in the hurricane of September, 1935. Hemingway's wrath at the authorities who had failed to act soon enough to rescue the men exploded in an article titled "Who Murdered the Vets?" [23]) A tall veteran who gets into conversation with Gordon provides Hemingway's commentary on the spectacle at Freddy's:

"These are the elite. The very top cream of the scum. . . . Well, Mr. Hoover ran us out of Anticosti flats and Mr. Roosevelt has shipped us down here to get rid of us. They've run the camp in a way to invite an epidemic, but the poor bastards won't die. . . . They've got to get rid of us. You can see that, can't you?"
"Why?"
"Because we are the desperate ones," the man said. "The ones with nothing to lose. We are the completely brutalized ones. We're worse than the stuff the original Spartacus worked with. But it's tough to try to do anything with because we have been beaten so far that the only solace is booze and the only pride is in being able to take it. . . ." [pp. 205–6]

What the tall man says is dramatized by a scene in the bar, the power of which rivals Zola's in such episodes.

On the sidewalk out front a pair of buddies are rolling, one of them banging the other's head on the cement "making a sickening noise." These two are a grotesque sample of sado-masochism. The one says that at noon he had hit his buddy on the head with a bottle fifty times. With his bloodied lips close to Gordon's ear, the other, a redhead, whispers his "secret": "It don't hurt. . . . Sometimes it feels good" (p. 203). Meanwhile two vets beat up a third. Congratulations are in order. "You cooled him this time." " 'When I hit him just then I felt his jaw go just like a bag of marbles,' the other said happily" (p. 205). Like Richard Gordon, the punch-drunk redhead has also lost a wife; he cannot remember where he saw her last or even what country she is in:

"But listen, buddy," said the red-headed one. "Wherever she is that little girl is faithful. . . .

"Sometimes . . . I think that she is maybe Ginger Rogers and that she has gone into the moving pictures." [pp. 211–12]

Red and a number of his buddies have venereal disease:

"That's all you guys ever talk about. The old rale. What difference does the old rale make?"

"None, the way we are now," one Vet said. "You're just as happy with it." [pp. 215–16]

Here in the jetsam of society, among the ruined ones, Hemingway says in effect, Eros is reduced to nothing but disease, perversion, violence, and sentimentality. But his feeling of disgust is mingled with angry compassion.

From the wretchedness of the veterans, Hemingway takes us to the millionaire vacationers and their love lives. His device, rather contrived, is to tell us something about the occupants of several yachts anchored in the waters through which passes the boat that is carrying the dying Harry Morgan.

On one yacht is a sixty-year-old grain broker whose business deals have driven to suicide more men than Harry Morgan ever killed. His conscience is serene; he is only uneasy about whether his income tax evasions will be discovered. "He had been admirably endowed for a speculative career," Hemingway explains, "because he had possessed extraordinary sexual vitality which gave him the confidence to gamble well" (p. 235). This gift, of course, he shares with Harry Morgan. But, unlike Morgan, he had never loved anybody, surely not his divorced wife or two sons. Against his doctor's orders, he is having a whisky, telling himself, "Only suckers worry"; and "as he drinks it, the speculator is not a sucker now; except for death" (p. 238).

Peacefully asleep on the *Alzira III* is "a pleasant, dull and up-right" family. Their wealth comes from a patent medicine cost-ing three cents a quart to make and selling in the pint for a dollar. Their "lovely" daughter Frances is engaged to a Yale man, a Skull and Bones man, who has been voted most likely to succeed and most popular. It will be a brilliant marriage. In fact, he may even be "a little too good for Frances . . . but . . . she may never realize it, with luck." For, Hemingway ex-plains, "the type of man who is tapped for Bones is rarely also tapped for bed . . ." (p. 239).

Hemingway has even less admiration for the Ivy League types on the next yacht. Bachelors in their thirties, Henry Carpenter and Wallace Johnston are a pair of M.A.'s from Harvard. Henry's income from his trust fund has dropped to two hundred dollars a month—too low for him to want to go on living. His "last stand" is Wallace, who owns the yacht and has "rather special pleasures." Henry's service is to please Wallace, so that he will not have to pay blackmail to busboys and sailors. By being a little difficult and coquettish this night, Henry hopes to stave off Wallace's boredom and be kept on a while longer. "Thus Henry Carpenter postponed his inevitable suicide by a matter of weeks if not of months" (p. 233).

On the next yacht and troubled by insomnia is Dorothy Hollis, whose husband, a Hollywood director, is too old and sick and whose lover, Eddie, is too drunk to give her the love she needs. Her thoughts about her own frustration include as much pathology as pathos. And for the first time Hemingway goes on the record as a writer who understands that the bitch-woman is made and not born:

I wonder how Eddie would be if we were married. He would be running around with someone younger I suppose. I suppose they can't help the way they're built any more than we can. I just want a lot of it and I feel so fine, and being someone else or someone new doesn't really mean a thing. It's just it itself, and you would love them always if they gave it to you. The same one I mean. But they aren't built that way. . . . If you're dark they want a blonde. Or if you're blonde they go for a redhead. Or if you're a redhead then it's something else. . . . I suppose I'll end up a bitch. Maybe I'm one now. I suppose you never know when you get to be one. . . . But women have a bad time really. The better you treat a man and the more you show him you love him the quicker he gets tired of you. . . . [pp. 244–45]

So, Dorothy Hollis gets to sleep with the help of masturbation and Luminol.

For the most part, then, the love lives of the affluent earn Hemingway's contempt. Yet, as he surveys our society from top to bottom, Eros, in A.D. 1937, seems everywhere an ailing god, the only exception being the Morgans. *To Have and Have Not* nonetheless sounds a new note: its author displays a wiser sympathy with women. If the sickness of a society is mirrored in the sickness of Eros, Hemingway now puts a larger part of the blame on the male of the species. There is nothing new in his sympathetic treatment of Marie; but Hemingway is also on the side of the more complex and sophisticated Helen Gordon. And though he does not much care for a narcissistic type like Dorothy Hollis, he is remarkably fair in presenting what is tender and affectionate in her and her clear-cut preference for monogamy.

In *To Have and Have Not* Hemingway had an amplitude of worthwhile materials and the chance of saying some penetrating or at least provocative things about America of the Depression years. If this book falls apart, the trouble is not with some error in esthetics or with Hemingway's unwonted haste in putting it together. It is, rather, that the novelist is at a standstill. The art he had perfected in the 1920's he has not been able sufficiently to develop, to experiment with, and to grow in for mastering new subjects and for meeting the demands of a new and different age. The advances made in *To Have and Have Not* are overshadowed by repetition of old stuff—especially in the characterization of the protagonist. Hemingway cannot shake off his fascination with a certain kind of hero. Harry Morgan is a brother of the much-admired matadors; he shares their courage, their grace under pressure, their arrogance, their stoicism, their *cojones,* and their pride in killing. He has been shaped by the conception of heroism worked out in *Death in the Afternoon*— a conception that had, as we saw, an element of criminal pathology at its core. That element predominates in Morgan; it makes him less admirable than the bullfighters because he is more sadistic: his talent is killing, not bulls, but men. Morgan is also less than the matador because he cannot, by any stretch of the imagination, be called an artist. In *Death in the After-noon* Hemingway thought he had found in the matador the type of tragic-artist-hero. From this conception, the artist has now been split off. We are left with a hero who is a killer, and an artist who is degraded into the figure of the despised writer, Richard Gordon.

This conflict of Hemingway's remains unresolved in *To Have and Have Not.* Consciously, it seems, he did want to be the writer *engagé* and to write a novel of social protest. Why, then, did the fury which fires the career of the protagonist here lack heat enough to become fused with the rest of the metal? Because in his heart Hemingway was back where he had been when he gave us *Death in the Afternoon.* For him this period ends as it began. What most deeply engages his passion—the intensity he seeks and realizes—is Morgan killing and being killed. It is the old *aficionado* studying the gorings so he can capture "the feeling of life and death I was working for."

Chapter IV

Beyond *Nada:*
Fiction on the Spanish Civil War

Not the bull ring, but war, best provides that sought-for "feeling of life and death." By the time *To Have and Have Not* reached the best-seller lists, its author was at the front in Spain. There was never any question about his commitment as a foe of fascism. The question is whether out of his war experience Hemingway could make a story in which he would view life as more than the struggle of a solitary against desperate odds. Could he give us a hero who might exemplify anything other than lonely integrity and stoic courage—a man pitting himself against organized hatred and destruction, not to test his individual strength, but because he has a vision of a possible world where men might work together?

For answers, we have Hemingway's next two works, both of them products of his involvement in the Spanish cause: *The Fifth Column* (1938), the only play he ever wrote; and *For Whom the Bell Tolls* (1940), his biggest novel. Undoubtedly, the plunge into action, action with a social purpose and for a cause great enough to liberate his idealism, was more than a tonic for Hemingway. He shook off the malaise that had dogged him during the Depression years. What he saw and felt of Spain's agony also pushed him as a fictionist into new directions.

He not only tried his hand as a playwright; he also turned out a novel which in spirit, scope, and style is markedly different from his earlier ones. He had made the recovery that eluded him in *To Have and Have Not.*

At first glance, however, his participation in the conflict seems to have done more good to Hemingway's conscience and mood than to his art. For, if we are hoping for evidence of growth in *The Fifth Column,* we have to look closely and sympathetically. Composed in besieged Madrid in the fall of 1937, it is a poor example of dramaturgy. Too much of it is the Hemingway we are impatient for him to outgrow. Although the dialogue is often witty and lively, it is no longer easy to know just when to laugh. Now that the secret agent has become a cliché in movies, fiction, and television, it is almost irresistible to read *The Fifth Column* as a parody of its kind.

The love-and-war plot centers on the counterespionage activities of an American correspondent, Philip Rawlings, who poses as an irresponsible playboy. By day he faces danger and death; by night he makes love to Dorothy Bridges, a writer for magazines. His apprehensions that she might eventually lead him to slacken in his work cause him to break up the affair. The nobility of his renunciation of love in favor of duty is not very impressive, however, for we know that the hero's former girl friend, Anita, a "Moorish tart," has re-established herself in his hotel room and is at the moment having a nice warm bath.

Plainly Hemingway has not yet given up exploiting his legend. Philip Rawlings seems to be the author himself, very little disguised from his appearance in the public prints. Rawlings' lingo and wit, his reputation as a rough-romping international playboy, his hard drinking and hard loving are stock items. His overmasculine swagger first amuses, then embarrasses, and finally grates upon the nerves.

In contrast, Hemingway presents a woman whose type has never before appeared in his fiction. Dorothy Bridges represents the kind of woman we are producing in considerable numbers

now: well-educated, talented, wanting a career, yet not necessarily out to beat men at their own game. Yet he does little to
explore Dorothy's complexity or to dramatize her individuality.
He permits a few interesting qualities to emerge, only to deny or
undercut them later. For example, having given us a leading lady
adventurous enough to take an assignment in Madrid and intelligent enough to write for magazines, he then insists that we
regard her as stupid. She is supposed to be so little aware of
what is going on as not even to suspect that Philip is involved in
the war. In one scene we see her calmly sit through a bombardment with him. Later, when she comes upon a dead man and
asks who shot him, she is treated like a wilting violet. "Maybe
he shot himself," the hero snarls. "It's none of your business.
Get out of here. Didn't you ever see a dead man before? Aren't
you a lady war correspondent or something? Get out of here and
go write an article. This is none of your business" (p. 38).[1] Not
surprisingly, Hemingway is more at ease and alive in his treatment of Anita. She is another of his primitives, whose love is
available and without consequences. Her earthy candor about
herself and others is refreshing, and she speaks a marvelous
pidgin English.

The central conflict of the play is supposed to be love against
duty. True enough, we do not doubt Philip Rawlings' courage,
competence, and loyalty to his cause. On the other hand, there
is no dramatization or articulation of the cause to which he is
dedicated. We must take on faith, as in a grade-B Western
movie, that the good guys are fighting the bad guys. The two
moments which are intended to enlighten us add nothing but
sentimentality. Once, when the hero hears the Comrades singing "Bandera Rossa," he says, "The best people I ever knew
died for that song" (p. 63). Again, when a Fascist bombardment begins and we hear a child scream, Philip explodes: "The
swine! They timed it for the minute the cinemas are out." As
another shell explodes and a dog yelps down the street, Max,
another agent, explains: "You hear? You do it for all men. You

do it for the children. And sometimes you do it even for dogs . . ." (p. 79).

If the cause is not so convincing as the hero's adherence to it, the love which conflicts with his duty is even less credible. The affair that develops is sensual and sentimental only. We note the shallowness of Philip's feelings when he tells a superior officer: "I'd like to marry her because she's got the longest, smoothest, straightest legs in the world, and I don't have to listen to her when she talks if it doesn't make too good sense" (p. 44). We have more doubts when he talks over the affair with Anita, who tells him he does not want to make a mistake "with that big blonde." "You know, Anita," he replies, "I'm afraid I do. I'm afraid that's the whole trouble. I want to make an absolutely colossal mistake" (p. 49).

Philip's worry that his involvement with Dorothy might make him waver in his duty is deepened by the arrival of Max, the German Communist whose face has been smashed into such ugliness by his Nazi torturers that the only way he can have a woman is with "some one that will give me a little something while she looks the other way" (p. 76). This time it is not the Hemingway lover who is wounded, but we are not spared the wounds of war, and they are not separated from love. In one scene, when Philip goes into Dorothy's bedroom and takes her into his arms, Max is in the adjoining room asleep; the stage directions specify this effect: *As he sleeps, the light shines on his face"* (p. 63).

Max, however, is a man of benevolence. When Philip decides he must break with Dorothy, Max tells him: "But remember to be kind. To us to whom dreadful things have been done, kindness in all *possible* things is of great importance" (p. 96). Instead, Philip chooses a way to reject her that is feline in its cruelty. When she asks if they cannot get away from Madrid and go to Saint Tropez, he leads her on:

Yes, and afterwards to Egypt and make love happily in all the hotels, and a thousand breakfasts come up on trays in the thousand fine mornings of the next three years. . . . We'd stay at the Crillon, or the Ritz, and in the fall when the leaves were off the trees in the Bois and it was sharp and cold, we'd drive out to Auteuil steeple-chasing. . . . Would you like to go to Hungary, too, some fall? You can take an estate there very cheaply and only pay for what you shoot. . . . And have you ever been to Lamu where the long white beach is, with the dhows beached on their sides, and the wind in the palms at night? Or what about Malindi where you can surfboard on the beach. . . . And have you ever been out to the Sans Souci in Havana on a Saturday night to dance in the Patio under the royal palms? . . . [pp. 97–98]

Then, having woven his spell, he tells her they will not go anywhere. "I've been to all those places and I've left them all behind," he declares (p. 98). He will not take her with him, he says, because she is useless, uneducated, a fool, and lazy. When she says at least she is not useless, he replies: "Oh, yes. *That*. . . . That's a commodity you shouldn't pay too high a price for" (p. 99).

If Philip in his petty sadism hurts Dorothy more than the break necessitates, he is also supposedly hurting himself. Yet his sacrifice is phony; he suffers no real torment or real loss. In the Preface, Hemingway remarks of the play: "If it has a moral it is that people who work for certain organizations have very little time for home life" (p. vi). But the play contains no reference to home life, or anything like a couple responsibly living and working together. There is no genuine love-duty conflict in *The Fifth Column* because the love exerts no strong pull. Naturally, a fighter sick of war dreams of escape, but what places and good times this hero dreams about! It is not love Philip Rawlings gives up, but only an endless round of recesses —a life of grown-up play, self-indulgence, and finally boredom. When Dorothy explodes: "Now get out of here. You conceited, *conceited* drunkard. You ridiculous, puffed-up, posing braggart" (p. 99), she is scarcely overstating the case.

To be sure, we smile with Hemingway at the spanking he

gives his hero in this episode. In fact, since *The Fifth Column* is the most frivolous of his fictions, it cannot be taken seriously. Its chief value at this period of Hemingway's career is to signalize, though faintly, a promise of new growth. The sentimentalism is regrettable; but with Hemingway that is the price to be paid for sloughing off the puerile misanthropy of, say, *The Green Hills of Africa*. If Philip Rawlings' political idealism is mindless and takes the form of horseplay and cops and robbers escapades,[2] it is at least a step beyond the visceral anarchism of a Harry Morgan. We are still in what Saul Bellow called "an era of hardboileddom"; nonetheless, the fact that Hemingway has begun now to discard the iron that habitually has armored his heart points to the chance of a deeper and freer exploration of the passions. At least, his decade-long obsession with death is undergoing a change. For instance, whereas Harry Morgan was exhilarated by dealing out death, Philip Rawlings says he is sick of it. Though *The Fifth Column* lacks any hint of clear vision of a world where men might work together, perhaps we can label it a preliminary sketch for Hemingway's one and only attempt to project such a vision in what was to be his most ambitious novel.

There was one other preliminary sketch for that work, with no fumbling at all. From Barcelona in April of 1938 Hemingway cabled a little story called "Old Man at the Bridge." It sounds the opening notes of *For Whom the Bell Tolls*. In their retreat, a Loyalist officer comes upon the last refugee from San Carlos. He is a man of seventy-six who stayed to take care of two goats, eight pigeons, and a cat. He has no family and says he is "without politics." He has walked twelve kilometers already and now is too exhausted to go on. The old man's whole concern is for his animals; the pigeons can fly away, and the cat can take care of itself. "But the others. It's better not to think about the others." The officer urges him to try to go on; at any moment the enemy may open fire. The old man rises, sways, then sits down again. Nothing can be done about him, on this Easter

Sunday as the Fascists advance. But the low gray clouds mean that their planes are not up. So the narrator concludes: "That and the fact that cats know how to look after themselves was all the good luck that old man would ever have" (p. 80). The classic perfection of Hemingway's art here makes comment inane. If the anguish of Spain's little nobodies stirred a compassion of such power, it is no wonder that at least one critic at the time considered Hemingway obviously the man to write "the great book about the Spanish War." [3] His own views were then less pretentious. "The nobility and dignity of the cause of the Spanish people," he wrote in 1938, would call for "many plays and many novels . . . and the best ones will be written after the war is over." [4]

Only two years later he gave us *For Whom the Bell Tolls*. It would be an amazing performance if for no other reason than that it came so soon after the end of the fighting in Spain. But it is a remarkable book for more fundamental reasons. Whatever its flaws, *For Whom the Bell Tolls* marks a new departure for its author.

The change in Hemingway's heart worked also a change in his esthetics. In the matter of style, everyone readily saw and appreciated that he had risked an experiment. In the dialogue, where he used an English at once colloquial and archaic, he tried to capture the form and feel of the earthy yet often dignified speech of the Spanish peasants. [5] Against his typical understatement, we have a more fluid and heightened style as fitting for the epic spirit which he felt in this story of the ordeal of the Spanish people. The wealth of detail is another novelty. Instead of omission, of suggestiveness by implication, Hemingway adds and becomes explicit, pausing to develop the many facets of a situation or a personality. The power comes not through spare selection but in massive cumulation. In general, the result is a gain to his art. He has devoted nearly five hundred pages to seventy hours of action—all of it concentrated on the hero's blowing up one bridge behind the Fascist lines with the help of a small band of guerrillas—and produced a narrative which almost never drags and very seldom bulges.

For Whom the Bell Tolls is proof of growth in Hemingway for reasons that lie deeper than its style and technique. Granted, we have the standard materials: a world of danger and violence, with pain and death everywhere, and in the midst of war a pair of doomed lovers. Still, in the handling of these familiar subjects a different Hemingway emerges, a man better acquainted with his fellow creatures, alive to their dignity, saner in his judgment. This is also the first novel in which he has moved outside himself. Though the author is identified with Robert Jordan and though we find in him certain aspects of Hemingway's own life and character, the hero has not been drawn in his creator's image, much less according to the legend. In other respects, too, Hemingway has broken out of his former subjectivity. He has, as Edmund Wilson remarks, succeeded "in externalizing in plausible characters the elements of his own complex personality." [6] The result is that, for a Hemingway novel, this one is unique in the number, range, and variety of its characters. Of these, about a dozen are treated in depth as individuals and in their relationships with one another.

As to what sort of story Hemingway tells: if we loosely term it a historical novel, then *For Whom the Bell Tolls* has unmistakable shortcomings. It hardly provides a comprehensive interpretation of the Spanish Civil War, nor does its central event epitomize that conflict. [7] Naturally we do not demand of a foreign novelist a broad and deep understanding of the Spanish people. It can be argued—as it has been by the Spaniard Arturo Barea, who fought for the Loyalists and knew Hemingway personally in wartime Madrid—that some of the incidents are unlikely and that some of the characters behave implausibly. [8] It is difficult for an American reader to challenge Barea when, for example, he informs us that the guerrilla fighters, who were from the Castilian mountain villages, would never have accepted as their leaders a Pablo or a Pilar, who are outside creatures and hangers-on at the bull rings. Yet if Barea somewhat undermines our faith in Hemingway's verisimilitude, our enjoyment of the novel need be spoiled no more than we are disturbed by the clock in Shakespeare's *Julius Caesar*.

It is likewise not very fruitful to regard *For Whom the Bell Tolls* as a political novel. True, political questions bear directly on the mind and fate of the protagonist—a matter to be gone into later. It is misleading, though, to suppose, as readers sometimes do, that Hemingway is propagandizing a specific cause. It is an error of partisanship to argue that, because the worst villain in the piece is a Loyalist, Hemingway has been unfair to the Republic. It is more to the point to question his incomplete explanation of the Loyalists' defeat, and, for instance, to wonder why he scarcely touches on the failure of other democratic nations to come to the aid of the Republic. Yet neither these political blind spots nor Hemingway's inadequacies as a historian are crucial to what is right and wrong with this novel.

Our central concern here is with his criticism of life. In Aristotle's terms, what we ask of Hemingway is far less the specific truths of history than the poet's truth about the human condition. If in *For Whom the Bell Tolls* he made a new venture in style and technique and scope—and in his conscious intent to be affirmative—the question is: has he developed a fuller vision of life? And is there now any essential difference in how he views and treats those constants in his universe, love and death? It has often been argued that the eloquent and moving statements of the hero about his commitment to democracy are canceled out by the drama of death and defeat which engages our imagination. The ending of the tale is bleak, perhaps disheartening; but are Robert Jordan's final actions only a futile gesture? Is it all *nada* as before?

Has anything happened to the Hemingway conception of heroic manhood? In particular, what sort of hero is Robert Jordan? In several ways he reminds us of earlier Hemingway protagonists. Like Nick Adams, he is an outdoorsman from the

Midwest, has been shocked by an encounter with violence at too early an age—in fact, he has witnessed the same Negro lynching described in an interchapter of *In Our Time*; and he is tormented by recollections of his father's suicide. Like Frederic Henry, he is brave under fire; and like Jake Barnes, he is shrewd in his understanding of other people. He relishes the pleasures of sex and drinking, maintains a stoic mastery of his worries and fears, and is impressive in his practical abilities. He is, like Harry Morgan, skillful with weapons; and he can also be "very cold" in the head. And like Philip Rawlings he has volunteered his services to the Loyalist cause.

Of all the Hemingway men Jordan is about as near as we come to an intellectual and a mind with some awareness of politics and history. He is unique in other ways, too; he lacks several features we have come to expect in a Hemingway hero. He is no hunter, does not like to kill animals, and is too young to have fought in World War I. Nor has he been wounded; he is the one lover in the novels who suffers no physical hurt until the finale. Comparatively speaking, he is also less at war with himself than are the earlier Hemingway protagonists. He is clearly the most mature and sober-minded of all the heroes so far, and Hemingway has treated him with a fine balance of sympathy and detachment.

A professor of Spanish on a year's leave of absence, Jordan has been caught up in the war "because it had started in a country that he loved and he believed in the Republic" (p. 163). No Communist, he is an anti-Fascist merely, under the command of a Russian general only because *pro tempore* the Communists "were the only party whose program and whose discipline he could respect" (p. 163). His work as a partisan is difficult for him, not only because it means risking his own life, but also because it brings extra danger to those who work with him and shelter him. His present assignment to dynamite a bridge at the start of a Loyalist offensive is especially painful. He knows at the outset that it will be hard to blow up this bridge and harder still to escape afterward; later he realizes that, even if successful, the operation will be futile, for the offensive is doomed to fail. And he has just acquired some compelling reasons for wanting to stay alive, having fallen in love with Maria. In other words, the love-duty question is not spurious as it was in *The Fifth Column*.

Romantic love in wartime naturally brings to mind *A Farewell to Arms*. Yet the purport and value of the love between Jordan and Maria are the antithesis of the love between Frederic Henry and Catherine Barkley. Even in the safety of Switzerland when the odds seemed not too much against them, that couple had never thought of the future, nor dared to imagine a lifetime together. Though there is far less chance that Jordan and Maria will survive, though the moment is terribly important to them, too—these lovers think and dream of a future as man and wife. Nor are Jordan and Maria so isolated. Aside from the circumstance that they are fighting for a cause they believe in, they are very much a part of other people; the guerrilla band helps them, and they help it. More important: where the obverse side of Frederic Henry's love was boredom, emptiness, and death, now love is much more on the side of life. Thus far, then, has Hemingway's understanding of the possibilities of Eros been metamorphosed. On one occasion the lovers' union is described as "an alliance against death"—a view that is sane, not merely in human, but also in simple, biological terms. Here, too, Hemingway makes love for a woman no threat to a man's integrity in the work he is devoted to. Jordan tells Maria: "I love thee as I love all that we have fought for. I love thee as I love liberty and dignity and the rights of all men to work and not be hungry . . ." (p. 348).

The soundness of these ideas does not free Hemingway from his old faults in dramatizing a love relationship. Given the circumstances, we are willing to take on faith the love at first sight and the high pitch of the romanticism. But the sleeping-bag episodes are embarrassing rather than moving; and, as usual,

HEMINGWAY: THE INWARD TERRAIN

Hemingway dodges the give and take that go on between a real man and a real woman. His idealized sketch of Maria contrasts sometimes ludicrously with the realism of his portrait of Jordan. Hemingway is not interested in her character except as the figment of a dream. Once, after he has made love to her, Jordan's fantasies take this shape:

Maybe it is like the dreams you have when some one you have seen in the cinema comes to your bed at night and is so kind and lovely. He'd slept with them all that way when he was asleep in bed. He could remember Garbo still, and Harlow. Yes, Harlow many times. Maybe it was like those dreams. [p. 137]

Such pubescent mooning over Hollywood stars cannot stir the poignant response Hemingway is fumbling for.[9] One critic has called Maria an "amoeba-like little Spanish girl";[10] the label is harsh but fairly accurate. She comes alive only when she recounts the horrors she has been through and when she struggles against their consequences.

Interestingly, it is the encouragement and maneuvering of Pilar that brings the love to consummation. It is her gypsy notion that only three times in a lifetime can the act of sexual love make one feel that "the earth moved." For Jordan and Maria, the earth moves that afternoon when they make love in the heather on a hillside. And of their last night together Maria says, "I am thankful too to have been another time in *la gloria*" (p. 379). Jordan, who is not much given to gypsy lore or mysticism, has some hard-headed second thoughts about that ecstasy. He wonders if it is not merely "the urgency and the lack of time and the circumstances" which have brought an unusual intensity to a commonplace experience. Still, after their last embrace, he is thinking that Maria did say *"la gloria."*

It has nothing to do with glory nor La Gloire that the French write and speak about. . . . It is in Greco and in San Juan de la Cruz, of course, and in the others. I am no mystic, but to deny it is as ignorant as though you denied the telephone or that the earth revolves around the sun or that there are other planets than this. [p. 380]

Such ruminations may be laughed at or deplored, but neither reaction bears on what is happening to Hemingway here. Whether or not it may be silly to wax mystical about sexual love, the writer who makes a mystique out of love is a saner man than the one who makes a mystique out of death. We have moved a world away from the philosophy of *Death in the Afternoon*.

To be sure, for all his honest sensuality, Hemingway has made the loving couple as mistily abstract as Pelleas and Melisande. On the other hand, if we regret that Maria is more symbol than woman, her symbolic function, at any rate, is plain enough: through Jordan's love she is restored to life and health; through her love Jordan has had an experience rich enough so that he can die feeling he has lived fully. His ending is not so black as the image of Frederic Henry walking away from the hospital in the rain. In sum, though Hemingway cannot and never will outgrow romanticizing his heroines, he has at least reached a conception of love which not only makes the human lot more endurable but which also gives him a chance for further development as a novelist.

He has arrived at this point in *For Whom the Bell Tolls* without any blinking at the destructive impulses in our common humanity. Indeed, quantitatively this novel contains more killing than any of the others. Man the killer still preoccupies Hemingway but not in the way that has dominated his imagination for so long. Instead of throbbing to the killer's prowess, Hemingway now explores his psychology and discovers that killing is a less simple matter than his earlier writings indicated.

Of the many who kill in this book, the most fascinating is Pablo; and he is a far cry from the heroic matador delivering the "Godlike gift of death." The most complex and ambitious characterization in all of Hemingway's fiction, Pablo is most of the time repulsive. Since he is the wily leader of the guerrilla band, Jordan must find a way to deal with him if the bridge is to be blown. More than any of the others, Pablo grasps the danger of the operation. His opposition springs from defeatism and something else; he wants to protect his comfortable hideout and the supply of horses he has been procuring by fair means and foul. Pilar tells Jordan that Pablo can no longer be trusted. Once he was a good man, she says; but now he is "terminated"; and she adds that he is also being destroyed by drinking and by a "sickness" for Maria.

When there is a showdown on the bridge question and the rest of the band sides with Jordan, Pablo backs down and surrenders his leadership to Pilar. She is described at this moment as "proudly and confidently holding the big spoon as authoritatively as though it were a baton," a phallic suggestion of a reversal of the roles of the sexes (p. 56). Defeated, Pablo leaves the cave to go out and talk with his horses, like a lovesick boy wallowing in self-pity: "Thou art no woman like a rock that is burning. Thou art no colt of a girl with cropped head and the movement of a foal still wet from its mother. Thou dost not insult nor lie nor not understand. Thou, oh thee, oh my good big little pony" (p. 64). That night Pablo cries wretchedly, grieves that the band has turned against him, and tells Pilar he is afraid to die.

Not until Pilar gives her account of how the Loyalists took a certain village under Pablo's leadership, killing the *guardia civil* and massacring the Fascists, do we begin to understand why Pablo is so sick in spirit. As a depiction of cruelty, Chapter Ten is among the most harrowing episodes in the novels of our century. What Pilar witnessed that day revolted her whole being. That night, however, Pablo tells her that he liked all of it. Significantly, he has no desire then for sexual union: "It is true, Pilar, I am a finished man this night" (p. 128). Pablo's love of killing evidently makes him incapable of making love. The contrast with Harry Morgan is striking.

It is old Anselmo who underscores the point. He recalls the "great days" of Pablo as a *guerrillero* "when he scourged the country like a tartar and no fascist post was safe at night. And now, he is as finished and as ended as a boar that has been altered . . . and, when the altering has been accomplished and the squealing is over you cast the two stones away and the boar, that is a boar no longer, goes snouting and rooting up to them and eats them" (pp. 193–94). This time it is not *cojones* that have produced a killer. It is sadism; and such sickness has made Pablo less of a man sexually and has became a kind of self-cannibalism. The whetting of his sadism—once he even blinded a wounded *guardia civil*—has evidently intensified Pablo's self-absorption; the self-absorption is accompanied by melancholy; to ease the melancholy he drinks heavily; and when drunk he becomes sentimentally remorseful about the people he has slaughtered.

The relative ease of his situation before Jordan's arrival has swelled Pablo's greed for horseflesh. The glutting of his blood-lust, compounded with avarice, has wrecked Pablo's integrity in the work of war. He is no longer a heroic fighter, nor reliable to the Republic, nor trustworthy to his own band. The night before the bridge is to be blown he steals and destroys the detonators and exploders; then, near dawn, he comes back, bringing reinforcements from another mountain band. "Having done such a thing there is a loneliness that cannot be borne," he explains of his return. "Thy predecessor the famous Judas Iscariot hanged himself," is Pilar's comment (pp. 390–91). Pablo fights well enough that morning; but when his part is done, he coldly murders his new comrades, takes their horses, and rejoins his group. He makes Jordan aware of one of war's bitterest ironies: that, however right the cause, one must ally oneself with the greedy, the treacherous, the sadistic, and the murderous.

As a killer, Pablo's foil is sixty-eight-year-old Anselmo, who kills only because his convictions have forced him to take sides in the war. His Christian and liberal idealism never allows him to forgive himself. Alone on guard duty, he thinks:

If we no longer have religion after the war then I think there must be some form of civic penance organized that all may be cleansed from the killing or else we will never have a true and human basis for living. The killing is necessary, I know. . . . But I think any one doing it will be brutalized in time. . . . In those who like it there is always a rottenness. [pp. 196–97]

When he has to shoot a sentry, Anselmo cries, blaming himself for "blubbering . . . like a woman," yet feeling as if he has struck down his own brother.

Like Anselmo in dignity, courage, courtesy, and dedication to the cause is El Sordo. He is, however, closer to other killers we have known in Hemingway's fiction; the act can bring him a fierce joy. Though the council of war which he and Jordan hold lays bare the desperation of their plight—combining Sordo's and Pablo's bands will still leave them short of horses and men— Sordo, unillusioned, is willing to do his part at whatever cost. But worse luck is added. Snow falls the night they go out to steal horses, and the Fascists easily track Sordo's men and attack them. The five survivors make it to the top of a hill, where it is only a matter of time before they will be wiped out by mortar shells or planes. Sordo, not afraid to die, only angry at being trapped, relishes the puzzlement of his enemies who cannot know if any are still alive on that hilltop. His last stand reminds us of episodes in *The Song of Roland*. As the Fascist captain, to drive on his men, steps out into the open, shouting, "Shoot me! Kill me!" Sordo laughs silently. He lines up this perfect target:

Look at him stride forward. . . . This one coming now makes the same voyage I do. Come on, Comrade Voyager. . . . Come right along. . . . Look, he has a moustache. What do you think of that? . . . He is a captain. . . . With pale blue eyes that don't focus. Close enough. Too close. Yes, Comrade Voyager. Take it, Comrade Voyager. [p. 319]

"Gently" he squeezes the trigger, the body crumples, and Sordo in his ecstasy laughs so hard "that he thought the top of his head would burst" (p. 319). Then the planes come, and it is all over.

Another sort of killer is the foul-mouthed, good-hearted Agustín. He burns so with a desire to kill his enemies that he can barely hold himself back from firing at a cavalry patrol that comes within his range. Later, he tells Jordan: "And when I saw those four there and thought that we might kill them I was like a mare in the corral waiting for the stallion" (p. 286). Agustín's remark sets Jordan to musing on the difference between Spanish and non-Spanish killers:

We do it coldly but they do not, nor ever have. It is their extra sacrament. Their old one that they had before the new religion came from the far end of the Mediterranean, the one they have never abandoned but only suppressed and hidden to bring it out again in wars and inquisitions. They are the people of the Auto de [*sic*] Fé; the act of faith. [p. 286]

If we seem to be veering toward the philosophizing of *Death in the Afternoon,* Jordan's next thought indicates that this Hemingway hero does not congratulate himself on the sadistic elements of his own make-up: "Stop making dubious literature about the Berbers and the old Iberians and admit that you have liked to kill as all who are soldiers by choice have enjoyed it at some time. . . . Don't lie to yourself. . . . You have been tainted with it for a long time now" (p. 287).

Jordan can kill coolly and efficiently. For the most part, however, the killings sadden him. When he cuts down the young cavalryman from his sleeping bag, Jordan acts as if from a conditioned reflex. Later, as he looks over the youth's papers, letters from a devout mother and a hysterically anxious fiancée, "I guess I've done my good deed for today, he said to himself. . . . I'm sorry, if that does any good" (p. 303). He tells himself he must "drop it," but he cannot. More than any of the earlier Hemingway heroes, he is given to examining his conscience: "Don't you know it is wrong to kill? Yes. But you do it? Yes. And you still believe absolutely that your cause is right? Yes. . . . But you mustn't believe in killing, he told himself. You must do it as a necessity but you must not believe in it" (p. 304). Of the twenty he has killed, only two he is sure were Fascists. He worries that such probings into guilt may make him unsteady at his job, yet he struggles to keep his head "absolutely straight." "No man has a right to take another man's life unless it is to prevent something worse happening to other people" (p. 304). Only thus far can reason resolve his dilemma, and it brings no ease to his heart: "You have no right . . . to forget any of it nor to soften it nor to change it" (p. 304).

It is at the end that Jordan thinks most about killing and being killed. The survivors have made their escape, and he has forced Maria to flee with them, trying in those desperate moments to reach through her stunned grief and explain the mystery of their love: "But if thou goest then I go with thee. It is in that way that I go too. . . . Not me but us both. The me in thee" (pp. 463–64). Jordan is alone to die now, alone with his own thoughts. When his broken leg begins to hurt so severely that he thinks he might faint and then could be captured, questioned, and possibly tortured by the Fascists, he considers suicide. "It would be all right to do it now," he tells himself. Then he reconsiders: *"And if you wait and hold them up even a little while or just get the officer that may make all the difference"* (p. 470). He holds on; the enemy cavalry approaches; soon their leader is only twenty yards away. His target is Lieutenant Berrendo, the most humane of the Fascist officers. "Completely integrated now," Jordan waits for the kill, and the novel ends.

During these last moments Jordan's thoughts about his father's suicide comprise the most directly autobiographical features Hemingway has put into his characterization. "I don't want to do that business that my father did. . . . I'm against that," the hero says (p. 469). On the night before the offensive, Jordan had endured a sort of Gethsemane. In his doubts and fears he had wished he might talk with his grandfather, who had fought through the Civil War and survived to fight Indians. Yet, if there should be a hereafter where they could meet, both of them "would be acutely embarrassed by the presence of his father" (p. 338). Hemingway's private pain pierces through when his hero makes these admissions:

> I'll never forget how sick it made me the first time I knew he was a *cobarde*. Go on, say it in English. Coward. It's easier when you have said it and there is never any point in referring to a son of a bitch by some foreign term. He wasn't a son of a bitch, though. He was just a coward and that was the worst luck any man could have. Because if he wasn't a coward he would have stood up to that woman and not let her bully him. [pp. 338–39]

We are close to the heart that created "The Doctor and the Doctor's Wife" and "My Old Man." The family recollections end with this summing up: "He understood his father and he forgave him everything and he pitied him but he was ashamed of him" (p. 340). So, Jordan's quarrel with his father has not really come to an end—nor has Hemingway's.

In this connection it is interesting to note how Hemingway's mixed feelings about his own father went into the creation of two contrasting father figures in *For Whom the Bell Tolls*. Pablo, as the leader of the guerrilla band, is one; he is powerful and smart, but he is also dangerous, cowardly, and never to be relied on. Into the characterization of Anselmo went Hemingway's filial warmth and respect, and even such tenderness as we saw in "My Old Man." Aside from the fact that Anselmo, like Hemingway, Sr., has been a great hunter, there are more meaningful emotional disclosures. Anselmo's reliable presence always does good to Jordan's heart. As Jordan says good-bye to the band and each goes off to his particular post for the bridge-blowing, his mind goes back to an earlier farewell when he left his father to go off to school for the first time. With moist mustache and teary eyes Jordan, Sr., had embarrassed the boy with his pious platitude: "May the Lord watch between thee

and me while we are absent the one from the other" (p. 405).
Remembering "the wetness of that farewell," Jordan all the
more appreciates the spirit of old Anselmo. Very simply, each
says to the other, "Until soon" (p. 410).

Ambivalence has also gone into the portrait of the mother
figure, Pilar. Sometimes the characterization of Pilar is marred,
especially when we hear not her voice but Hemingway's. The
most egregious gaffe is Jordan's amazement at her virtuosity in
recounting the massacre—since he, too, has come upon the open
secret: that she has done it in Hemingway's best manner.
Nevertheless, Pilar remains the most vivid, interesting, and
fully realized woman in all his fiction. To be sure, Pilar is often
stagy, sometimes operatic, a creature of romance, like something
out of Sir Walter Scott modernized for our century. But her
complex and many-sided nature, her vitality, conquer our
imagination.

She is earthy, tough, foul-mouthed, bitter, zestful, and big-
hearted. Unlike Pablo, she never vacillates in her courage or in
her devotion to the Republic: "I believe in it with fervor," she
tells Jordan, "as those who have religious faith believe in the
mysteries" (p. 90). When he first encounters her, he sees a
big woman about fifty years old, "almost as wide as she was
tall . . . [with] a brown face like a model for a granite monument" (p. 30). It is at this meeting that Pilar, practicing her
gypsy lore, reads Jordan's palm, finding in it the sign of his
early death. This stock device of romance is not out of keeping
with her make-up; and of course it runs like a leit-motif through
the narrative.

Though barren, Pilar is very much a maternal creature. And
like other mothers in Hemingway, she is strong-willed and bul-
lying. She takes away the leadership of the band from Pablo,
returning it only when she wishes. Before becoming Pablo's
woman, she had lived with a bullfighter, tubercular, many-
scarred little Finito, to whom she had been as much mother as
mistress. Her relations with Maria are predominantly maternal;

she has cared for the girl since her rescue from the Fascists. And she is Maria's counselor in matters of love. In part, too, she functions as a mother figure for Jordan. He relies on her advice and experience in dealing with the *guerrilleros;* and when he wires the bridge, his nerves are steadied by thinking of her resoluteness. Perhaps she also satisfies an unconscious filial wish of Jordan's: as the adoptive "mother" of Maria, she not only approves but encourages and abets his union with the girl.

At first Pilar seems to take a kind of supervisory interest in their affair. She wants it for Maria, for it is Pilar's belief that the experience of being raped by the Fascists will be wiped out if Maria finds real love. Pilar also arranges that, after the three of them visit El Sordo, she will leave Maria and Jordan alone.

On this trip Pilar reveals much of her complex emotional life. She has become involved in the young lovers, and her feelings are mixed. Part of her moodiness on that occasion springs from jealousy. Their youth and their love increase her self-awareness. She is moved to tell them about her own love life:

"Do you know how an ugly woman feels? Do you know what it is to be ugly all your life and inside to feel that you are beautiful? . . . I would have made a good man, but I am all woman and all ugly. Yet many men have loved me and I have loved many men. It is curious. . . . Look at the ugliness. Yet one has a feeling within one that blinds a man while he loves you." [pp. 97–98]

She reminisces about Valencia, where she spent her happiest years, enjoying to the full the life of the senses and of love. But the grim conference with El Sordo has depressed Pilar, and she rages with the thought that she may have to die in the hills. Suddenly her anger explodes upon Jordan, and it is mixed with envy and sexual jealousy: "Take thy little cropped-headed whore and go back to the Republic. . . . And I suppose that you'll go to Valencia together and we can eat goat crut in Gredos" (p. 150). She promptly apologizes for her outburst, explaining, "I have an evil temper" (p. 154).

That Pilar's torment is a complicated one is indicated by the next incident. In her strong, tough nature is a generous admixture of masculinity. Now, as she caresses Maria, who has put her head in Pilar's lap, the dialogue takes on certain overtones of lesbianism:

"Yes, he can have thee," Pilar said and looked at neither of them. "I have never wanted thee, but I am jealous."

"Pilar," Maria said. "Do not talk thus."

"He can have thee," Pilar said and ran her finger around the lobe of the girl's ear. "But I am very jealous."

"But Pilar," Maria said. "It was thee explained to me there was nothing like that between us."

"There is always something like that," the woman said. "There is always something like something that there should not be. But with me there is not. Truly there is not. I want thy happiness and nothing more. . . . Listen, *guapa*, I love thee and he can have thee, I am no tortillera [lesbian] but a woman made for men. . . . I do not make perversions. I only tell you something true. Few people will ever talk to thee truly and no women. I am jealous and say it and it is there. . . ." [pp. 154–55]

A moment later Pilar is smiling and teasing Jordan that she might take the girl away from him. He says she cannot. " 'I know it,' Pilar said and smiled again. 'Nor would I wish to. But when I was young I could have' " (p. 156).

All of this forms a rather unusual prelude to the love-making of Jordan and Maria that afternoon. Afterward, his head seems very clear; and he thinks he understands Pilar's conduct:

She made things easier so that there was last night and this afternoon. She is a damned sight more civilized than you are and she knows what time is all about. . . . She took a beating and all because she did not want other people losing what she'd lost and then the idea of admitting it was lost was too big a thing to swallow. [p. 168]

But Jordan has no sooner credited her with uncommon generosity than Pilar does something to anger and embarrass him.

When the lovers meet her on the way back to the cave, she at once presses Maria to tell her "one thing of thy own volition" (p. 173). Although her persistence about such an intimacy riles Jordan, the woman's peculiar curiosity strikes him as neither "predatory" nor "perverted" (p. 173). Hemingway's phrasing, however, is notably ambiguous: "There was a spreading, though, as a cobra's hood spreads. He could feel this. He could feel the menace of the spreading. But the spreading was a domination, not of evil, but of searching" (p. 173).[11] As if hypnotizing the girl, Pilar gets Maria to admit that for her the earth moved. Jordan's anger goes when it appears to him that Pilar's curiosity is neither evil nor morbid: "It was only wanting to keep her hold on life. To keep it through Maria" (p. 176).

To wish to keep one's hold on life through someone else is not the same thing as trying to live that person's life or to exercise absolute control over it. Like the mothers in the stories, Pilar has a strong need to dominate; unlike them, Pilar's need is guided by intelligence and springs from a vigorous involvement in life and from a powerful individuality. Its effect is neither "predatory" nor destructive. With Jordan, we respect Pilar's strength; but even in banter she is never allowed to lord it over him. She is the last mother figure who appears in Hemingway's fiction, and the only one he treats sympathetically. Insofar as he could through his art, Hemingway has progressed to this point in resolving the love-hate feelings which he evidently felt toward his own mother.

Also through Pilar, Hemingway characteristically interweaves Eros and Thanatos. Besides the palm-reading and such, we have Chapter Nineteen, which might be labeled "The Smell of Death." A gaudy tour-de-force, this chapter is made tolerable by Hemingway's romanticizing the subject as a curiosity of gypsy lore. Pilar contends that some gypsies have a preternatural olfactory sensitivity by which they can tell, from the odor of certain persons, that they are soon to die. When Jordan rejects it all as gypsy nonsense, she specifies the gruesome and nauseous

ingredients which come nearest to what the gypsies perceive—
"the smell," she declares, "that is both the death and birth of
man" (p. 256).

Throughout *For Whom the Bell Tolls* are many instances
of such interweaving.[12] There is an obvious bit of symbolism
when the gypsy, Rafael, kills a pair of rabbits he comes upon
copulating in the snow. More interesting, psychologically, is
Maria's hysterical reaction when Jordan kills the solitary cavalryman; as the band rushes to protect themselves against the coming
of more enemy horsemen, Maria clings to Jordan, crying, "Not
love me now?"

> "*Dejamos.* Get thee back. One does not do that and love all at the
> same moment."
> "I want to go to hold the legs of the gun and while it speaks love
> thee all in the same moment."
> "Thou art crazy. Get thee back now." [p. 270]

Love and the *nada* of death are also adumbrated even in the
episode when the earth moved. For Maria, lying on her back,
the sunlight on her eyelids makes everything "red, orange, gold-
red . . . all of it, the filling, the possessing, the having, all of
that color, all in a blindness of that color." For Jordan, facing
the earth, "it was a dark passage which led to nowhere . . .
always and forever to nowhere" (p. 159). And again, El Sordo,
sprawled behind the dead body of a horse, fights his last fight on
a hill which to him seems "shaped like a chancre. Or the breast
of a young girl with no nipple" (p. 309).

In the linking of love and death, as one student of the book
has pointed out, horses also have a symbolic function in this
novel, a function related also to their literal and dramatic uses.[13]
Nothing more needs to be said about Pablo and horses, nor
how hoofprints lead to El Sordo's premature defeat. Maria's
loveliness is more than once likened to that of a colt. Her joyous-
ness after love-making she once expresses in this metaphor: "In
my happiness I would like to be on a good horse and ride fast

with thee riding fast beside me and we would ride faster and faster, galloping, and never pass my happiness" (p. 161).

Traditionally, the horse has had two opposite symbolic meanings. He has been a funerary beast—and is so imaged, for instance, in Emily Dickinson's poem, "Because I could not stop for death"; and the stallion embodies virility. Such symbolism resonates through the fate of Robert Jordan. The horse he obtains when he shoots the cavalry scout is the same big gray, a gelding, which he mounts after the bridge is blown. When the tank shell knocks the horse down, it falls upon and breaks Jordan's leg. So the double irony is that the castrated horse gives the hero his symbolically castrative wound.[14]

That wound brings death to Robert Jordan. And we are brought back to the central and most difficult question about For Whom the Bell Tolls. We may rejoice in Hemingway's effort to escape his nihilism. But can we take his hero's sacrifice as an affirmation of the cause of democracy, or of some greater cause? Or does Jordan never achieve enough stature to make his death anything beyond the Byronic gesture of one more self-absorbed Hemingway hero? The truth may lie somewhere between these two views.

What has so often been objected to is that the affirmations are verbalized while the death and waste are dramatized. Unquestionably, it is the anguish and destruction of war which Hemingway feels most deeply and which his art is best equipped to realize. It is also true that his hero is possessed by no easy and steadily burning faith in the Loyalist cause. Jordan is a complex and never a one-idea man. Sometimes he tells himself he has no politics. Again, he can say, "If we win here, we win everywhere," or can think of his bridge "as the point on which the future of the human race can turn." Sometimes he has an almost religious conviction:

You felt, in spite of all bureaucracy and inefficiency and party strife something that was like the feeling you expected to have and did not have when you made your first communion. It was a feeling

of consecration to a duty toward all of the oppressed of the world. . . .
You felt an absolute brotherhood with the others who were engaged
in it. [p. 235]

In another mood he will be grim about those on his side: "If
you had three together, two would unite against one, and then
the two would start to betray each other" (p. 135). Nor can we
say that Jordan is wholeheartedly committed to the government
for which he fights, or to any system of government, or that he
believes a new social dispensation will provide a brave new
world. He dies without any tidy ideological certainty and well
aware that his death may be useless even in this particular and
local battle for democracy. Yet, if Jordan and his comrades afford us small reason to exult over the coming victory of democracy, we should hardly single out Hemingway for blame—
or expect him to salvage "the liberal imagination." Most of
the twentieth-century masters—Mann, Lawrence, Kafka, Eliot,
O'Neill, Faulkner—have, as toward society, a comparable lack
of faith.

At any rate, Hemingway's chief concern is not politics. He
is, rather, concerned with the possibility of man's achieving and
maintaining dignity. On the other hand, since he has placed his
protagonist in a specific historical situation, Hemingway's conscious intention was to create a hero on a scale large enough to
represent the moral and political defeat of the Spanish people.
So, if Robert Jordan's heroic death is to reach toward tragic
significance, then we might expect him to embody and compre-
hend the historical events that victimize him. Precisely that
comprehension Jordan lacks. He thinks *about* the forces that
seal his doom, but he never thinks *through* them; their workings
are on the periphery of, but never absorb, the hero's mind. For
example, Jordan admires the cynical and lucid brain of the
journalist Karkov as he admires the hard-headed competence of
General Golz; but he does not join such men in their unillusioned grasp of what is going on.[15]

True, the novel evinces Hemingway's own awareness of the

confoundings and contradictions of the Loyalists' predicament. One thinks of the boy Joaquin on El Sordo's hilltop, quoting La Pasionaria and then, as the Fascist planes come, shifting suddenly into an Ave Maria and the Catholic "Act of Contrition"; and of the marvelous account of Andres carrying through night and danger and red tape his fatal message, to be held up by the psychopathic André Marty; and of how, when at last the message reaches Golz, too late, the general speaks into the phone while the bombers roar overhead: *"Bon. Nous ferons notre petit possible,"* and hangs up (p. 430). None of this figures really in the mind of Robert Jordan. "You're a bridge-blower now. Not a thinker" (p. 17), he tells himself. Under the immediate circumstances that self-admonition was a practical necessity. Yet we feel Hemingway expects us to admire his hero for exactly this tough-minded pragmatism—as, rightly, we do admire Jordan for the idealism he feels and articulates and finally proves with his life. The consequence is that, when we come to his finale, Jordan seems less a figure representing the issues he has been caught up in than a man working out a personal matter of how to act with honor.

Is Jordan, then, a mite ground by a juggernaut into senseless extinction? I think the answer here must be no. If his death lacks tragic grandeur, Hemingway has not failed to give it considerable significance. We have already seen what Jordan's death means in private terms: he has undergone an education; can die more easily because he has known love; and can die, if not reconciled to his father's suicide, at least feeling he has compensated for the guilt and shame that deed laid on his own heart. Jordan's death also has meanings well beyond these private ones —meanings which we see more plainly now that a quarter of a century has passed since the story was published, and we have become habituated to wars and revolutions and the mega-death-dealing bomb and the increasing mechanization and dehumanizing of our lives. If we look at the bigger forces that defeat Jordan and consider how he met them, we may understand better what sort of affirmation Hemingway has succeeded in making here.

In the broadest sense, Jordan's plight is analogous to that of many high-minded men today, men who do not necessarily face gunfire. Given a difficult but evidently unavoidable assignment with the odds against its successful completion, lacking the men and wherewithal he needs, ruled by a hierarchy he has not chosen and in whose competence and probity he can have no great confidence, working with associates some of whom may willy-nilly undo his best efforts, entangled in a faceless bureaucracy for whose operations somehow no one is responsible, unable to communicate with those who seem to make the decisions, Jordan is, in sum, trapped by circumstances beyond his control. That he does not fully understand diminishes his stature, but it also makes him more broadly representative of the plight of modern man. And what Jordan does do makes him heroically representative: without the solace of religion, without faith that his cause will eventually win, without even much hope that his immediate task will have practical consequences, Jordan still chooses to act. He takes the one honorable course that is open to him.

His is more than an act of courage. It is an act which affirms the possibility of human dignity and decency. If in *For Whom the Bell Tolls* Hemingway has anything to say about the conduct of life, it is that such dignity is not only necessary but also possible. This conviction he bodies forth in a hero who is not an anarchical individualist but one among several persons who feel and think and act with unselfish dedication to something outside their own lives.

Chapter V

The Last of the Heroes:
Novels of the Fifties

When he published *For Whom the Bell Tolls* the novelist was in his forty-second year. Though there was more of the old Hemingway in that work than we might wish, it also exhibited tremendous creative energy. One had reasons to hope, in 1940, that the author had come upon new veins for his art and that he might be resuming his distinguished career as a fictionist. Instead, he published not a single piece of fiction for a decade. When at last we get his next novel, it turns out to be his worst failure. It was not that in *Across the River and into the Trees* Hemingway had merely stopped growing—or blundered by chancing something beyond his gifts. He seems to have painfully unlearned his craft and gone backward in every way. This book reads like one written by an aged adolescent recording his boyish dreams in a first novel.

As to what has gone wrong, we will probably never get an explanation satisfactory to everybody. And it is hardly enough to know that, when he finished *Across the River and into the Trees* in Venice in the winter of 1949–50, Hemingway was so ill with an infection resulting from a hunting accident that apparently he feared he was going to die.[1] For the sickness which went into this book's making was not a matter of streptococci.

There is a sickness of spirit here worse than anything that afflicted Hemingway in the 1930's. In none of his other books has his morbidity displayed itself so nakedly or worked such havoc with his art.

It is possible now to see that by his early forties, with his big book on the Spanish Civil War, Hemingway had virtually completed his work in fiction. What followed was only this fiasco; the novella, *The Old Man and the Sea*; and the posthumous memoirs, *A Moveable Feast*. From the late 1940's on we had rumors and reports that he was working on a big book about "the Land, the Sea, and the Air." [2] What may yet be unearthed among Hemingway's literary remains and brought to print we cannot at present be sure. But it is doubtful that any unpublished work of his last twenty years will appreciably alter the nature of his achievement. Evidently, these are the years of the long decline in his creativity, a decline hastened by the combination of external circumstances and inward forces. [3]

On the surface the decade began with adventure, and one gets the image of robust health and hardihood. Shortly after he married his third wife, Martha Gellhorn, the couple went off in January of 1941 to report on the wars in China. Then, a few months after America entered World War II, Hemingway transformed his cabin cruiser, the *Pilar*, into a Q-boat; and for a year and a half with a crew of nine he patrolled the waters off Cuba in search of Nazi submarines. When these suicidal adventures produced boredom, he went to Europe in the spring of 1944. With RAF pilots he flew a number of missions. On D-Day he crossed the channel to the Normandy beaches in an LCV(P) craft. From the twentieth of July until the German collapse he fought on European soil—in his own unorthodox style. Allegedly a war correspondent, Hemingway wrote only enough dispatches to keep from being sent back to the States; nearly got himself court-martialed for violating the Geneva Convention, which forbids correspondents to carry weapons; in his jeep ranged far ahead of the advancing First Army, making con-

tact with French guerrillas and sending intelligence reports back
to the division commander; on the nineteenth of August set up
headquarters and found himself taking charge as commanding
officer at Rambouillet, thirty miles from the French capital; on
the road to Paris got a tongue-lashing from General Leclerc,
whose armored division had been given the honor of first entering the French capital—because, it seems, the Hemingway ir-
regulars were impatient with the niceties of military protocol;
and by August 25 had so far "liberated" the Ritz that, when one
of his friends went to the entrance, he recognized Hemingway's
jeep driver, who issued the invitation: "Papa took good hotel.
Plenty stuff in cellar. You go up quick." The bloody climax
came in November of 1944 when for eighteen days Hemingway
was in Huertgen Forest, sharing the hardships and horrors endured by the regiment of his friend, Colonel "Buck" Lanham,
whose outfit suffered 80 per cent casualties.[4] We also have the
story told by the artist John Groth who visited "Task Force
Hemingway," a farmhouse on the Siegfried Line so close to
enemy pillboxes that German patrols sometimes reached the
farmyard. There, one night during dinner, German 88's broke
in, shattering the window and putting out the lights; everyone
hit the floor and groped for helmets—supposedly; when at last
candles were lit, Groth was amazed: "Hemingway was still
seated at the table, his broad back to the window, helmetless,
eating." [5]

Out of all this came two or three dispatches in which once
again Hemingway proved that he could make of war reporting
a genuine art.[6] For the rest? No doubt his adventures are romantic and gallant. They enlarge his legend in big, bold colors
and should liven the pages of his biography. But once in the
midst of combat one battle-weary G.I. asked the writer, "What
are you doing here if you don't have to be here?" The reply
was, "Lots of money." [7] To be sure, that is not the answer, nor
did Hemingway mean it to be. Surely, though, that is the question: what drove this novelist, in his forties and seemingly at

mid-career, to seek heroism on Europe's battlefields? For nearly half a decade the best of Hemingway's time and energy, heart and brains, went into fighting. He won decorations, publicity, the affection and respect of the G.I.'s and their officers. On his own terms he could say he was studying war—which, he once remarked, was "one of the major subjects and certainly one of the hardest to write truly of." The irony is that all the heroics and the suffering in no way helped him as a fictionist to write "truly" about the subject. He himself had doubts: while the buzz bombs were terrifying London, he wrote that "sometimes it doesn't seem the right man in the right place and I have thought some of leaving the whole thing and going back to writing books." [8] Long afterward he told himself, "You will never again interrupt the work that you were born and trained to do until you die." [9] But this promise was made in 1956, when it was too late. For his World War II exploits seem to have taken a frightful toll out of his art and to have drained, if they did not shatter, his creative personality.

To act is easy, to think is hard. Almost too patly Hemingway demonstrates Goethe's truism. Like his earlier confrontations with violence, Hemingway's encounter with the hell of war afforded an escape from his inner hell. All through his writings we have seen his desire for dangerous action in which one can prove himself a man among men. The obverse side of it we have also noted: his fear of women or, more precisely, his dread of any feminine softness in his own make-up. In the 1920's he managed to control his anxieties and compulsions and make use of them in his fiction. In the next decade they threatened to swamp his art, though he struggled with his sickness and tried, however uncertainly, to understand it. But the Hemingway who fought World War II did little self-questioning. If the world would applaud a man risking his life against totalitarianism, was not that reason enough to stop worrying over his intellectual and moral perplexities and his emotional confusion? In good conscience he could put himself in a kill-or-be-killed situation and be at one with a fighting and exclusively male world. Yet such desperate remedies worked the opposite of a cure. For Hemmingway the real victory was his neurosis; the real defeat was his art.

We have the ruins in *Across the River and into the Trees.* That book is such a disaster that it almost calls for the services of a pathologist rather than the analysis of a critic. Its central mood, one of peevish self-pity, is fit for burlesque. One academically brilliant suggestion is that it be read in this way and that we regard the bragging hero as in the literary tradition of the *miles gloriosus* which begins with the comedies of Plautus.[10] That would be interesting, had not Hemingway so clearly intended that we take his novel seriously.

The most frequent complaint is that he has repeated himself, unconsciously, to the point of ludicrous self-parody. Once again we have the hero, now fifty years old and the veteran of two world wars. Once again we have love and war, and love defeated by death. Colonel Richard Cantwell's teen-age Italian countess, Renata, is more than ever a dream girl. Again we have the gusto in drinking and eating, in hunting and love-making, in virile camaraderie. What we can regret is that Hemingway had here the seeds of two works the world will never see: a joyous account of his love affair with Italy and a mordant history of his experiences in and reflections on World War II. What he did not have in him was another love story.

Nonetheless, he tried, feverishly, to be affirmative, to say a good word for love. Rarely has Hemingway given such free rein to his tenderness and affection, or so often dropped his guard. But the self-criticism that must be at work in any satisfactory artistic creation has been lulled asleep. As a result we have Hemingway's most self-indulgent performance. What is intended to be good-heartedness slops over, regularly, into gush; what is intended to be manliness hardens into brittle posturing. The famous manner has become a set of mannerisms.

Freud, we recall, compared the artist to the day-dreamer. Each indulges in fantasies that flatter his self-love. When the day-dreamer asks us to share his reveries, we are bored and offended by their display of raw egoism. The artist, on the other hand, pleases us because, though his fantasies rise from the same kind of self-absorption, he can by his gifts conceal their origins. His discipline and technical mastery, his devotion to formal require-ments, enable him to disguise and elaborate his fantasies and get them into patterns that win our acceptance. All too nicely, *Across the River and into the Trees* illustrates Freud's theory. In fact, it is closer to being an outright daydream than a novel. As such, it fails to charm—except for the word painting of the weathers and waters of Venice—and it never earns our sympa-thies.

What we are offered is a curious study in the psychology of dying, all of it focused on one character. Though scarcely a beautiful youth, Colonel Cantwell is Narcissus. He looks into the mirror at his face and body, both the worse for wear, and likes what he sees:

He did not notice [are we sure he did not?] the old used steel of his eyes nor the small, long extending laugh wrinkles at the corners of his eyes, nor that his broken nose was like a gladiator's in the oldest statues. Nor did he notice his basically kind mouth which could be truly ruthless. [p. 112]

As to the other personages in the story, their only function is to reflect the colonel's peeves and affections, his pride and preju-dice, his crotchets and lucubrations. Hemingway has placed his most acutely self-conscious protagonist in a maze of mirrors. The effect is both comical and exasperating.

Even Cantwell's pleasures can irk us. His delight in eating and drinking is that of a snob. When he revels at being the darling of headwaiters, bartenders, and concierges, the reader sees far less a man of the world than a sophomore come to the big city for a week-end. The promptitude with which gourmet food and bottles of wine are produced for the colonel by adoring puppets is dream stuff. Hemingway also takes us into the dream world of adolescence when he has his ill and aging hero knock out two young, husky sailors who have ogled his sweetheart. It is true, sometimes the Colonel suspects he is a boy. Addressing the portrait of Renata, he promises: "I'll be the best God-damned boy you ever witnessed today. And you can tell your principal that" (p. 173). At the same time, he is even more proud of his "wild boar blood" (p. 65).

Equally comic is the sentimentalizing of the hero's war experiences. Of his divisional insignia Cantwell confesses: "We wore a four-leaf clover, which meant nothing except among ourselves, who all loved it. And every time I ever see it the same thing happens in my inner guts" (p. 248). And are we to keep a straight face when, of his accommodations at the Gritti, we are told: "it was a defensive, rather than an attacking bathroom, the Colonel felt" (p. 111)? We hover on the edge of sweet tearfulness whenever Hemingway writes of the *maître d' hôtel*, who had been wounded in the first World War and who also suffers a cardiac condition. The *Gran Maestro* has "a long and loving face with the grey eyebrows over the softly hooded eyes, and the ever happy face of the old soldier who is still alive and appreciates it." The understanding between these two old soldiers is perfect. When the Colonel and Renata sit down to eat:

They were at their table in the far corner of the bar, where the Colonel had both his flanks covered, and he rested solidly against the corner of the room. The *Gran Maestro* knew about this, since he had been an excellent sergeant in a good company of infantry, in a first-rate regiment, and he would no more have seated his Colonel in the middle of a room than he would have taken up a stupid defensive position.

"The lobster," the *Gran Maestro* said. [p. 115]

What dream is more romantic than a ride with your girl over the canals of Venice? In the space of a brief gondola trip, this much-scarred, prematurely old hero, with his seriously ailing heart, achieves three orgasms with his nineteen-year-old *contessa*. Alas! We are not willing to suspend our disbelief.

We could pity the Colonel as a luckless lover; but since his affair is sheer wish-fulfillment, we feel none of his heartbreak. And are we never supposed to ask why a beautiful Venetian aristocrat should fall headlong in love with a long-winded bore she knows is soon to die? When the obstacle to romantic love is death, then that love, as in the Tristan legend, is allegedly transfigured. But there is no death and transfiguration here. What we do have is Hemingway's ultimate demonstration that the sort of romantic love he has clung to since *A Farewell to Arms* leads down a dark alley to nowhere.

Renata is the last and the most impossible of his heroines. After Brett Ashley, each of them—except for Dorothy Bridges, who is pointed at rather than characterized—has become more brainless. The emptiest of all is Renata. The self-absorbed hero never tries to understand her because, like his creator, he is not interested in her. Cantwell is in love only with the emotions she stirs in him. If we agree that in *For Whom the Bell Tolls* Hemingway had arrived at a more mature *idea* about love even though he could not realize it fictionally, now he has dropped even that promising idea. The best measure of how far he has regressed here is provided by the love affair, which is in every respect inferior to that of Frederic Henry and Catherine Barkley.

Indeed, in his fiction, Hemingway, we must conclude, can put up with very few representatives of womankind. First of course are those he feels most easy toward, his inferiors, the primitives and earthy ones such as the little Indian Trudy and Harry Morgan's wife. Next are those he makes most interesting, those with the masculine qualities of Brett and Pilar. Psychologically related to them are his bitch-women like Margot Macomber. Finally we have the women who regard themselves as mere appendages of the man they love and totally submerge their identity in him. Out of these never-never creatures Hemingway fashions his romantic heroines. Extensions of the masculine ego, they never represent actual women, nor anything more than a narrow sector of the love experience. They are remote from life because love is remote from their creator's imagination—or, more accurately, because in the world of Hemingway's fiction aggressiveness regularly predominates over the erotic. His deepest commitment is to the exclusively masculine.

Naturally, then, his last romantic hero gets his greatest satisfaction when Renata listens to his tales of war. The Colonel's opinions on a wide variety of generals and politicians and writers, his "inside dope" on certain military operations—these might pique our interest in another kind of book, but not in this one. To be sure, by indulging in these splenetic digressions Cantwell is supposed to be purging himself of hate and bitterness so that he may die at peace with himself. Yet we are never shown how these confessions bring to fruition "his always renewed plan of being kind, decent, and good."

Obviously, as he wrote *Across the River and into the Trees*, Hemingway was trying to get out of his system the horror and shock he had been through in World War II, especially the nightmare of Huertgen Forest.[11] The therapy, though, seems to have failed as surely as does the art. For the novel is the product of a disintegrating personality. Its author has not yet made his way out of his sufferings, nor mastered his materials, nor gained his perspective. All of this is concentrated in his hero. Of course Hemingway is not Cantwell, yet never before and at such length has he put so much of himself into a protagonist with so little disguise. To mention only a few items: Cantwell is Hemingway's own age, has had Hemingway's marital woes, has many of Hemingway's scars and concussions, has Hemingway's hypertension and his hobbies, and in general his experiences in both world wars parallel Hemingway's.[12]

That the author was near to being inwardly shattered as he worked on this novel explains some of the oddities of his hero. Plainly symptomatic are the jangling juxtapositions we encounter in Cantwell's love talk, both to Renata and in his monologues about their love. Side by side, unresolved, unrelieved, are tenderness and toughness, the *dolce affetuoso* and the hard-boiled obscene. The bounty of cuss words we accept as correct for the battlefield and the barracks. In the situations where Hemingway has often used them, however, he has made them not so much offensive as silly and phony. Unlike Robert Jordan, Cantwell can be tender only if, at the same moment, he sounds off like a juvenile delinquent—as if, at least verbally, he is honor-bound to defend his virility. To write about love in military metaphors is of course to follow a venerable tradition. It becomes silly, though, when, for example, to Renata's question, "Don't you feel better to be loved?" Cantwell explains:

"I feel as though I were out on some bare-assed hill where it was too rocky to dig, and the rocks all solid, but nothing jutting and no bulges, and all of a sudden, instead of being there naked, I was armoured. Armoured and the eighty-eights not there." [pp. 128–29]

The sweet rough talk is embarrassing when, as Cantwell sighs over the girl's portrait, he felt like "a General now again, early in the morning . . . and with Valpolicella, knew as absolutely as though he had just read his third Wassermann that there was no eff-off in portrait . . ." (p. 173). We are informed that for the Colonel sexual love and its ecstasies comprise "the only mystery that he believed in except the occasional bravery of men" (p. 153). What we experience, though, is not the Colonel's faith, but his befuddlement; for his typical manner of connecting the two mysteries is by the tiresome way of the obscenely tough.

Significantly, the same kind of language expresses this same kind of ambivalence whenever the Colonel talks or thinks of art and literature. Explicitly, he is the most cultivated of the Hemingway heroes, the one most frankly in love with beauty and most obviously delighting in art. In a random glance through the pages of *Across the River and into the Trees* we find Cantwell mentioning painters like Giotto, Piero della Francesca,

Bruegel, Mantegna, Titian, Tintoretto, Goya, Velasquez. In music, we have references to Bach, Wagner, and Pablo Casals. Among the writers the Colonel alludes to are D'Annunzio, Browning, Byron, T. S. Eliot, Rimbaud, Whitman, Verlaine, Villon, John Webster, and, most importantly, Dante and Shakespeare. But Cantwell can allow his interest in art and beauty to escape his lips only when it is well laced with hard-guy lingo. His Puritan fear that such sensitivity might unman him is most egregiously summed up in this silliness: "Did you ever read King Lear, Daughter? [he asks the portrait] Mister Gene Tunney did, and he was the champion of the world. But I read it too. Soldiers care for Mr. Shakespeare, though it may seem impossible. He writes like a soldier himself" (p. 171). Evidently Shakespeare is admissible only for military reasons and because a pugilist once approved of him. Even Cantwell's bitterness toward his approaching death and toward what he calls his sad and sometimes his dirty "metier of war" must be similarly expressed. Recalling how "old Hieronymus Bosch really painted" death's "ugly face," he adds: "But you can sheathe your scythe, old brother death, if you have got a sheath for it. Or he added, thinking of Huertgen now, you can take your scythe and stick it up your ass" (p. 254).

The Colonel's pleasure in the art and scenic beauty of Italy is contrasted with the insensitivity of his driver, T/5 Jackson. Cantwell scorns this average G.I. Despite Jackson's combat infantryman's badge and Purple Heart, he is "in no sense a soldier." The Colonel has none of Robert Jordan's sympathy for the common man as soldier. In fact he is about as misanthropic as was the author of *Green Hills of Africa*. The G.I.'s aggravate him, and he rages against his military and political superiors. Only a happy few are permitted within his circle of snobbery.

For decades critics have noticed that most Hemingway characters fit into either one of two contrasted groups: call them the insiders and the outsiders. In the first are those depicted sympathetically—the heroes, tutor figures, and such—all who share

183

certain attitudes and values and of course follow the code. These in the Hemingway scheme prove the morally superior ones. Toward the others, their foils—Robert Cohn is the most familiar example of the outsider—we are expected to feel contempt, sometimes too readily. In *Across the River and into the Trees* Hemingway drives his peculiar dualism to such quirky extremes as to make it both ludicrous and paranoiac. The hero and four other grizzled, scarred ex-soldiers belong to a Secret Order "so inane," remarks one critic, "that it would have embarrassed Tom Sawyer." [13] The leader of this private club of old boys is known as the Cherry Buster; and *El Ordine Militar, Nobile y Espirituoso de los Caballeros de Brusadelli* has been named after a war profiteer who had once accused his young wife "publicly and legally through due process of law, of having deprived him of his judgment through her extraordinary sexual demands" (p. 57). For himself, Cantwell privately rephrases the secret of the order in these terms: "I'd rather not love anyone . . . I'd rather have fun" (p. 71).

Indeed, the only people the Colonel can really care for are those who have been severely wounded:

> Other people were fine and you liked them and were good friends; but you only felt true tenderness and love for those who had been there and had received the castigation that everyone receives who goes there long enough.
>
> So I'm a sucker for crips, he thought. . . . And any son of a bitch who has been hit solidly, as every man will be if he stays, then I love him.
>
> Yes, his other, good side said. You love them. [p. 71]

Nowhere else in his writings has Hemingway revealed at such length and so unmistakably his obsessional linking of love and wounds. Hemingway's own scars were innumerable, some of them dating from boyhood. He was in three serious car accidents: one nearly cost him his arm; another, during a London blackout, required fifty-seven stitches in his scalp, stitches he himself pulled out on the way to Normandy on D-day. In her

New Yorker sketch in May, 1950, Lillian Ross reported this bit of conversation Hemingway held with an old friend he had just run into:

"Wolfie, all of a sudden I found I could write wonderful again, instead of just biting on the nail. . . . I think it took a while for my head to get rebuilt inside. You should not, ideally, break a writer's head open or give him seven concussions in two years or break six ribs on him when he is forty-seven or push a rear-view-mirror support through the front of his skull opposite the pituitary gland or, really, shoot at him too much." [14]

One student of the matter has reported: "In combat alone Hemingway was shot through both feet, both knees, both arms, both hands, and the scrotum, and has been wounded in the head six times." [15] His friend Malcolm Cowley declares that Hemingway carried scars "literally from the crown of his head to the sole of his right foot . . . recording different events, so that the story of his life is engraved on his body." [16]

His worst wound is the same as Colonel Cantwell's. The biographical facts are these: at Fossalta, on the bank of the Piave River, Hemingway was hit on the night of July 8, 1918, by an Austrian trench-mortar shell; and the three Italians with him were killed, their legs blown off. When Hemingway regained consciousness, one of the men was still alive and screaming. Somehow the American picked him up and carried him back; but on the way the man died and Hemingway was hit again, machine-gunned in the foot and knee. "I knew that I was hit and leaned over and put my hand on my knee," Frederic Henry reported. "My knee wasn't there. My hand went in and my knee was down on my shin." The pride Hemingway took in his hurts he showed on his return to Oak Park after the war when, during a speech at his old high school, he is reported to have "held up a pair of shrapnel-riddled trousers for the students to see." [17]

Colonel Cantwell takes a like pride in his scars. Studying his face in the mirror: "He looked at the different welts and ridges that had come before they had plastic surgery, and at the thin, only to be observed by the initiate, lines of the excellent plastic operations after head wounds" (pp. 111–12). Again, when he looks "critically and truly" at the reflection of his nude body: " 'You beat-up old bastard,' he said to the mirror. . . . The gut is flat, he said without uttering it. The chest is all right except where it contains the defective muscle" (p. 180). The Colonel, however, is not satisfied to contemplate his wounds in the privacy of his bathroom. He wants the rest of the world to pay proper deference to them. Consider the incident when he is walking along the street and thinks that a couple of young fellows behind him are talking about him, discussing his gray hair, his limp, and "their absolute certainty that I can no longer make love." He maneuvers to stand in their path and stare them down: "They stopped and he looked at them both in the face and smiled his old and worn death smile" (p. 187). We do not blame the Colonel for disliking young smart alecks. But what most enrages him is this:

. . . couldn't those badly educated youths realize what sort of animal they were dealing with? Don't they know how you get to walk that way? Nor any of the other signs that combat people show as surely as a fisherman's hands tell you if he is a fisherman from the creases from the cord cuts. [pp. 187–88]

It is not his limp but the Colonel's wounded hand that occupies most of our attention. Connotations of religion and sacrifice are fixed to the hand when Renata tells her lover that every night for a week she has been dreaming of that hand, "and it was a strange mixed-up dream and I dreamed it was the hand of Our Lord" (p. 84). Considering Hemingway's fascination with martyr-heroes, this reference to the Crucifixion story is not uncharacteristic of him. At any rate, during the love scenes we are seldom allowed to forget that hand. Renata fusses over it tenderly and tells the Colonel what his heart desires: "I love your hard, flat body and your strange eyes that frighten me when they become wicked. I love your hand and all your other wounded places" (p. 141). Another wish is fulfilled when, as they make love in the gondola, the Colonel says:

"I'm going to run my hand through it [her hair] and make it unkempter still."
"Your hurt hand?"
"Yes." [pp. 151–52]

Then under the blanket he caresses Renata, where "there was no wind nor nothing; only his ruined hand that searched for the island in the great river with the high steep banks" (pp. 152–53). In this business of the wound eroticized, we are reminded of Harry Morgan caressing his wife with his stump. The imagery of the river and its banks, however appropriate, also bears resemblances to the nightmare recollections of Nick Adams—the screen memory of the place where Nick and his creator got their first bad wound. It is curious, too, that on this night of romance, the Colonel—for evidently the same reason Frederic Henry could not resist bringing up the subject with his sweetheart—must talk of venereal disease.

In a later scene, while the lovers lie together, Renata asks Cantwell to put his hand on her:

"My good or my bad?"
"Your bad," the girl said. "The one I love and must think about all week. I cannot keep it like you keep the stones." [p. 226]

The reference is to the pair of emeralds she has given to him as a gift of love. These he keeps in his pocket, and they are often caressed by the bad hand. Since there are two of them and since one of the common synonyms for testicles is stones, Renata's gift involves sexual symbolism. In this *Liebestraum*, the green stones are a prescription or talisman against castration anxiety.

Equally interesting to the pathologist are the boozy, insomniac hours the Colonel devotes to mooning over and talking to the portrait of Renata which he has in his hotel room. Even this painting has behind it a history of wounds, disfigurement, and sexual abnormality. When Renata gives Cantwell the portrait, she tells him about the artist: "He is a very good painter, but he has false teeth in front because he was a little bit *pédéraste* once and other *pédérastes* attacked him one night on the Lido. . . . He is a man now, of course, and goes with very many women to hide what he is . . ." (p. 96).

Throughout the story Cantwell frequently addresses Renata as "Daughter." Once she asks him:

"Did you ever have a daughter?"
"No. I always wanted one."
"I can be your daughter as well as everything else."
"That would be incest."
"I don't think that would be so terrible in a city as old as this and that has seen what this city has seen." [p. 98]

Renata, it seems, whispers to the Colonel's heart of incest permitted. She fulfills other wishes, too. It is hardly surprising that the muddled hero is never quite sure of her real sex. As they are together in bed on one occasion, Cantwell tells her, "I wish the hell you were a soldier with your straight true brain and your beauty memory." "I would wish to be a soldier if I could fight under you," she answers (p. 231). The hero has just about gone back to the polymorphous perverse when he soliloquizes: " 'Portrait,' he said. 'Boy or daughter or my one true love or whatever it is; you know what it is, portrait' " (p. 173).

When Renata takes up the subject of his approaching death, Cantwell's characteristic reply is:

"That is one thing we do alone. Like going to the bathroom."
"Please do not be rough."
"I meant I would love to have you with me. But it [dying] is very egotistical and an ugly process." [p. 228]

In the Colonel's mind, death and defecation are regularly connected. Once, while he and Renata are kissing, he reflects "how close life comes to death when there is ecstasy. . . . Yes, ecstasy is what you might have had and instead you draw sleep's other brother. Death is a lot of shit, he thought" (p. 219).

Cantwell's attitude toward excrement and death, his attitude toward his wounds (each wound may be regarded as a partial death), the pride he takes in them, the grief he feels for them, the self-love he invests in them—in fact, the essence of all the feelings Hemingway and his heroes have had about their wounds —all of this culminates in *Across the River and into the Trees.* What is surely one of the more bizarre incidents in modern fiction occurs in the third chapter of this novel. Going back to Fossalta and determining by triangulation the precise spot where he (and Hemingway and Frederic Henry) first met death, Cantwell squats low and relieves his bowels. What morbidly intense feelings in a writer to so memorialize a wound received thirty years before! For both the obsessed author and his obsessed heroes, here is the climax of their compulsion to go back again and again to the scene of the trauma. "A poor effort," the Colonel comments. "But my own." Then to "complete the monument," he digs a hole in the earth there and puts into it a ten-thousand-lire note—twenty years of the pension he has been receiving from the Italian government:

It's fine now, he thought. It has merde, money, blood; look how that grass grows; and the iron's in the earth along with Gino's leg, both of Randolfo's legs, and my right kneecap. It's a wonderful monument. It has everything. Fertility, money, blood and iron. [pp. 18–19]

Into the tomb of fertile mother earth goes manure mingled with the limbs hacked off by the iron weapons of war. With this ceremony Cantwell epitomizes his love and his hate, his tenderness for his comrades in arms and his outrage against the violation of their flesh, his reverence for his wounds—and his disgust with them. For the other side of the Colonel's pride in his wounds is his shame. The lost limbs and the lost kneecap are the wounds of a symbolic castration. At long last the embar-

rassing joke played by Mars on Jake Barnes is luridly illuminated. The bitter paradox is that at the very moment of virile
pride, the assertion of heroism, the hero is emasculated. He wins
the badge of shame.[18]

So we arrive at the absurd, and the absolute dead end for the
Hemingway hero. At the time, however, his creator was not
aware of this fact. Shortly before its publication, he had felt
that *Across the River and into the Trees* might be his best book.
"I think I've got 'Farewell' beat in this one," he told Lillian
Ross. But when the critics lambasted his wild boar—or bore?—
of a hero, Hemingway in 1951 wrote to an army friend: "Down
with turning the other cheek. The nonfighting folk hate the
fighting people." He was also under a delusion when he added,
"Truly you know I was the only writer of the U.S. who fought
and now I am ostracized for it." [19] Such touchy egoism is com-
pounded of hurt, hostility, and feelings of persecution.

It was perhaps too painful for him immediately to accept the
extent of his failure here. For in characterizing Cantwell, Hemingway had drawn heavily upon the legend he had invested so
much in. Besides, the excesses in this novel throw into new
perspective his other heroes. Regularly they have been divided
creatures: outwardly virile, self-reliant, brave, hard; inwardly and
unconsciously dependent, fearful of sexual love, and dreading
any tender feeling as effeminate and corrupting. Now, by
dropping his guard and abandoning anything like critical self-
awareness in the portrayal of Cantwell, Hemingway knocked
down the façade. He permits us to see the reality: his Colonel
is a sad and bitter invalid, incapable of love, with nothing much
now to be heroic about, with only a few transparent defenses
and delusions to mask his fear and his emptiness. With this poor
wreck of a hero, Hemingway unwittingly punctured a myth and
created a protagonist with more than his share of the ills of
ordinary humanity.[20]

It must have taken courage for Hemingway ultimately to see
what he had done and to accept the verdict of the critics. Those

who are unmoved by or even regret his heroics on the battlefield must still admire the aging and unwell writer who faced
the crucial question of how to begin again. Considering the ri-
gidities in a personality like Hemingway's, one could hardly
expect the mold to be broken to make way for new growth.
Yet he could still learn, and he did. He turned away now from
subjects he knew he could not handle. If this amounts to a
rejection of large areas of life, we have a compensation. For
Hemingway also learned how to salvage what was precious from
a lifetime of thinking about the possibility of heroism and of
dignity in the conduct of life. The proof came a brief two years
later.

With *The Old Man and the Sea* Hemingway surprised us
that somehow he had regained control of his art. Out of his
inner conflicts as man and artist he achieved a harmony which
makes this, in a classical sense, the sweetest and most serene of
his works. To be sure, we have something of the story as before:
a hunt after big game, a test of manly courage, a proof of grace
under pressure, and a theme like that of "The Undefeated." One
can call it "a late work by a tired writer"; and one can complain
that its style lacks the fresh power of the youthful author.[21]
Another loss might also be regretted: that the Hemingway skill
in stripping a narrative down to essentials has resulted in certain
oversimplifications; the hero this time is for the most part un-
involved with any person other than himself. Still, whatever its
shortcomings, *The Old Man and the Sea* will stand in relation
to the body of Hemingway's writings as *Billy Budd* does to Mel-
ville's.

Both authors explored the power of blackness. In each of
these books they tried, near the end of their careers, to say "yea"
to life. Whether or not Hemingway wins us over to an affirmation, we have here his most philosophical story. A tale of adventure, this is one of those fictions where the meaning and the
action are one. It comprises Hemingway's summa—the summa
of his lifelong preoccupation with the enigmas of evil, of hero-

ism, and of love. His subject is man in nature and the nature of man. In his depiction of the seascape he can express the love of beauty that so abashed him in Colonel Cantwell. But for all his description of nature's loveliness, Hemingway never lets us forget the Darwinian struggle going on beneath and above the Gulf waters. Against such naturalism, we are made continually aware of Santiago's fellow feeling for nature's creatures. His tenderness toward them reminds us of Francis of Assisi. This dualism is embodied in the old Cuban fisherman.

Santiago is unique among Hemingway heroes. More by chance than by choice is his manhood challenged. He is not on a battlefield or in a bull ring or meeting a lion's charge or otherwise facing the likelihood of sudden death, nor is he recovering from a wound. With a long streak of bad luck behind him, Santiago at the start is more like, say, a farmer who has had a series of bad harvests. His predicament is that of average humanity in its day-to-day effort to keep going. That is why he is more representative of the human race than any other Hemingway character. In fact, his is the sort of figure so far absent from Hemingway's fiction.

He is not a desperate man and is without inward violence. He is more or less at peace with himself and not at war with his world. Long ago he "attained humility" and yet suffered "no loss of true pride" (pp. 13–14). Santiago's physical courage is incidental to the routine need of earning his daily bread. Since what he endures is not edged by masochism, it never exacerbates our nerves. Naturally, we feel with Santiago his hurts; but these occupy us, as they do him, more as practical impediments than as badges of heroism.

Of all the Hemingway protagonists, he is closest to nature, feels himself a part of nature; he even believes he has hands, feet, and a heart like the big turtles'. At first he seems a simple man, another primitive. Under this guise, however, we have a remarkably sensitive and contemplative person. He by no means lives an unexamined life. He asks the eternal questions. We can easily imagine another old fisherman undergoing Santiago's ordeal with equal physical courage and yet never having the surface of his mind or conscience troubled. On those vast blue waters Santiago is a speck of intense human consciousness. And the essence of his ordeal is spiritual—a question of what shall a man believe. The essential courage he demonstrates is moral, even intellectual, courage in his ceaseless self-examination.

What comes of his self-examination, this inquiry into the nature of man, these questions put to the universe? On the Gulf waters Santiago meditates on the drama of love against hate and of life against death which nature perpetually stages for us. He thinks the little sea swallows have a harder life than our human one because "the ocean can be so cruel." But the ocean is not necessarily an antagonist. Santiago regards it "as feminine and as something that gave or withheld great favours, and if she did wild or wicked things, it was because she could not help them" (p. 30). He watches a man-of-war bird trying to catch one of the flying fish while they are being pursued by a school of dolphin. Though always Santiago feels affectionate kinship with creatures who must prey on one another, he knows he in his turn must prey on them. These musings—the torment of their ambivalence and of their ambiguities—are dramatized in his struggle with the big fish.

Santiago hooks his marlin at noon, and all the rest of that day and all of the following night the creature tows his skiff farther from land. He thinks then about the time he caught one of a pair of marlins; how "the hooked fish, the female, made a wild, panic-stricken, despairing fight that soon exhausted her"; how the male stayed with her; how, after Santiago had landed her, "the male fish jumped high into the air beside the boat to see where the female was and then went down deep. . . ." Among the marlins, this was "the saddest thing" Santiago had ever seen. These reflections stir guilt in him simply because he is a fisherman. "But that was the thing that I was born for" (pp. 49–50), so he answers his doubts. Then in words that might remind us of the marriage vow: " 'Fish,' he said softly, aloud, 'I'll stay with you until I am dead' " (p. 52). Then, a little later: " 'Fish,' he said, 'I love you and respect you very much. But I will kill you dead before this day ends' " (p. 54).

As the hours grind away and his hand bleeds from a line burn and the other hand stiffens and cramps, he eats some raw fish to regain his strength. "I wish I could feed the fish, he thought. He is my brother. But I must kill him and keep strong to do it" (p. 59). When the marlin jumps and for the first time shows its huge size, Santiago tells himself he must never let the fish know how strong it is. "But, thank God," he adds, "they are not as intelligent as we who kill them; although they are more noble and more able" (p. 63). As the day wears on and Santiago wears down, he reflects: "Man is not much beside the great birds and beasts. Still I would rather be that beast down there in the darkness of the sea" (p. 68).

Everywhere are signs of Eros and its antagonist death. When he is being pulled through an island of Sargasso weed "that heaved and swung in the light sea as though the ocean were making love with something under a yellow blanket" (p. 72), Santiago catches and kills a dolphin that flaps "wildly in the air. . . . in the acrobatics of its fear . . ." (p. 72). While the duel with the marlin continues through the second night, his conscience puzzles over these killings: "Then he was sorry for the great fish that had nothing to eat and his determination to kill him never relaxed in his sorrow for him" (p. 75). Of these painful mysteries he can only tell himself: "But it is good that we do not have to try to kill the sun or the moon or the stars. It is enough to live on the sea and kill our true brothers" (p. 75). When the old man manages to doze a little, though, he does not dream of killing; he dreams of a vast school of porpoises in their mating time, and he dreams of lions as playful and harmless as lambs.

By sunrise of the third day the marlin begins to circle. Santiago, though faint and dizzy, is able to pull the tiring marlin closer to the boat. Yet again it swims away: "You are killing me, fish, the old man thought. But you have a right to. . . . Come on and kill me. I do not care who kills who" (p. 92). So, in this mortal battle, fish and man become one, killer and killed become one. To be sure, we think of Hemingway's bullfighters, and it is significant that, before he could possibly know its sex, Santiago identifies the marlin as male. The Freudian will see— correctly enough—that once more we have, symbolized, the oedipal clash of male against male, the big beast of the sea as fierce and noble as the bull.[22] Still, even in this ambivalence, we have nothing like the sickly caressing of the dead kudu in *Green Hills of Africa*. Rather, the larger context might remind us of Emerson's paradoxes in "Brahma":

> If the red slayer think he slays
> Or if the slain think he is slain,
> They know not well the subtle ways
> I keep and pass, and turn again.

At last comes the chance, and Santiago drives the harpoon into the marlin's heart: " 'I am a tired old man. But I have killed the fish which is my brother . . .' " (p. 95). Then he lashes the great carcass to his skiff and begins the long trip back to land, believing his lacerated hands will mend quickly in the salt water: "The dark water of the true gulf is the greatest healer that there is" (p. 99).

An hour later the first shark hits—a giant mako. Santiago succeeds in putting his harpoon into the mako's brain. This time he is pure killer, kills with hate, and we infer both the masoch- ism and the sadism: "He hit it with his blood mushed hands driving a good harpoon with all his strength. He hit it without hope but with resolution and complete malignancy" (p. 102). But the shark has already succeeded in mutilating the marlin, and it is as if Santiago himself has been hit. He fights his de- spair: " 'But man is not made for defeat,' he said. 'A man can be destroyed but not defeated' " (p. 103).

Unquestionably, this is the explicit moral of *The Old Man*

and the Sea. But immediately Santiago has an afterthought: "I
am sorry that I killed the fish, though" (p. 103). He tells himself he has no "understanding" of sin, yet he wrestles with his
conscience: "Perhaps it was a sin to kill the fish. I suppose it was
even though I did it to keep me alive and feed many people."
He tries to justify what he has done: "You were born to be a
fisherman as the fish was born to be a fish. San Pedro [Saint
Peter] was a fisherman as was the father of the great DiMaggio"
(p. 105). Such reflections bring no comfort:

You did not kill the fish only to keep alive and to sell for food, he
thought. You killed him for pride and because you are a fisherman.
You loved him when he was alive and you loved him after. If you
love him, it is not a sin to kill him. Or is it more?
"You think too much, old man," he said aloud. [p. 105]

He is troubled even about killing the mako:

"I killed him in self-defense," the old man said aloud. "And I
killed him well."
Besides, he thought, everything kills everything else in some way.
Fishing kills me exactly as it keeps me alive." [p. 106]

Then he checks these gloomy musings by reminding himself
that it is the love of the boy Manolin which also keeps him
alive. Clearly, this Hemingway hero is no self-destroyer, nor
death-obsessed. Santiago is philosophical: he is thinking about
death, not morbidly agonizing over it.

When more and still more sharks come—ugly shovel-nosed
galanos—he fights them off and kills them with his oars, with
a club, even with his tiller. By sunset they have eaten away half
his trophy; by midnight nothing is left of the marlin but the
bones. Exhausted, Santiago spits into the ocean: " 'Eat that,
galanos, and make a dream you've killed a man' " (p. 119). He
is "beaten now finally and without remedy," though somehow
he manages to sail his skiff and the great skeleton back to his
home port. He is grateful that the boat is sound and the current
is helping. "The wind is our friend, anyway, he thought. Then

he added, sometimes. And the great sea with our friends and our enemies." He wants only bed and sleep. "It is easy when you are beaten, he thought. I never knew how easy it was" (p. 120).

If we ask what are the meanings of the old man's experience, Hemingway himself has explained: "I tried to make a real old man, a real boy, a real sea and a real fish and real sharks. But if I made them good and true enough they would mean many things." [23] For symbol-searchers that announcement has sometimes provided *carte blanche*. Certain things in *The Old Man and the Sea* are of course suggestive beyond literal fact. For some readers these deepen the spiritual resonances of the story, enhance its overtones. Still, even those items which are symbolic are subordinated to the conventions of realism as Hemingway has typically practiced it. That is, at his best, in this novella as elsewhere, Hemingway does not impose any elaborate symbolic patterns; rather, his images and symbols are organic, growing out of their fictional context.[24]

It is easy for close readers to point to analogies between Santiago and Christ. Everyone remembers the fisherman's hurt hands and recalls in particular how, when Santiago first sees the sharks, he makes "a noise such as a man might make, involuntarily, feeling the nail go through his hands into the wood" (p. 107). Yet in this instance, and in Santiago's stumbling climb beneath the weight of his mast up the hill to his shack at the story's end, his identification with Christ is at most tentative. These tenuous links between the Crucifixion and Santiago—especially when we recall Cantwell and Jake Barnes and the other martyr-heroes—spring from Hemingway's absorption in his own father-son conflict: the son's need to keep his father's love and at the same time to overthrow and replace him. Freud's view of the Crucifixion as a supreme example of this ambivalence seems relevant to the body of Hemingway's writings: that is, Christ crucified expiates the crime committed against the Father; but the Son, taking the guilt on his shoulders, becomes God himself beside the Father, in a sense replaces the Father.[25] How Hemingway in *The Old Man and the Sea* sought reconciliation with his own father image we will consider presently.

Only those who insist on seeking in literature support for their own religious convictions or yearnings will be satisfied with interpreting the story, in any doctrinal sense, as a type of Christian allegory. Aside from the intricacies of symbolic analysis, almost any doctrinaire religious reading of *The Old Man and the Sea* will push us into some awkward positions. For Hemingway has not given us a man who relies much upon his religion; Santiago hardly gets from Christianity the sort of consolation a committed believer does. And only the parochial-minded will argue that his virtues are distinctively Christian. He is humble, compassionate, conscientious, patient, loving, and feels kinship with and reverence for living creatures. These virtues, however, are by no means the exclusive teachings of Christianity. If at the end Santiago's resignation may be called Christian, we must admit that other religions and philosophies also teach resignation, even renunciation of this world.

Whether Santiago can be labeled a tragic hero in anything like an Aristotelian sense is a problem that arises when we examine the question he puts to himself: What defeated him? Did he err? If he erred, it is not prideful individualism but practical necessity—his bad luck for over eighty days—that impels him to risk going far beyond the regular fishing grounds. Since in this he never overestimates his physical and moral strength, we cannot call his venture foolhardy. In the heat of battle with the marlin, naturally Santiago's pride grows, but his is hardly the overweening sort that drives a man out of his place in the order of things and angers the gods. At the moment of the actual kill he feels no pride. And he is not punished for *hubris*. He suffers for two reasons: by a lucky accident he hooked such an extraordinary fish; and, second, by going out so far he consequently increased the likelihood of sharks getting his trophy. The coming of the sharks does not surprise him. When he looks for a reason why he has lost, he can only say, " 'I went out too far' " (p. 120). That is all he knows. That is all we know. With good luck he got his fish; with better luck he might have escaped the sharks. The old man was not rebelliously challenging the nature of things. Nor does he glimpse, as heroes of classic tragedy sometimes do, a fresh awareness of his own nature or some new insight into the workings of the universe. His pride in his skill is part of healthy self-love, the normal pride anyone should take in worthwhile work. From the beginning, Santiago knew himself well enough, and he knew the law of kill-or-be-killed. His only lesson is that defeat is easier than he thought it might be.

This book, however, is neither nihilistic nor pessimistic. No other work of Hemingway comes so near to reconciling us to the human lot. Frederic Henry thought that the world "kills the very good and the very gentle and the very brave. If you are none of these things you can be sure it will kill you too but there will be no special hurry." Santiago is very good, very gentle, very brave; but he has not been killed in a hurry. At the end he is asleep, dreaming of his happy lions, with the boy who loves him watching at his side. He inspirits us, too, because he is genuinely heroic. In *Across the River and into the Trees* Hemingway had laid bare in all its inanity the image of military heroism in our century.[26] Now, with his old fisherman, he reaffirms heroism in a form we can believe in and be satisfied by. Since Santiago's ordeal comes by way of mankind's daily toil, his heroism is more broadly based than, say, Anselmo's in *For Whom the Bell Tolls*. And because that heroism is unforced and unassuming, Hemingway has nowhere else given us a better example of its dignity.

More striking in a Hemingway hero, the hard strength of Santiago's manliness is instinct with tenderness. Of his humanity we are never in doubt. He seems always to have known what Harry Morgan glimpsed only in his death agony: that "No man is an *iland*." Robert Jordan's solidarity with humanity remains at best problematic. In contrast with the other Hemingway protagonists, the love that binds Santiago to nature and to other human beings is always realized. He is lonely but not alienated. He has not rejected the world, nor has he cut himself off from his fellows.

Hemingway makes plain enough the values of the love realized in *The Old Man and the Sea*. In effect, he tells us that there are persons like Santiago who have love in their hearts. He sees much love also in the nonhuman world. But alive as the hero is to the love in himself and in nature, he is equally alive to the pain and violence and killing which are inherent and inescapable in the natural world. Though he is tormented that he, too, must bring pain and death, at least Santiago knows that the love he feels is somehow allied with the love in nature. Before this paradox Hemingway does not flinch. It permeates every page of his story; it is writ large in every ambiguity and ambivalence of Santiago's adventure with the marlin.

In *The Old Man and the Sea* Hemingway has succeeded in expressing tenderness—without the tight lips or the oblique implications. Colonel Cantwell's expression of love's tenderness fails because the author was subjectively entangled with his hero. There are no such fumblings and false notes here, although the aging Hemingway was something of a Santiago himself. He, too, had fished for big ones in the Gulf Stream, and sharks had eaten away one of his own great catches. But now he does not slip into exploiting the legend of Papa the great sportsman.[27]

Nevertheless, it is Hemingway's deeply personal involvement which gives this novella throughout a convincingness lacking—except in a few of the stories—in all his other writings since *Winner Take Nothing*. Here at last he has found—and found a way to realize in fiction—the warmth and kindliness of love. A love that affords a reprieve against violence, pain, and death gives this story its poignancy. Part of Hemingway's success also comes from his attitude toward his subject. It required the disciplined love of the artist to create a hero who, without too much self-love or too much self-hate, can still interest us.

Granted, Santiago is not presented as a figure complexly involved in his society. Mostly we see him as a man alone with nature and alone with himself. Not that his community is indifferent to Santiago or he independent of it. On his way back he reflects: "I hope no one has been too worried. There is only the boy to worry, of course. But I am sure he would have confidence. Many of the older fishermen will worry. Many of the others too, he thought. I live in a good town" (p. 115).

Yet Santiago is without a real home. His wife has been dead so long that, though he keeps a couple of religious remembrances of her, he no longer dreams or thinks of her. He has no woman, no family, no children. All his personal love is directed to the boy. And Manolin is another man's son.

Manolin's function is to heighten our sympathy for and increase our understanding of Santiago. The boy appears only at the beginning and at the end of the narrative. In the central drama he can be of no practical help, though repeatedly Santiago wishes the boy were with him. Before the old man sets out, Manolin fetches him food and bait and helps him carry his gear. After the ordeal, he is the first to see the old man, finding him asleep. His mangled hands make the boy cry, and he is not ashamed of having other people see his tears. The special tenderness in Manolin's solicitude for Santiago goes further than what we expect of affection between age and youth or the reciprocal love between master and apprentice. He adores Santiago as the boy narrator of "My Old Man" adores his father. It is not only his worries that Santiago may not eat enough, or his carefulness about the blanket when the old fisherman sleeps. For a boy scarcely in his teens, Manolin has astonishing tact when it comes to helping Santiago maintain certain little fictions to sustain the dignity of the elderly—like that about the cast net, which he knows has been sold, and the pot of yellow rice and fish, which he knows does not exist. Clearly, in his sympathy, love, and admiration for Santiago, Manolin takes on something of the role which in the earlier fictions has been performed by passive heroines like Maria and Renata.[28]

What complicates the figuration of this father-son relationship is the fact that Manolin dislikes his own father and prefers Santiago. Beyond this, Hemingway offers no explanations of the boy's unusual devotion to the old man. Possibly Hemingway had other reasons to put Manolin into his story, emotional reasons he was not fully conscious of. And perhaps here we can begin to understand some of the hidden depths of the power of this story. At least this much seems likely: Hemingway, himself an aging and fine fisherman, could identify with Santiago; at the same time he could identify with Manolin. So he was able, in his fantasy and in this fiction, not only to recapture something of his own adult experience but also to relive some of his own childhood. Is not Hemingway telling again the story of himself as a little boy, whose father was a big fine fisherman and gave him his first rod when he was three—the father whose suicide later so burdened him? From the psychologist's point of view, we might remark that here Hemingway resolves a basic conflict —at least insofar as he has made a work of art out of his own mixed feelings toward his father. By this light, too, we may understand the recurring dream of his youth which so pleases Santiago:

He no longer dreamed of storms, nor of women, nor of great occurrences, nor of great fish, nor fights, nor contests of strength, nor of his wife. He only dreamed of places now and of the lions on the beach. They played like young cats in the dusk and he loved them as he loved the boy. He never dreamed of the boy. [p. 25]

Playful and affectionate cats are all that is left now of the fierce beast, symbols of the terror and hate inspired by the father, which once stalked the child's nightmares. So, the controlled sweetness and hard-won serenity that charm us in *The Old*

Man and the Sea are rooted in this reconciliation with the image of the father.

Thus far has Hemingway gone toward affirming the power of Eros in this, his farewell book. By his testimony, love does exist and is a stay against death. But the only viable personal love is love among males, cut off from women, from family ties, from parental responsibilities, from the complications of society.[29] True, Santiago is not wholly an isolate. Yet, mostly he is alone in the wilderness—the Gulf waters being for Hemingway all that was left of our American wilderness. So, in the tradition of American letters, his old fisherman takes his place along with figures like Natty Bumppo, an old trapper alone on the prairies, dying among the Pawnees, loving Hard-Heart and loved by him as earlier he had loved Chingachgook of *The Last of the Mohicans*.[30]

"We live by accidents of terrain, you know. And terrain is what remains in the dreaming part of your mind."

Across the River and into the Trees

Epilogue

When the news flashed around the world that on Sunday, July 2, 1961, Ernest Hemingway was dead, everybody was shocked. He had long been so alive and big to the imagination that momentarily we had to struggle with our disbelief in the established fact: he had killed himself, like his father before him. But perhaps we should not have been oversurprised. Those who had read him attentively could hardly have missed certain omens in his masochistic obsession with death. Some few might have remembered how, nearly thirty years before, he had almost threatened suicide when he declared publicly that, if he had spent less time killing animals, he might have shot himself. That Hemingway had often been hurt and more often exposed himself to the likelihood of being killed was common knowledge. The pattern, psychologically, spells an extraordinary need for punishment, the sort of need that usually comes from overwhelming feelings of guilt. And the extreme end product of self-punishment is self-destruction.

To be sure, these remarks, superficial and sketchy, tell us virtually nothing about the terrible complexity of Hemingway's tragic end. Yet the biographical facts of his last decade do not contradict them; and the details make depressing and, finally, anguished reading. We witness his accelerating decline, physically and emotionally—then the finale with the blasts of the double-barreled shotgun. It appears now that the author was ailing from the time he composed *Across the River and into the Trees.* Our first knowledge came only in the public way. After *The Old Man and the Sea,* no more fiction was published except a pair of stories in the centenary issue of the *Atlantic,* both about blind men and a distillation of the blackest *nada.*[1]

Glancing backward, we recall hearing that he was too ill to accept the invitation of President-elect Kennedy to the Inauguration of 1961. Not long before that, news leaked through that Hemingway was in the Mayo Clinic, being treated for hypertension, a liver ailment, and diabetes. We did not know then how many months he had spent there and that he was also afflicted with a deep depression.[2] Earlier, in September, 1960, we read in *Life* magazine his two installments about Spanish bullfighting, *The Dangerous Summer*; what pleasure we took in their genial humor was spoiled by our realization that in returning to old haunts and hobbies Hemingway was reworking a vein he had exhausted long ago. There had been another visit to Spain, in the winter of 1956–57; at that time a Madrid physician found rather alarming heart symptoms in the writer.[3] Before that, in October, 1954, came the announcement that Hemingway had won the Nobel Prize, but the following December he was not well enough to go to Stockholm and give his speech of acceptance.

What made still bigger headlines were the reports that twice within less than one week in January of 1954 Hemingway and his wife were in airplane crashes in Africa. Obituary notices, which he later read, appeared in papers around the globe.[4] The irony, however, is not that his demise, like Mark Twain's, was prematurely announced, but rather that we did not know the appalling extent of his injuries. What he went through was enough to kill a younger, perhaps also a stronger, man. Yet he kept up a show of bravado. In fact, he not only tried shortly afterward to resume his safari despite constant pain; he also tried to help put out a forest fire when he was still so disabled that he stumbled, fell into the flames, and burned once again his freshly healed skin.[5]

Whatever view we take of the motives behind this recklessness, Hemingway never recovered from his African ordeal. The damage done to his body took its toll of his spirit, too. Besides, since he was the sort of man who could scarcely tolerate middle age, let alone growing old, he probably resented his aging as a personal insult.[6] Indeed, to judge from the photographs after those air crashes, his decline was startling in its swiftness.[7] In those photographs, too, we sometimes see eyes that look frightened, almost pleading—eyes that have looked on too many horrors.

Our impression is of a man ever more desperate and driven. Fitfully he crosses and recrosses the ocean. He must go back to France, to Spain, to Africa. There he visits Philip Percival, the white hunter of *Green Hills of Africa*. At Pamplona he tries to convince himself that the San Fermín fiesta is like old times; he shows his wife the bridge Robert Jordan had blown up and the hilltop where Sordo died. He follows the corridas from city to city, seeking the same dark elation, but now the late hours and the wining and dining exact too high a price of an ailing body and spirit.[8]

Merely to touch on these details is to be involved in the legend. The memory is so fresh, we are so close to the man and the writer, that it is still difficult to separate the legendary from the literary figure. Perhaps it is too early by some decades for any firm assessment of Hemingway's place in the history of letters. How his reputation may rise and fall in the years ahead is anyone's guess. Yet in the light of the present study—and this book is only one contribution to the critical siftings his work must go through—a certain summing up, however tentative, is in order.

First and unmistakably, Ernest Hemingway emerges as a world figure in several senses of that term. Aside from the fact of the Nobel award and the publicity, he has made his mark on the consciousness of twentieth-century man. Because of what he wrote and did, we cannot help seeing ourselves and our world, at least sometimes, through lenses he has focused for us. His influence here is vast and unmeasurable. At least one President of the United States is to be counted among his admirers.[9] One of the shapers of our policy in the Cold War was possibly thinking of the old *aficionado* when he likened his job to that of the bullfighter.[10] And when we spread downward into other manifestations of our culture, we have the Hemingway influence on the magazines and popular fiction, on the comics, the movies, and television. There may be something of Hemingway in the acting styles of, say, Paul Newman and Marlon Brando. And is it going too far to find the Hemingway thing, so cunningly rigged by the wizards of Madison Avenue, in that plethora of rugged masculinity which, out of the picture tubes and the slick magazines, entices us to consume to the uttermost? Naturally, we cannot trace or demonstrate such influences with any precision, and it goes without saying that Hemingway is neither to be credited nor blamed for all this. He only expressed and unwittingly encouraged something that was already there.

So of his Americanness in general. His writings reinforce and give voice to what so often has been said are American traits: the rebellious impatience with the past, the ambivalent attitude toward culture, the leeriness of all theory—above all, the peculiarly American pride in hard-headed pragmatism. When we are urged by so many who set themselves up as pundits in our nuclear age to accept as the best wisdom available, as the ultimate realism, a kind of settled, gloomy toughness in staring at the hardest of facts, we cannot help thinking of the world outlook reflected in Hemingway's works.

To turn to matters less speculative: in literature Hemingway's reputation and influence are international and have been established since the 1920's.[11] That his limited vocabulary and simple syntax make him easy to translate is by no means the whole story. In post-Fascist Italy, he has taught the neorealists. In France, he has influenced writers as different as Camus and Malraux; and it is hard to imagine what Graham Greene might have been like without the example of Hemingway. Aside from his sovereignty in the short story both at home and abroad, among the American novelists who have learned from him are James Jones, John O'Hara, James T. Farrell, Nelson Algren, and Norman Mailer.

His importance, however, is not merely as an exponent of things American nor as the mouthpiece of a certain transient mood or the model for a temporary stance—nor merely as an influence upon other writers. In the future he will be read or not read for the intrinsic values of his writings. These will endure for whatever was both new and true in them.

What was new was indisputably the style; it was absolutely his own, fresh, essentially inimitable; and esthetically it carried out a task no other writer had attempted. What was also new was the Hemingway kind of short story. He took that genre a step beyond any of his predecessors, and we can be sure that at least a generous dozen of the stories will last as long as people read the English language. About his novels we cannot be so certain, though even in the poorest of them are passages that can never stale. But all of the novels are flawed. The only one probably never to be shaken from its position as a major classic is *The Sun Also Rises*. Not quite so sure to last is *A Farewell to Arms*. For future readers, its love story will be less winning; and, superb as are the chapters on war, they do not give us an experience whose intensity and meanings are comparable to those of *All Quiet on the Western Front*. *For Whom the Bell Tolls* is great in its ambition but only almost great in its achievement, because Hemingway failed to fuse his theme with his epic materials. As has often been remarked, his best gifts were not those of the novelist; he was seldom at ease in creating a group of characters, dramatizing their relationships, and developing their meanings over a span of time. Rather, he is an artist of still life; the breadth and dynamism of the novel is not his forte. Put differently, he is better in the short story because his is the talent of the lyricist rather than of the dramatist.

As to what was true in Hemingway: we cannot shrug off his dark reading of our human condition. He tried without flinching to face the destructive urges in our common humanity. He gazed open-eyed at the harsh actualities of our warring world. He showed us how man-made forces can reduce man to a thing, then to a nothing. He will never allow us to forget the presence of terror, panic, pain, and death—against the facile liberalism and the proud scientism which pretend to have nostrums for every ill flesh is heir to. And whether or not he has helped us toward understanding it, he makes us alive to the violence of our inner nature.[12]

As artist and moralist, the paradox of Hemingway is that his strengths and weaknesses seem to have one and the same root. Of the famous style, we sense that great cunning and tremendous force of will have won simplicity out of complexity. In the long run, however, the style can do only certain things: it cannot penetrate the labyrinths of the psyche; it cannot argue or think; when it goes beyond its bounds, it oversimplifies or slips into its own kind of pseudo-rhetoric. By its very nature, too, the Hemingway short story must leave unexplored many areas of human concern.

The same paradox dogs Hemingway the moralist. When it comes to teaching us how to live in his and our world, he can point only to his hero. In creating his hero Hemingway sought to win from the death drive itself some affirmation of human dignity. This is what we admire in him and what moves us so deeply. And yet that hero's usual virtue is physical courage in the midst of swift action. Such heroism is not enough for us. Too readily it can be debased, slip down to the bravado and brainless violence of the young hoodlum scared to be called "chicken." The other kind of heroism, which puts a man to a long test, to be hurt, worn down, until little is left but his spirit—this kind suited neither Hemingway's temperament nor his art.[13] Though admirable, the famous code is not nearly enough for us now. In essence, it was almost too old-fashioned from the start: a handful of virtues, valuable, shining, but garnered out of an earlier and simpler world.[14] For Hemingway's own generation—anyhow, for the characters in his novels and stories—it was a temporary expedient, imposing, if not a meaning, at least a style upon their lives in the 1920's. For youth today, however, for the youngsters needing a moral equivalent of war—for the ones who have opted out, for the ones who sacrifice comfort and safety in fighting for civil rights, or for the ones who risk security and careers to ask questions of the dogmatists of *Realpolitik*—Hemingway has little to say if anything at all.[15]

We need to know why. From an artist who saw and experienced so much, from a witness who earned of Edmund Wilson the label "gauge of morale," why are we left with a criticism of life that is so truncated? In part, the power of his art came from his uncanny genius for omission. Now ever more plainly we see the price: he omitted so much that he has left us only a "brilliant half-vision of life." [16] That half-vision scarcely grew with the years or with his experience. In his writings the incapacity to develop it shows plainest, I think, in his treatment of love and in his attitude toward culture. This is not to say that in his own life he failed in love, nor to imply that his art was not a subtly cultivated one, much less to assert that the man himself lacked cultivation—for Hemingway was a better linguist, thinker, reader, and art lover than most of his commentators. Rather it is that throughout his writings we see his mixed feelings toward love and culture, and what predominates is fear of these two fundamentals. The fear was strong and must have gone deep. However it worked on him, it turned Hemingway into more of a narrow specialist than he might have been. Here was his essential failure, and it was a failure of nerve. The critic's task is to probe that nerve.

It is a commonplace that Hemingway's fiction is marked by a paucity of ideas, a shortcoming which has not much harmed greater writers. But Norman Mailer—who happens to admire the Hemingway brand of courage—goes deeper when he charges that Hemingway "pretended to be ignorant of the notion that it is not enough to feel like a man, one must also think like a man." [17] The scorn of intellectualism—his shocked reaction against the professorial rhetoric and lofty abstract idealism of, say, Woodrow Wilson—stood Hemingway in good stead in the 1920's.[18] After that, the times signaled him to break out of it and move on. But he could never fully outgrow his attitude because the exclusion of intellect from his writings was no mere response to a hostile climate of opinion.[19] He would not think because he feared thinking would unfit him for heroic action.

We must respect in Hemingway that his determination to earn and keep his full share of masculine humanity took priority over his concern with being an artist. That demanding program has certain affinities with Emerson's "American Scholar." Emerson's definition, which might be applied to the artist as well as to the intellectual, was "Man Thinking." To measure Hemingway by this standard—and his life and career suggest it—he dodged the *Thinking* and clung to a cruelly limited conception of what being a *Man* calls for.

His fiction affords us certain insights into the origins of this distrust of thinking. For almost any boy, first impressions of the larger world of work, struggle, and adventure are acquired through his father. When the father is a man of science, a physician, as was Nick Adams' father and as was Hemingway, Sr., we might expect the boy in the normal course of things to feel that somehow intellectual enterprise and manhood are quite naturally connected. Almost nowhere in Hemingway's writing do we have an indication that the sort of intellectual activity embodied by such a father can be considered manly or even interesting. Nick Adams' father is weak and unmanly, and for Nick as for Robert Jordan his cowardice is finally proven by suicide. Except for hunting and fishing, the father as a guide and model is not to be trusted. Unless we count old Santiago, what is absent from the fiction is any sense of intellectual adventure, any awareness that thinking can call for hazards worth taking, demand the best in a man, and put him through a severe test. We find the opposite; masculinity and intellect are split apart. So, what drives Hemingway is not philosophical skepticism that rationalism may breed dry rot, but a fierce contempt for intellect as a form of weakness. Wherever intellect is present in Hemingway's books, it is regarded askance or yoked with cowardice. In other words, he dreaded that *Thinking* might unman him just as he dreaded that the *Man* in him might be devoured by the artist.

This same prejudice permeates his view of culture. We have seen that, for all the rigor of dedication to his own art, a part of him held the arts suspect. Esthetically, he could justify his disvaluing of the resources of culture because his aim in fiction was to capture the immediacy and authenticity of direct experience.[20] To travel light, however, he threw off too much. The cost to him as man and artist was that he could find in culture neither an armor against nor a weapon with which to fight a hostile world. Nor is it with Hemingway just a revolt against a ruined past. It is an anxiety toward culture as something that might soften his manliness. That anxiety also reaches back to his boyhood. In the household at Oak Park, Illinois, art was represented by the feminine. His mother, Grace Hall Hemingway, was more than a talented singer with a good musical education. She had a remarkable voice, sang a concert in Madison Square Garden, and was offered a contract by the Metropolitan Opera Company. Although she gave up this career to marry, she continued to sing, compose, and teach; later she became enough of a painter to have her pictures exhibited in several cities, to sell them for good prices, and even to have one-man shows.[21] Whatever her actual shortcomings as a mother— and evidently she had enough[22]—the point here is that no mother in her son's fiction ever has comparable gifts. The few mother characters that do appear have one quality in common: all are domineering. Whether she is Krebs's mother or Nick Adams', she is a threat: she has unmanned the father and may do the same to the son. Whatever love she gives is problematic. The anxiety Hemingway evidently felt toward his mother he came in time to project onto all of her sex—at the very least it limited his portrayal of women. When he fled her domination, he was struggling to assert and prove his manhood. It was a struggle in which art and culture, bound up in his heart with the maternal and the feminine, were the losers.

In sum, from that first battlefield every human being fights on, Hemingway emerged a casualty. The oedipal conflict left grievous scars. Then, in rejecting the world of both his parents, he intensified his jeopardy. After the fierceness of his revolt against their Victorianism,[23] he could rely only on what was in himself: on the one hand, his sexual and aggressive drives and, on the other, the puritanic conscience which was drilled into him. In one form that conscience came out in his devotion to style. In another form that conscience, burdened by a largely unconscious hostility toward his parents, made for an abnormal sense of guilt. To appease that inward tyrant, a towering penance was necessary. Couple this need for punishment with an equal need to assert masculinity, and we see why in Hemingway's own life, as in the careers of his heroes, the supreme test of virility is the capacity to take blows.[24] In his writings, the sad and ironic result is that the hero is less the man who does things than the man to whom things are done—the man who is passive and thus, unconsciously, feminine. Such conflicts went into the making of the artist and, finally, into the breaking of the man. We are a long way, however, from any final word about them.

For anything like a full or coherent elucidation of these and other puzzles in Hemingway's personality we must await the biographer who can assimilate and order the mass of available data and bring to it both the awareness of the literary critic and the disciplined insight of the psychiatrist. It may be some time before we get this ideal combination, and the book we are hoping for. The present study is neither a biographical nor a psychiatric one. Yet if my critique has found in Hemingway's work features that might be termed neurotic, it raises questions about the connection between these features and his last years of illness and violent death. Such questions will inevitably occur to readers of A. E. Hotchner's *Papa Hemingway*.[25] My own book, begun before 1962, was substantially completed before the appearance of that best-seller. When I read it, I was, like most students of Hemingway, not very surprised. For one thing, it contained much that was already in print; for another, it seemed to fill out the climactic details of an emotional illness already discernible in Hemingway's writings. Hotchner's account of the suicide and its immediate antecedents looked like the finale of a drama that had been in the making for decades. Without entering the controversies over *Papa Hemingway*, I can only state that no responsible-minded scholar will put much faith in such an undocumented book—except where Hotchner's evidence is corroborated by more trustworthy authorities.[26] If we are to look into the self-destruction of Hemingway's last years in the hope of pointing to a few relevant considerations, our best procedure is to draw from several reliable sources and to use Hotchner only with great care.[27]

First and obvious is the bitter irony that Hemingway, whose style of living and of writing demanded youth and vigor, aged prematurely and rapidly lost his physical health. Just as obvious, the melancholy and malaise that were always in him, despite the celebrated bonhomie, more and more had their way—until during the winter and spring of 1960–61 he went into a depression so deep that hospitalization and twenty-five electric shock treatments were considered necessary.[28]

If in his wretchedness Hemingway ever came to feel that those who were not wholly for him must be wholly against him,[29] that looks like a morbid exaggeration of something we have seen

critic named Hal. In malicious zest Hemingway cuts down these enemies, sometimes with a bludgeon, more often with a rapier. More space goes to Gertrude Stein and the Scott Fitzgeralds than to any other figure, three sketches apiece. As Hemingway gives his own version of the break with Miss Stein, his fear-hatred of homosexuality seems to be at the core of it; behind this tangled business may also be his mixed feelings toward any kind of mother surrogate. The good love is with Hadley, Hemingway's first wife. Her foil is Zelda Fitzgerald, a portrait of the bitch-woman destroying both the masculinity and the genius of her husband. And surely, whether fact or fiction, the anecdote on "A Matter of Measurements" must already be established as one of the best drolleries among the curiosities of literature. Still, when Hemingway tries, empirically, to reassure the naïve Scott that he is normal—against the torment of Zelda's complaint that her husband's "measurements" made him sexually inadequate and so brought on her first breakdown—we do not have to go very deep to see in the joke a projection of Hemingway's own castration anxiety.[37]

On the familiar Hemingway themes of women and money and integrity, the final chapter is the most revealing. Here the melancholy darkens into remorse that for fame and wealth he sacrificed love and innocence. Hemingway is deliberately cryptic in his confession. The setting shifts from Paris to the snows and ski trails of the Austrian Alps. There he found Eden with Hadley and his work on *The Sun Also Rises*. He grew a beard then and let his hair go uncut; and we are not surprised when this creator of martyr-heroes recalls that in this high white fairy-land the peasants called him "the Black Christ" (p. 206). Into his coda Hemingway weaves strains reminiscent of *A Farewell to Arms* and the tortured memories of Harry of "The Snows of Kilimanjaro." A "nightmare winter" broke into the idyl, a "murderous summer" followed, and a trusted friend turned out to be a Judas. Like a "pilot fish," he led "the rich" into the company of the young writer. Against their spell Hemingway was helpless; and when they tempted him to read from his novel-in-the-making, he yielded "like a trained pig in a circus who has finally found someone who loves and appreciates him for himself alone" (p. 209). Their flattery fed his heart; their price was the violation of his artist's integrity. Another intruder arrived, "another rich," a young unmarried woman; and "unknowingly, innocently" she set out to marry the husband. Thus, the eternal triangle, the break-up of his marriage, the death of his first married love.[38] Fame was close to Hemingway, and the gall of remorse was already his intimate: "All things truly wicked start from an innocence. So you live day by day and enjoy what you have and do not worry. You lie and hate it and it destroys you and every day is more dangerous, but you live day to day as in a war" (p. 210).

The wonder is that out of such battles within Hemingway won so many victories. Those conquests, not his derring-do, were the essential heroism of the writer and the man. We have always relied on his courage to seek out and set down uncompromisingly those truths which were his own province. That is why we have trusted him for "news from the fighting fronts of modern consciousness."[39] Whenever he swerved from this course, he forgave himself less readily than we do.

Of his outward enemies, perhaps the worst was fame. Like Byron or D'Annunzio or—coming closer to home—like Jack London and Stephen Crane, Hemingway was doomed to create a legend. His ill luck was to be a creature of a time and clime whose adulation can be cruel. For all his wariness, he never found a way, as did Faulkner, to protect himself from the limelight; he needed applause—too much;[40] so that the mask he wore in public he came at times to mistake for his own face.[41]

The other kindly foe in the outward world was war. If, arguably, he was breaking new ground in For Whom the Bell Tolls, at the moment of that very promise, conscience and the legend and his own aggressiveness combined to lure him into combat in World War II. These exploits, as we saw, drove him backward rather than forward. The first World War brought the wound at Fossalta. For the eighteen-year-old youngster that wound was a proof that the world was as bad as he had anticipated, in fact worse. What that blast effected was a hellish fusion of the blackness already in Hemingway with the blackness outside. The shock—as we read of it in "Now I Lay Me"—revived a long-buried trauma of early childhood. The consequences were apparently twofold. It revealed to him one mystery: that Eros and Thanatos could be united; but it barred him from glimpsing that happier mystery, both sexual and spiritual, where love can be "dying-in-one-another in order to be born into a new life." [42]

In the second place—and this was another block to growth—as Hemingway tried to pull himself out of it, he was compelled again and again to return to the experience of his wounding, as if by reliving the anguish he might somehow master it. Thus driven and obsessed, he must repeat himself, in his writings repeat his themes, motifs, character types, images, symbols, rhythms. [43] His art seldom gets free of his neurosis. What further impoverishes his work is the narrowness of life represented in it. We do not complain that he broke with conventional realism here; on the contrary, we naturally prize Hemingway's success in achieving his conscious intent: to show meticulously not how things are but what the feelings are in respect to those things. [44] Rather, our regret concerns those feelings; for Hemingway has an abnormally tense grip on outward reality because such reality is for him only a sort of check or umpire for the whelming emotions within, his relentless unconscious struggle: combativeness versus passivity, aggression versus self-punishment, rebellion versus repentance. What oppresses us in Hemingway's narrowed representation of life is its fierce exclusiveness. My complaint is not so much that he left untouched vast reaches of human experience. Rather, the charge is against an ever present implication in his writings: that for enduring this nightmarishly confined world no honest man can hold to any other possible virtues and values than those Hemingway insists upon. We recoil against such dogmatism. And finally we are wearied by a fictional world that has become so repetitive and even predictable.[45]

With Hemingway his life and his art are inextricable. We know that in his own life he acted out themes and motifs frequent in his fiction. Toward the end his obsessions won their long war against both his emotions and his art. In his final decade his repetition compulsion swells to a crescendo.[46] More and more he must turn backward in time—as if to recapture the past.[47] Four times during these years he visited Spain. There he made friends with the handsome young matador, Ordoñez, son of the bullfighter on whom he had modeled Romero of *The Sun Also Rises*. But this is not the Spain of the 1920's, and the repetition in *The Dangerous Summer* depresses us. He became involved with Ordoñez, a sort of manager, counselor, and wound-dresser for him. When Ordoñez' right arm was badly hurt by a bull and against doctor's orders he returned to the ring within twenty-four hours to give one of his best faenas, and when the elderly *aficionado* cabled to *Life*'s editors his admiring account, we hear the melody as before.[48] It is the old Hemingway in more than one sense. We did not know it then, but now we know it was a *danse macabre*. His work was done. He had used up his great spirit. The big robust body had failed him—and so had fame.[49] He deserved peace. He had earned it, and he took it—the hard way.

There is a photograph of him taken in Spain in the summer of 1959; it haunts the memory and hurts the heart. Hemingway is seated at a bedside. The big chest and the shoulders sag. His balding head—the beard white as snow—is bent down. On the bed lies Ordoñez, his right leg exposed from the coverlet. Hemingway is absorbed in contemplating that leg. In his right hand he holds a cloth, which might be a newly removed bandage. He is grave. Tenderly, reverently, his left hand reaches out toward the young hero's wound.[50]

Notes

In these notes the works cited most frequently have been abbreviated as follows:

Baker, *The Writer*   Carlos Baker, *Hemingway: The Writer as Artist* (3rd ed.; Princeton, N.J.: Princeton University Press, 1963).

Baker, *His Critics*   *Hemingway and His Critics*, ed. Carlos Baker (American Century Series; New York: Hill and Wang, 1961).

Baker, *Critiques*   *Ernest Hemingway: Critiques of Four Major Novels*, ed. Carlos Baker (Scribner Research Anthology; New York: Charles Scribner's Sons, 1962).

McCaffery   *Ernest Hemingway: The Man and His Works*, ed. John K. M. McCaffery (Cleveland and New York: World Publishing Company, 1950).

Weeks   *Hemingway: A Collection of Critical Essays*, ed. Robert P. Weeks (Twentieth Century Views; Englewood Cliffs, N.J.: Prentice-Hall, 1962).

Young   Philip Young, *Ernest Hemingway: A Reconsideration* (University Park and London: Pennsylvania State University Press, 1966).

Quite often a critical essay on Hemingway has appeared in more than one publication; when that is so and when the essay in question is included in one of the collections listed above, I have as a rule cited only the collection. There the reader may find when and where the particular essay was earlier, or originally, published.

Chapter I

1. Hemingway's father committed suicide in 1928. The year before, Hemingway and his first wife, Hadley Richardson, were divorced. This story originally appeared in *Scribner's Magazine*, XCIII (1933), 204–8.

2. I am indebted to Joseph DeFalco's critique of this story in *The Hero in Hemingway's Short Stories* (Pittsburgh, Pa.: University of Pittsburgh Press, 1963), pp. 27–33.

3. So in fact, it was; for it first appeared in the *New Republic* as "Italy," L (May 18, 1927), 350–53. The Guy of the story is Hemingway's friend and traveling companion, Guy Hickok.

4. For a Christian interpretation of erotic symbols and motifs here, see William Bysshe Stein, "Love and Lust in Hemingway's Short Stories," *Texas Studies in Literature and Language*, III (1961), 234–42.

5. In his Preface to *The Short Stories of Ernest Hemingway*, p. v.

6. In his brief commentary on this story, Carlos Baker remarks of Hemingway: "His preoccupation is rather with the healthy norm of ordinary sexual behavior." See pp. 139–40 in his *The Writer*. This statement is hard to understand unless by "preoccupation," Dr. Baker means Hemingway's ideal ethical preference.

7. This is one of the central insights of Karl A. Menninger's *Man against Himself* (New York: Harcourt, Brace & Co., 1938), a medical discussion of self-mutilation and suicide.

8. Pp. 78–82.

9. For a general discussion of love and death in Hemingway's writings, see Richard Drinnon, "In the American Heartland: Hemingway and Death," *Psychoanalytic Review*, LII (1965), 5–31 [149–75]. His comment on "A Way You'll Never Be" is on pp. 9–12 [153–56]. As Drinnon points out, the dream images symbolize

the female genitals and are an expression of the longing for death.

10. A discerning treatment of the repetition compulsion and of Hemingway's primitive ritualism is in Young, pp. 164–71.

11. See his "Nightmare and Ritual in Hemingway," in Weeks, pp. 40–51. Originally, this essay was the Introduction to *The Portable Hemingway* (New York: Viking Press, 1945).

12. As Nick is making coffee he remembers arguing with Hopkins about how to make a good brew. He recalls that Hopkins was "the most serious man Nick had ever known"; that he played polo; that he became a millionaire overnight; that they called his girl "the Blonde Venus." Interestingly, when Hopkins left the fishing camp on the news of his sudden wealth, the gifts he gave his pals had, symbolically, certain sexual implications: the phallic, to Nick, who gets Hopkins' .22 caliber Colt automatic pistol; perhaps the voyeuristic when Bill gets his camera. But they never again saw Hopkins. As Nick drinks the coffee now, it tastes bitter and he laughs. "It made a good ending to the story," he thinks. The story is cryptic enough. Evidently because it stirs painful memories— tinged with envy or jealousy?—Nick stops his reminiscences (pp. 217–18).

13. In Weeks, p. 41.

14. That the Nick Adams of this story had had experience in war we know only from some of the interchapters of *In Our Time*, where, fittingly, "Big Two-Hearted River" is the final story.

15. My interpretation of this story owes something to Nancy Hale, "Hemingway and the Courage To Be," *Virginia Quarterly Review*, XXXVIII (1962), 620–39.

16. There is enough evidence on the strict moralism of Hemingway's father in Leicester Hemingway, *My Brother, Ernest Hemingway* (Cleveland, Ohio: World Publishing Co., 1961, 1962).

17. On both the ethical and psychological implications of Doctor Adams' dealings with the half-breed, DeFalco is penetrating and comprehensive. See *The Hero in Hemingway's Short Stories*, pp. 33–40.

18. Carlos Baker has supplied us with the relevant biographical data in the *New York Times Book Review*, July 26, 1964. The portrait of Hemingway's own mother, as we have it in Constance Cappel Montgomery's *Hemingway in Michigan* (New York: Fleet

Publishing Company, 1966), is scarcely flattering. See especially "Twenty-first Birthday," pp. 172–82.

19. Painful as this story is, the actuality was evidently worse. For accounts of how harshly the author was treated by his parents when he returned home as a wounded veteran, see the following: Constance Cappel Montgomery, *Hemingway in Michigan;* Marcelline Hemingway Sanford, *At the Hemingways: A Family Portrait* (Atlantic Monthly Press Book; Boston: Little, Brown and Company, 1961, 1962); and Leicester Hemingway, *My Brother, Ernest Hemingway.*

20. Young (p. 165) tells us that once, when Hemingway was asked the name of his psychoanalyst, the writer replied with a laugh, "Portable Corona, No. 3." Hemingway was contemptuous of Freudianism in *Death in the Afternoon,* pp. 53–54. And he seems to have taken a dim view of what he called Philip Young's "trauma theory of literature." The phrase is quoted by George Plimpton in "An Interview with Hemingway." This interview appeared originally in the *Paris Review,* XVIII (Spring, 1958), and is included in Baker, *His Critics,* pp. 19–37.

21. Compare the passage from the short story with this: "I died then," Hemingway told his friend Guy Hickok. "I felt my soul or something coming right out of my body, like you'd pull a silk handkerchief out of a pocket by one corner. It flew around and then came back and went in again and I wasn't dead any more." This is quoted by Malcolm Cowley in "A Portrait of Mr. Papa," *Life,* January 10, 1949, and reprinted in McCaffery, p. 47.

Chapter II

1. This paragraph is indebted to Baker, *The Writer,* pp. 37–39.
2. Perhaps the best known essay making this interpretation is Mark Spilka's "The Death of Love in *The Sun Also Rises,*" in Baker, *His Critics,* pp. 80–92.
3. See *"The Sun Also Rises*—But No Bells Ring," in Robert Stallman's *The Houses That James Built* (East Lansing: Michigan State University Press, 1961), pp. 173–93.
4. Baker, *The Writer,* p. 78.
5. The quotation is from McCaffery, p. 52.

6. This paragraph is indebted to Isaac Rosenfeld's excellent essay-review, "A Farewell to Hemingway," *Kenyon Review*, XIII (1951), 147–55.

7. Though I cannot accept his over-all argument, for an interesting treatment of love in Hemingway's writings, with particular emphasis on the Tristan motif, I recommend Robert W. Lewis, Jr., *Hemingway on Love* (Austin & London: University of Texas Press, 1965).

8. On the question of romantic love, *A Farewell to Arms* nicely illustrates the general argument of Denis de Rougement's *Love in the Western World*, trans. Montgomery Belgion (rev. and augmented ed.; Garden City, N.Y.: Doubleday and Co., 1957, Doubleday Anchor book).

Chapter III

1. In his essay "Hemingway: Gauge of Morale," McCaffery, p. 245. Wilson's essay appeared earlier in *The Wound and the Bow* (New York: Oxford University Press, 1941).

2. See Callaghan's *That Summer in Paris* (New York: Coward-McCann, 1963), especially chap. xv.

3. For a discussion of Hemingway's esthetics, see Carlos Baker's treatment of *Death in the Afternoon*, chap. vii, especially pp. 150–61, in his *The Writer*.

4. It argues a certain coarseness in Hemingway's sensibility here that he mistakes the thrills of watching matadors for feelings of immortality. To watch bullfighters, lion tamers, and death-defying aerialists or high-wire artists does of course give to one's nerves a more powerful sensation than, say, listening to Beethoven's *Ninth Symphony*. But surely the quality of the emotion Beethoven stirs in us points to very different meanings and values.

5. On the relation between Hemingway's and Waldo Frank's treatment of the bullfight, see Baker, *The Writer*, pp. 150–52.

6. For an extensive analysis and critique of this story, see John Portz, "Allusion and Structure in Hemingway's 'A Natural History of the Dead,'" *Tennessee Studies in Literature*, X (1965), 27–41; another critique is John A. Yunck's "The Natural History of a Dead

Quarrel: Hemingway and the Humanists," *South Atlantic Quarterly*, LXII (1963), 29–42.

7. See Stephen A. Reid, "The Oedipal Pattern in Hemingway's 'The Capital of the World,'" *Literature and Psychology*, XIII (1963), 37–43. Quite helpful on the larger significances of bullfighting to Hemingway is Richard Drinnon's "In the American Heartland: Hemingway and Death," *Psychoanalytic Review*, LII (1965), 5–31 [149–75].

8. The crudity of Hemingway's psychology here is blatant. Men who harm their health by consorting with diseased prostitutes are scarcely "thinking only of the woman."

9. Young, p. 97.

10. Edmund Wilson has remarked of *Green Hills of Africa* that it "must be one of the only books ever written which make Africa and its animals seem dull. Almost the only thing we learn about the animals is that Hemingway wants to kill them" (McCaffery, p. 246).

11. On the emotional meanings which big-game hunting had for Hemingway, see W. M. Frohock's "Violence and Discipline," in McCaffery, pp. 262–91.

12. *Portraits and Self-Portraits*, collected and illustrated by Georges Schreiber (Boston: Houghton Mifflin, 1936), p. 57.

13. This point has been made by Earl Rovit in his *Ernest Hemingway* (Twayne's United States Authors Series; New York: Twayne Publishers, 1963), pp. 70–71.

14. My interpretation of this story is considerably indebted to Stephen A. Reid; see Note 7 of this chapter.

15. An interesting psychological discussion of this story is that of Lewis in *Hemingway on Love*. I am somewhat indebted to the critique in his chap. v, "The Eternal Triangle."

16. The manifest content of this dream is relatively simple: the fearful image of the lion was obviously stimulated by the crisis of the preceding day. Symbolically, the dream of being threatened by a lion expresses the anxiety of being killed or hurt by the father.

17. Characteristically, Hemingway does not tell us explicitly what happened. He merely gives us the results the next morning: that is, Macomber's frank realization of his hatred for Wilson.

18. See Young's discussion, pp. 74–78.

19. See Baker, *The Writer,* p. 229.

20. Regarding *To Have and Have Not,* Carlos Baker has written, "He [Hemingway] told [Maxwell] Perkins that he did not consider it 'a real novel' " (*ibid.,* p. 205).

21. The history of the publication is traced by Carlos Baker (*ibid.,* pp. 203–5).

22. On the literary lineage of Harry Morgan, see Young, pp. 198–200; and Baker, *The Writer,* pp. 210–11. My discussion of this novel has been helped at some points by Lewis, *Hemingway on Love,* chap. ix, "Hollow and Sick."

23. *The New Masses,* XVI (September 17, 1935), 9.

Chapter IV

1. All quotations from the play are from *The First Forty-nine Stories and the Play The Fifth Column* (Modern Library ed.; New York: Random House, 1938).

2. My phrasing here is close to Young's, p. 103.

3. The critic was Cyril Connolly, who made the statement in *New Statesman and Nation,* XIV (October 16, 1937), 606 (quoted by Baker, *The Writer,* p. 223).

4. In his Preface to *The First Forty-nine Stories and the Play* . . . , p. vi.

5. An important essay on the particular experiment in style is Edward Fenimore's "English and Spanish in *For Whom the Bell Tolls,*" in McCaffery, pp. 205–20.

6. In his "Hemingway: Gauge of Morale," in McCaffery, p. 257.

7. This novel stirred mixed responses. Among the more important essays on it, the following are suggested: James Gray, "Tenderly Tolls the Bell," pp. 226–35; Edwin Berry Burgum, "Ernest Hemingway and the Psychology of the Lost Generation," pp. 308–28, both in McCaffery; and these, included in Baker, *Critiques:* Lionel Trilling, "An American in Spain," pp. 78–81; Alvah C. Bessie, "Review of *For Whom the Bell Tolls,*" pp. 90–94; Allen Guttmann, "Mechanized Doom: Ernest Hemingway and the American View of the Spanish War," pp. 95–107.

8. His essay "Not Spain But Hemingway," in Baker, *His Critics*, pp. 202–12.

9. Leslie Fiedler's comment here is that "Hemingway has written the most absurd love scene in the history of the American novel . . ." (*Love and Death in the American Novel* [New York: Criterion Books, 1960], pp. 304–5).

10. The phrase is Edmund Wilson's in his footnote to "Hemingway: Gauge of Morale," in McCaffery, p. 254.

11. Psychologically, such telescoped imagery is interesting: that is, the fearsome cobra is of course a male symbol; but here it is associated with defensive feelings toward a domineering mother figure.

12. In chapter viii of his *Hemingway on Love* Lewis has made an impressive study of these interweavings.

13. On the love-death ambivalence Lewis is perceptive in his treatment of the symbolic function of horses here (*ibid.*, pp. 157–66).

14. On this event, Lewis comments: "The horse crushes his left leg; ironically, the gelded (incomplete, undeveloped) symbol of eros administers the symbolically castrative wound. . . . In effect, Jordan is a fisher-king, a sacrificial hero, just as the horse has traditionally been a sacrificial embodiment of the god of vegetation. In order to insure fecundity of life, life must be taken. Eros is killed for the sake of eros" (*ibid.*, p. 165).

15. On the death of Jordan, Lionel Trilling has written: "Yet Hemingway, we may be sure, intended that the star-crossed love and heroic death of Robert Jordan should be a real tragedy, a moral and political tragedy which would suggest and embody the tragedy of the Spanish war. In this intention he quite fails. The clue to the failure is the essential inner dullness of his hero . . . he does not in himself embody the tensions which were in the historical events he lived through. . . . Consider as an illuminating detail the relation which Hemingway establishes between Robert Jordan and the leaders he admires, Golz the general and Karkov the journalist. Both are cynical and exceptionally competent men, wholly capable of understanding all the meanings of the revolutionary scene. . . . [But Jordan does not] really want to understand as his friends do. He wants, he says, to keep his mind in suspension until the war is won" ("An American in Spain," in Baker, *Critiques*, p. 79).

Chapter V

1. Baker, *The Writer*, p. 265 fn. and p. 335; Young, pp. 114 and 144–45; Cowley in McCaffery, p. 35 fn.

2. Baker, *The Writer*, pp. 265 and 330; Young, p. 144; Cowley in McCaffery, p. 35.

3. See John W. Aldridge, "Two Poor Fish on One Line," an essay-review occasioned by the publication of a paperback edition of *The Old Man and the Sea*, in *Book Week*, June 20, 1965, pp. 16 and 19, in the *New York Herald Tribune* and *Washington Post*.

4. This account of Hemingway's activities in World War II follows Cowley's in McCaffery, pp. 35–41. I am also indebted to Young, pp. 142–44. Part of Hemingway's own account we find in his war correspondent dispatches; some of these are included in *By-Line: Ernest Hemingway; Selected Articles and Dispatches of Four Decades*, ed., William White (New York: Charles Scribner's Sons, 1967).

5. John Groth, "A Note on Ernest Hemingway," in McCaffery, pp. 19–24.

6. I am thinking of two particularly in *By-Line: Ernest Hemingway*—"Voyage to Victory" and "War in the Siegfried Line."

7. *By-Line*, p. 386.

8. *Ibid.*, p. 360.

9. *Ibid.*, p. 470.

10. See Kermit Vanderbilt, "The Last Words of E. H.," *The Nation*, CCI (October 25, 1965), 284–85.

11. Baker has written: "Even as late as 1949, when he turned aside from his major task to work on his novel of Venice, the traumatic effects of his life in the second world war still rankled in his mind. The story of Colonel Cantwell emerged as a way of exorcizing what for Hemingway still had the aspect, and the terrorizing atmosphere, of a recent nightmare" (*The Writer*, p. 260).

12. See the parallels pointed to by Young, pp. 115–17.

13. The phrasing is David Gordon's in "The Son and the Father: Patterns of Response to Conflict in Hemingway's Fiction," *Literature and Psychology*, XVI, Nos. 3, 4 (1966), 122–38. At several points in this chapter I have found Gordon's excellent essay very useful.

14. Reprinted as *Portrait of Hemingway* (Avon Books; New York: Hearst Corporation, 1950, 1961), p. 77.

15. Young, p. 163.

16. McCaffery, pp. 44–45.

17. Charles A. Fenton, *The Apprenticeship of Ernest Hemingway* (New York: Viking Press, 1954), p. 70.

18. On this paradox Richard Drinnon's entire article is most illuminating: "In the American Heartland: Hemingway and Death," *Psychoanalytic Review*, LII (1965), 5–31 [149–75]. See especially p. 18 [162] where he writes: "In battle itself, one band of buddies strains against another, striving to penetrate each other. 'If soldiers seduce civilians on their own side into the inexplicit homosexuality of army life,' writes Miss Brigid Brophy [in her *Black Ship to Hell* (London: Secker and Warburg, 1962), p. 48] 'they practice violent seductions on the other side. Or, rather, it is a case of reciprocal seduction.' The seducers hold on to their manly faith in their own inviolability until they too are hit solidly, 'as every man will be if he stays'; the seduced are the crips, the mutilated, the temporary or permanent *castrati*.

"To be sure, battle is much more and much else than a violent expression of manly love and hate. But *one* dimension is such and it is from here that you have some insight into the mysterious wound trauma of Hemingway and his heroes. First there was the inexplicit homosexuality of martial society and then there was the violating wound. Try as they would—even to holding up shrapnel-riddled trousers for social approval—Hemingway and his heroes could not shake the feeling that these war wounds were somehow Red Badges of Shame. Awake or asleep, each and every one asked over and over with Jake Barnes: Why did this have to happen to me? Underground emotions exploded in retort like land mines: Because he and the other had actively courted the seductive relationship with 'the man with the beard who looked at him over the sights of the rifle.'" "The man with the beard" is an image that appears near the end of "A Way You'll Never Be." Significantly, Hemingway, Sr., was a man with a beard.

Regarding Hemingway's wounding at Fossalta, Young has remarked on "his mingled disgust and reverence for that event of his life by which the whole may be known, and by which it was unalterably determined" (p. 120). Writing of the significance of Nick Adams' wound, Young calls it "an outward and visible sign of an inward and spiritual dis-grace" (p. 41).

19. Quoted by Richard Drinnon, "In the American Heartland," p. 26 [170].

20. This paragraph is indebted to Isaac Rosenfeld, "A Farewell to Hemingway," *Kenyon Review*, XIII (1951), especially 154–55.

21. The phrase is Nemi D'Agostino's, in "The Later Hemingway," in Weeks, p. 159.

22. On these matters, see Robert P. Weeks, "Fakery in *The Old Man and the Sea*," *College English*, XXIV (1962), 188–92. About the impossibility of determining the sex of a marlin before cutting the fish open—Hemingway's handling of which Weeks calls "fakery" —Richard Drinnon has explained: "In the case of the marlin Hemingway was forced to devise implausible stratagems: The death mystique, the dialectic of castrate or be castrated, made it absolutely essential that the armed enemies and animals and fish be males" ("In the American Heartland," p. 26 [170]).

23. *Time*, LXIV (December 13, 1954), 72.

24. On the symbolism vs. realism argument in Hemingway criticism, my general position is in accord with E. M. Halliday's "Hemingway's Ambiguity: Symbolism and Irony," in Weeks, pp. 52–71; and with Bern Oldsey's "The Snows of Ernest Hemingway," *Wisconsin Studies in Contemporary Literature*, IV, No. 2 (Spring-Summer, 1963), 172–98.

25. Pointed out by David Gordon in "The Son and the Father," pp. 136–37. The pertinent passage from Freud is in the third from the last paragraph of his *Moses and Monotheism*.

26. See Leslie Fiedler, *Waiting for the End* (Delta Book; New York: Dell Publishing Co., 1964), chap. ii, "War, Exile and the Death of Honor."

27. I disagree with Norman Mailer that this novella is "a bad piece of work." Mailer has declared: *"Only when one feels, more or less subliminally, the face of Ernest on the body of a Cuban fisherman does the fraud of the tale take on its surrealist truth."* In a footnote, he remarks with more point: *"But a work of affirmation must contain its moment of despair—specifically there must be a bad moment when the old man Santiago is tempted to cut the line*

and let the big fish go. Hemingway avoided the problem by never letting the old man be seriously tempted." Both quotations are on p. 19 of *Advertisements for Myself* (New York: G. P. Putnam's Sons, 1959).

28. Pointed out by Young, p. 125.

29. *The Old Man and the Sea* illustrates the general argument of Leslie Fiedler, *Love and Death in the American Novel* (New York: Criterion Books, 1960).

30. This paragraph is indebted to a valuable general study of the love-death ambivalence in Hemingway: Melvin Backman, "Hemingway: The Matador and the Crucified," in Baker, *His Critics,* especially p. 258.

Epilogue

1. "Two Tales of Darkness: A Man of the World; Get a Seeing-Eyed Dog," *Atlantic,* CC (November, 1957), 64–68.

2. Baker, *The Writer,* p. 345; Young, p. 269.

3. Baker, *The Writer,* p. 341.

4. *Ibid.,* p. 335.

5. *Ibid.,* pp. 333–35. Mrs. Hemingway was also injured but not dangerously. Baker tells us that in the first crash Hemingway suffered "a ruptured liver, a ruptured kidney, complete stoppage of peristalsis in the intestines, damage to the lower vertebrae and the sphincter muscle," and a concussion whose more obvious symptoms were a wound in the skull (out of which cerebral fluid oozed) and the affliction for a while of double vision and loss of hearing in one ear.

6. In his Introduction to *Critics* Baker gives us this quotation: " 'Because of his absolute youthfulness,' said one of his oldest and most admiring friends, 'he regards old-growing as an utter and complete tragedy . . . [and] he is not going to degrade himself by maturing or anything absurd of that sort. All the same, since he has a sense of costume, he will emphasize his decline in all its hopelessness by sprouting a white beard and generally acting the part of senex. We are going to get a lot of this inverted youth from [him] henceforth' " (p. 9).

7. See Young's description of Hemingway's photographs, pp.

148–49. Also useful on this matter is Leo Lania's *Hemingway: A Pictorial Biography* (New York: Viking Press, 1961), especially the photographs on pp. 112–28—those, if Lania is accurate, dating from early 1954 on. In one titled "Hemingway in Venice, 1954," he already looks prematurely old.

8. This account of Hemingway's last decade is indebted to Baker, *The Writer*, chap. xiii, "The Death of the Lion." See especially p. 343.

9. Besides the facts of the invitation to the Inauguration and John F. Kennedy's borrowing of the phrase "grace under pressure" as a definition on the first page of his book, *Profiles in Courage*, there was, Philip Young declares, "a remarkable affinity between the writer and the President." See Young's list of specifics, p. 273 fn.

10. In the cover story on him in *Time*, LXXXV (June 25, 1965), 26–29, McGeorge Bundy is quoted: "A politician's life is like a bullfighter's. . . . The bull can get him any day."

11. See, for instance, *The Literary Reputation of Hemingway in Europe*, ed. Roger Asselineau, (Lettres Modernes; Paris: M. J. Minard, 1965). The American edition was published the same year by New York University Press. See also the July 29, 1961, number of the *Saturday Review*, an issue devoted to Hemingway. And see in particular the intercontinental scope of "A Checklist of Hemingway Criticism," in Baker, *Critics*, pp. 279–98.

12. Apropos the large problems touched on here as they concern not merely Hemingway but modern literature in general, see the wonderfully illuminating essay, "The Fate of Pleasure," in Lionel Trilling's *Beyond Culture* (New York: Viking Press, 1965).

13. Where in all of Hemingway's published writings do we find admiration for a Socrates, a Michelangelo, a Bruno, a Milton, a Beethoven, a Thoreau, a Garrison?

14. On this question, Isaac Rosenfeld is penetrating: ". . . the old values were never seriously questioned, and such cliches as manliness, courage, and self-reliance remained unchanged. There is no objection to these values as such; the objection is to the meaning society has given them. Hemingway never examined their social meaning; he merely cut the traditional world of application out from under these values and put something unexpected in its place" ("A Farewell to Hemingway," *Kenyon Review*, XIII [1951], 149).

15. In *Advertisements for Myself*, Norman Mailer has leveled this charge against Hemingway: *"He's no longer any help to us, he's left us marooned in the nervous boredom of a world which finally he didn't try hard enough to change"* (p. 18). But for a spirited defense of the code see chap. viii, "Hemingway: Man, Artist and Legend," in Earl Rovit, *Ernest Hemingway* (Twayne's United States Authors Series; New York: Twayne Publishers, 1963).

16. The phrase is Alfred Kazin's, in McCaffery, p. 203.

17. In *Advertisements for Myself*, Mailer's next sentence is: *"Hemingway has always been afraid to think, afraid of losing even a little popularity"* (p. 18).

18. Harry Levin has written: "The realism of his generation reacted, not only against Wilsonian idealism, but against Wilsonian rhetoric" (Baker, *Critics*, p. 101). Another important essay on this question is Lionel Trilling, "Hemingway and His Critics," also in *ibid.*, pp. 61–70.

19. Though it scarcely looks for the emotional bases involved, the best essay on Hemingway's anti-intellectualism is Robert Evans, "Hemingway and the Pale Cast of Thought," *American Literature*, XXXVIII (May, 1966), 161–76.

20. Concerning Hemingway and fictionists like him, Alberto Moravia has remarked on "a lack of faith in the resources of culture, which the American writer sees as cramping and weighing down the immediacy and authenticity of direct experience." See his interesting article on Hemingway, "Nothing Amen," *Status* (November, 1965), pp. 28–29 and 89. The essay also appears in Moravia's *Man as an End: A Defense of Humanism* (New York: Farrar, Straus & Giroux, 1966).

21. These data on Hemingway's mother I have drawn from Marcelline Hemingway Sanford, *At the Hemingways* (Atlantic Monthly Press Book; Boston: Little Brown and Company, 1961, 1962), pp. 56–59 and 222–38.

22. In one of the most trying periods of the young Hemingway's life—when he had returned home, was still suffering from the more immediate effects of his war wound, had scarcely recovered from the rejection of his love by Agnes H. von Kurowski (the Red Cross nurse who became in part the model for Catherine Barkley), was trying to find his way and trying to write—his uncomprehending

parents actually drove him out of the home, the mother being the chief instigator of this harsh action. The story is told in careful detail by Constance Cappel Montgomery, *Hemingway in Michigan* (New York: Fleet Publishing Company, 1966), especially chap. xiv, "Twenty-first Birthday." See also chap. iii in Leicester Hemingway, *Ernest Hemingway, My Brother* (Cleveland and New York: World Publishing Company, 1961, 1962).

23. From the accounts available, our sympathies are not with the parents but with the son. Hemingway's fictional treatment of his return from the war, "Soldier's Home," actually softens the reality. Small wonder that, in his rebellion, he turned his back on the middle-class world once and for all.

24. Philip Young remarks: "But there is one thing that should be clear about him, and that is that more prominent in his life than anything else save the production of books has been the absorption of blows" (p. 164).

25. (New York: Random House, 1966).

26. See in particular Philip Young's devastating essay-review, "On Dismembering Hemingway," *Atlantic*, CCXVIII, No. 2 (1966), 45–49.

27. My chief sources are Young and Baker. I rely for some things also on Leslie Fiedler, since he and Seymour Betsky were evidently the last literary people to visit Hemingway. See Fiedler's account, "An Almost Imaginary Interview: Hemingway in Ketchum," *Partisan Review*, XXIX (1962), 395–405.

28. Young, pp. 269–70.

29. Young has written: "One remembers the terrible need for reassurance that caught Hemingway up during the months of acute depression in his last two years, when he felt that after all he had been knocked out and nothing he had ever written was worth a damn" (p. 290). This impression is confirmed by Fiedler in "An Almost Imaginary Interview."

30. *Papa Hemingway*, pp. 245–46 and 293.

31. *Ibid.*, pp. 266–70.

32. On Hemingway's overreacting to critics, see Philip Young's "Foreword: Author and Critic: A Rather Long Story." Edmund Wilson tells us that Hemingway "succeeded in delaying for several months the publication of a book of mine by getting out an in-

junction against the publishers." See his "That Summer in Paris," *The Bit between My Teeth* (New York: Farrar, Straus and Giroux, 1965), p. 523. The essay in question was the sympathetic "Hemingway: Gauge of Morale," in Wilson's *The Wound and the Bow* (1941).

33. In his article "The Christmas Gift," *Look*, XVIII (April 20 and May 4, 1954). The quotation is from the reprinting in *By-Line: Ernest Hemingway: Selected Articles and Dispatches of Four Decades*, ed. William White (New York: Charles Scribner's Sons, 1967), p. 455.

34. *Ibid.*, p. 460.

35. Precisely how much was written during these last years and how much was merely rewriting and polishing earlier notes, we do not yet know. In an introductory Note the author's widow tells us Hemingway began work on *A Moveable Feast* in the fall of 1957 and that he finished it in the spring of 1960. The story of the recovery of the Paris notebooks and of the writing of *A Moveable Feast* is told by Mary Hemingway in "The Making of the Book: A Chronicle and a Memoir," *New York Times Book Review*, May 10, 1964, pp. 26–27.

36. Quoted from the last sentence.

37. Since as writers Fitzgerald and Hemingway had many affinities, Hemingway might indeed have identified with him. He might also have envied Fitzgerald, who at the time was already an established and popular novelist. Though Hemingway is at once amusing and sympathetic, the joke is finally on Fitzgerald.

38. Again an expression of suicidal thoughts. When he returns from Paris where "the girl I was in love with" was then living, Hemingway confesses his feelings: "When I saw my wife again standing by the tracks as the train came in by the piled logs at the station, I wished I had died before I ever loved anyone but her" (p. 210).

39. The phrase is Harry Levin's in Baker, *His Critics*, p. 113.

40. For instance, Leicester Hemingway has remarked of his brother: "He needed uncritical admiration. . . . A little worshipful awe was a distinct aid. . . . I made a good kid brother when I was around" (quoted by Young, p. 274).

41. One of the best and most penetrating analyses of the effect

the legend had on Hemingway, psychologically speaking, is Edmund Wilson's "That Summer in Paris," in *The Bit between My Teeth,* pp. 515–25.

42. The phrase is from Karl Stern, *The Flight from Woman* (New York: Farrar, Straus and Giroux, 1965), p. 259.

43. The relations between Hemingway's compulsions and the repetition in his writings are illuminated by Bern Oldsey, "The Snows of Ernest Hemingway," *Wisconsin Studies in Contemporary Literature,* IV, No. 2 (Spring-Summer, 1963), 172–98. As to one of the obsessions, Earl Rovit has remarked that Hemingway took over "the role of what we might call 'jongleur of pain.'" See his *Hemingway* (Twayne's United States Author Series; New York: Twayne Publishers, 1963), p. 173.

44. Oldsey, "The Snows," p. 194.

45. See Robert Evans, p. 172, fn. 19.

46. On the repetition compulsion, see Young, pp. 164–71.

47. Baker, *The Writer,* p. 329.

48. *Ibid.,* p. 343.

49. Of the illness and old age which eventuated in his brother's suicide, Leicester Hemingway in his biography has remarked, "Ernest felt his own body had betrayed him" (p. 283).

50. This photograph appears opposite p. 209 in John Brown, *Hemingway* (La Bibliothèque Idéale; Paris: Gallimard, 1961).

Bibliographical Note, with a
Checklist of Selected Readings

For comprehensive surveys, the following bibliographical sources are invaluable: (1) Carlos Baker, *Hemingway: The Writer as Artist* (3rd ed.; Princeton, N.J.: Princeton University Press, 1963). In his extensive "Working Checklist of Hemingway's Prose, Poetry, and Journalism—with Notes," Dr. Baker includes the fiction and the nonfiction, both the collected and uncollected items of the Hemingway canon down to 1960. (2) Carlos Baker, ed., *Hemingway and His Critics* (American Century Series; New York: Hill and Wang, 1961). In the Appendix is a useful "Checklist of Hemingway Criticism," international in scope and ranging from the late 1920's to 1960. (3) Maurice Beebe, "Criticism of Ernest Hemingway: A Selected Checklist with an Index to Studies of Separate Works," *Modern Fiction Studies*, I, No. 1 (1955), 36–45. (4) Louis H. Cohn, *A Bibliography of the Works of Ernest Hemingway* (New York: Random House, 1931). (5) Earl Rovit, *Ernest Hemingway* (Twayne's United States Authors Series; New York: Twayne Publishers, 1963). In his Selected Bibliography this author includes a brief but very helpful annotated list of "Critical Studies." (6) Lee Samuels, *A Hemingway Check List* (New York: Charles Scribner's Sons, 1951). (7) Warren S. Walker, "Ernest Hemingway," *Twentieth-Century Short Story Explication* (Hamden, Conn.: Shoe String Press, 1961). (8) And finally, for students hoping to keep up to date on the huge bulk of Hemingway commentary there are the annual surveys in *American Literary Scholarship* (beginning with 1963), the annual bibliography in *PMLA,* the bibliography appearing each quarter in *American Literature,* and the items included regularly in *Abstracts of English Studies* and *The Explicator.*

In addition to the works specifically cited in my Notes, I am grateful for those listed below. All of the following critiques have been illuminating and useful to me, either by supplementing and clarifying my own views or by challenging them.

Aldridge, John W. "Hemingway: Nightmare and the Correlative of Loss," in *After the Lost Generation.* New York: Noonday Press, 1958.

Atkins, John. *The Art of Ernest Hemingway: His Work and Personality.* London, 1952; reissued with a new Preface, London: Spring Books, 1964.

Baker, Carlos. *The Land of Rumbelow: A Fable in the Form of a Novel.* New York: Charles Scribner's Sons, 1963.

Baker, Sheridan. *Ernest Hemingway: An Introduction and Interpretation.* American Authors and Critics Series. New York: Holt, Rinehart and Winston, 1967.

Brooks, Cleanth. "Ernest Hemingway: Man on His Moral Uppers," in *The Hidden God.* New Haven, Conn.: Yale University Press, 1963.

Brown, John. *Hemingway.* La Bibliothèque Idéale. Paris: Gallimard, 1961.

Clendenning, John. "Hemingway's Gods, Dead and Alive," *Texas Studies in Literature and Language,* III (1962), 489–502.

Colvert, James B. "Ernest Hemingway's Morality in Action," *American Literature,* XXVII (1955), 372–85.

Cooperman, Stanley. "Death and Cojones: Hemingway's *A Farewell to Arms,*" *South Atlantic Quarterly,* LXIII (1964), 85–92.

Cowley, Malcolm. "Papa and the Parricides," *Esquire,* LXVII (June, 1967), 100–1, 103, 160, 162.

Escarpit, Robert. *Hemingway.* La Renaissance du Livre. [Paris]: A.-G. Nizet, 1964.

Geismar, Maxwell. "Ernest Hemingway: You Could Always Come Back," in *Writers in Crisis: The American Novel between Two Wars.* Boston: Houghton Mifflin, 1942.

———. "Ernest Hemingway," in *American Moderns: From Rebellion to Conformity*. New York: Hill and Wang, 1958.

Grebstein, Sheldon. "Sex, Hemingway, and the Critics," *The Humanist*, XXI (1961), 212–18.

Hagopian, John V. "Symmetry in 'Cat in the Rain,'" *College English*, XXIV (1962), 220–22.

Hoffman, Frederick J. "No Beginning and No End: Hemingway and Death," *Essays in Criticism*, III (1953), 73–84.

———. "The War and the Postwar Temper," in *The Twenties*. 2nd ed. New York: Free Press, 1962.

———. *The Mortal No: Death and the Modern Imagination*. Princeton, N.J.: Princeton University Press, 1964, pp. 153, 208, 361 and *passim*.

Hofling, Charles K., M.D. "Hemingway, *The Old Man and the Sea* and the Male Reader," *American Imago*, XX (1963), 167–73.

Howe, Irving. "The Quest for a Moral Style," in *A World More Attractive*. New York: Horizon Press, 1964. See especially pp. 64–69.

Killinger, John. *Hemingway and the Dead Gods: A Study in Existentialism*. Lexington: University of Kentucky Press, 1961.

Moore, Geoffrey. "*The Sun Also Rises*: Notes Toward an Extreme Fiction," *A Review of English Literature*, IV, No. 4 (1963), 31–46.

Sanderson, Stewart F. *Ernest Hemingway*. Evergreen Pilot Books. New York: Grove Press, 1961.

Scott, Arthur L. "In Defense of Robert Cohn," *College English*, XVIII (1957), 309–14.

Scott, Nathan A., Jr. *Ernest Hemingway*. Contemporary Writers in Christian Perspective. [Grand Rapids, Mich.]: Eerdmans, 1966.

Sylvester, Bickford. "Hemingway's Extended Vision: *The Old Man and the Sea*," PMLA, LXXXI (1966), 130–38.

Tanner, Tony. "Ernest Hemingway's Unhurried Sensations," in *The Reign of Wonder: Naivety and Reality in American Literature*. London: Cambridge University Press, 1965.

Warren, Robert Penn. "Ernest Hemingway," *Kenyon Review*, IX (1947), 1–28.

White, William. "Father and Son: Comments on Hemingway's Psychology," *Dalhousie Review*, XXXI (1952), 276–84.

Index

For references to Hemingway's writings, see under Hemingway, Ernest: Works.